YOUR
MESSAGE
AND
THE MEDIA

Of related interest:

FACE THE PRESS

Managing the Media Interview

John B. J. Lidstone

LINDA FAIRBROTHER

YOUR MESSAGE AND THE MEDIA

The Complete and Practical Guide
to Media Relations

NICHOLAS BREALEY
PUBLISHING
LONDON

First published by
Nicholas Brealey Publishing Limited in 1993
156 Cloudesley Road
London N1 0EA

in association with
The Industrial Society
48 Bryanston Square
London W1H 7LN
Telephone: 071 262 2401

ISBN 1 85788 00 64

© Linda Fairbrother 1993

British Library Cataloguing in Publication Data
A catalogue record for this book is available from
the British Library.

Typeset by Dorchester Typesetting Group Ltd, Dorchester, Dorset
Printed in Great Britain by The Bath Press, Avon

CONTENTS

INTRODUCTION

WHO THIS BOOK IS FOR – THE PRESS PERSON

This book is aimed at people who are not public relations or media specialists but who want to use the media to get more publicity for themselves or their organisation.

It is for anyone who is taking on a media relations job who needs to find out how to deal with press and broadcasting. Media work may be the whole job or only part of it. So you could be one of the following:

- the marketing or advertising person who's suddenly told that 20% of the job is now going to be publicity;
- the new assistant to the full-time press officer;
- the secretary to the full-time press officer, who's going to help with queries and press conferences;
- the director who's going to be overseeing a small public relations department as well as sales, marketing, and advertising;
- the company spokesperson who'll be called upon to talk to the press for product launches or in a crisis;
- running your own small business;
- anyone involved in dealing with the media.

It is difficult to find a term which will cover all these people. They probably won't be full-time press officers or public relations officers (though there may be tips of interest to these people) so to call them 'press officers' might be misleading.

Nor will they necessarily be the spokesperson of their organisation, because many people who do the donkey work aren't allowed to actually make the quotes or appear on the screen. So the term used is the 'press person'. It's clumsy, but it allows for the fact that media work may be only part of your job, or that you aren't the person in overall charge of press relations.

Obviously there are both men and women who use the media, and who work as journalists and broadcasters. Rather than use the term 'he or she' all the time, the two are used interchangeably. For 'he' also read 'she', and vice versa.

'PRESS' VERSUS 'MEDIA'

There's a problem of what you call the whole world in which you as the press person will work. The trouble is that the word 'press' strictly covers only the printed word; while the word 'media' is usually taken to mean only radio and television. There isn't really a term which comfortably covers both. However, most organisations still call the person in charge the 'Press Officer' rather than the 'Media Officer', so for better or worse, the two terms are used more or less interchangeably in this book, except when it's obvious that a distinction is being drawn between them.

WHO THIS BOOK IS FOR – THE ORGANISATION

Nearly every organisation nowadays recognises the power of the media for good and ill. Whether you are making things, selling services, campaigning for a message, fund-raising, educating, or curing the sick, you can benefit from using the media.

You also have to recognise that the media may come to you whether you like it not. If you or your industry were to be involved in something controversial, then you'll find that it matters whether you can keep some control of what goes on. A ruined reputation lingers.

This book uses case studies and examples drawn from all sorts of organisations: industry, health, charities, small businesses, finance, etc. Obviously not all the techniques are going to be relevant to all organisations, but there should be ideas which can be adapted to your own circumstances.

WHAT'S IN IT

The aim is to cover all the basic principles that anyone trying to raise their profile in today's media needs to know. The approach is as practical and helpful as possible, so that it really is a comprehensive guide with lots of tips and techniques and case studies. It's slanted towards 'press (or media) relations' rather than 'public relations'. Press work is obviously part of public relations, but doesn't include sponsorship, advertising, public speaking, and so on.

At the beginning of each chapter is a summary, and at the end a checklist that asks the questions each press person should be able to answer with a 'yes'.

There's a section on crisis management: how to anticipate and prepare for trouble, and how to react if some horrible crisis comes your way. The last part deals with special aspects of particular fields: health, education, charities, etc.

Overall, it tries to answer all the questions a person new to media relations might want to ask, plus answering a few she might not even have thought of!

ACKNOWLEDGEMENTS

My main source for ideas and case studies has been my delegates on the various courses I run for The Industrial Society, both public courses and in-house. They also ask lots of questions, most of which I hope are answered in this book. So the biggest thank you goes to my course members over the years.

Many other people have helped me with those courses, and with information for the book. In no particular order, I'd like to thank: Christine Wright, Deborah Hall, Patrick Byrne, Nik Gowing, Deborah Hunt, Graham Lancaster, Alex MacDonald, Julian Dawton, Sue Heaton, Francis Baring, Stephen Milligan, Norman Parry, Wendy Elkington, and all those who have given their time and energy. My apologies if anyone feels misquoted: they'd better read the appropriate chapter on what to do ...

I would also like to thank all the papers and broadcasters who have given permission for quotations to be used. My apologies to those I was unable to contact.

Lastly, I must remember my family, who have had to put up with all the usual trials of having an author in the house.

PART ONE
GETTING ORGANISED

1

Why Bother with Media Relations?

- Everyone can benefit from better use of the media.
- Advertising costs a lot of money; editorial coverage is free.
- If you get it right, you'll keep more control of your message.
- Friendly, informed journalists are less likely to make mistakes about you and can help in a crisis.
- Media coverage is popular with employees.

SUPPING WITH THE DEVIL

IT is well known that all journalists have horns and a pointy tail. They are only out to get you, to report bad news, to misquote and misrepresent. Added to all that, they are ignorant, frequently drunk and probably fiddling the expenses.

Like most stereotypes, there may be some truth in this: there are reporters who will unscrupulously hound some unfortunate blonde seen talking in a night club with the latest football star, or twist your words on purpose to make a better story. Wensley Clarkson, a former reporter for the *Sunday Mirror*, wrote a fascinating – if repellent – account of his life as

5

a tabloid newsman (*Dog Eat Dog*, Fourth Estate, 1990). Without remorse, he describes how he walked uninvited into Oliver Reed's holiday villa and shouted questions through the keyhole of the bedroom about the young girl the actor was on holiday with. Not surprisingly, Mr Reed took umbrage at this and rushed at Clarkson in a fury, shouting out things like: 'We are just having a lovely time, it's no business of yours', and 'Her family know all about it, she hasn't been kidnapped'. These words shouted on the run became the basis for an 'Exclusive interview with Oliver Reed on his paradise retreat'. Some paradise, some retreat.

Such incidents make journalists unpopular, to say the least. They just about manage to stay ahead of politicians and lawyers for the title of 'least liked profession', but it is a close run thing. But tabloid bogies are in the minority, and most journalists are just doing a job, with all the ordinary foibles that most of us have. Some are people you would like to have a drink with, or even be friends with; some are poisonous or incompetent. Just like your colleagues at work, in fact. A journalist's job is to find and write a story that first his editor and then his readers will find interesting. If he gets things wrong, it is usually because of the pressure of working to tight deadlines. Or it may not be the fault of that particular journalist at all – someone else may have rewritten the copy.

SO WHAT IS SO GREAT ABOUT GETTING YOUR NAME IN THE PAPER?

Why put yourself to the risk of talking to the media at all? Surely better to stay well away from them all, just in case the devil lurking beneath decides to reassert himself? Well, using the media can have a number of advantages:

- free publicity;
- greater credibility for your product or service or message;
- more control of your message;
- insurance against disaster;
- a boost to internal morale;
- keeping up with your competitors.

Whether you sell double-glazing or industrial chemicals, aid to the Third World or to lost donkeys; whether you are trying to change people's minds on an issue or to publicise your local play group; whether you are large or small, commercial or voluntary, public or private; you will probably benefit by increasing your media coverage.

Free publicity

A cynical definition of the difference between advertising and public relations is that advertising costs money. And how! A colour page in a Sunday newspaper magazine will cost tens of thousands of pounds, and that just buys the space. Every day the advertising time in the middle of the evening television ten o'clock news generates around £1.5 million. So if your company is the subject of a feature article in your local paper, you are getting free what could otherwise cost hundreds of pounds.

Greater credibility

Although journalists as a profession regularly show up in surveys as mistrusted and disliked, it is ironic that the words that they write tend to be believed. How many times have you heard: 'Do you know, I read in the paper that…'? Rightly or wrongly, people give greater trust to the editorial part of a paper or radio than they do to the advertising. So if you proclaim in a glossy ad that your sausages are the best thing since the pig was domesticated, readers are going to put it to the test before accepting your invitation to lay in a lifetime's supply. But if the highly respected food writer proclaims that eating it has given her taste buds their best treat in the past year, her readers will come flocking to your shop.

More control of the message

One of the commonest questions about media relations is 'How do I retain control over what they print or say?'. The straightforward answer is that you can't. Journalists will pick up on what they think is interesting, and unfortunately their ideas of a good story or angle may not be yours. Why do journalists ignore how wonderful you are, and insist on trying to find out about your connection with animal testing or about a former employee who has been arrested as a mass murderer? The simple answer is that bad news is often more interesting than good. How fascinated would you be in a friend who kept phoning you up to tell you how wonderful his marriage, his job and his children are?

But it is amazing how much control you can keep if you plan ahead and get your targets right:

- if you choose a newsworthy angle in the first place, it is far more likely that the media will follow that angle and not go haring off to find another;
- if you target your story to the right places, it is far more likely that it will be used in the way you hope;
- if you get the wording and style right it is far more likely that your actual news release will be used verbatim. Perhaps not all of it will appear, but it is amazing how many stories appearing in a newspaper use practically the same words as the original release;
- if you practise your answers before an interview, you will get your main points across better and know how to avoid traps.

Insurance against disaster

Another question that people regularly ask about working with the media is: How can I keep them out of my hair most of the time, but make sure they are available and friendly when I need them? The short answer, again, is that you can't.

If your policy is to keep all journalists at bay, to treat them with suspicion and never initiate contacts or help with any enquiries, then don't be surprised if the pack turns on you when they smell blood. What do they have to lose by writing or broadcasting the most lurid story they can come up with?

On the other hand, any contacts you have made when things are going well, will stand you in good stead if crisis strikes. If you have shown that you are a useful source of good local stories, or that you are always available for a quote on matters relating to your industry, or that you are generally OK, then a journalist is less likely to be unfair or sensationalist if you are in some trouble, because he or she might lose something too – a valuable contact.

That's not to say that any journalist worth his or her salt will back off a 'good' disaster story just because they are friendly with the organisation concerned. But they are far more likely to be willing to hear your side of things, to ask for your comments, and to be favourably disposed towards your explanation of events.

So one of the facts of life about media relations is that you have to take the rough with the smooth. Time and thought spent now may turn out to be immensely important in two years' time, in a way you cannot foresee.

Boosting morale

Lastly, one of the most important aspects of getting your name in the media is the way that your employees (and the higher-ups) get a buzz out of it.

Anyone who has ever appeared on television, however fleetingly, will recognise the experience of one senior personnel manager who had a high profile in his organisation. In his spare time he was interested in collecting water colours, and happened to be at an auction which was being televised by the local television news. By chance he appeared for about five seconds on the evening bulletin, as one of the people bidding for a picture. The next morning, colleague after colleague commented on it. 'I felt rather disappointed,' he said. 'Week after week I see these people, talk to them, do things with them, but it was as if I only became real when I'd appeared on television!' People do get excited when their organisation is written about or talked about, and feel proud that their achievements have received 'recognition'.

Also don't forget that your competitors are probably doing their best to get in the papers too. If your customers are always reading in their trade paper intelligent quotes from your competitor about the state of the industry, but it seems that you are never good enough to be quoted, what do you think are the conclusions they'll draw?

CASE STUDY Good Habits

The most unlikely organisations may find that press publicity pays.

A Benedictine convent was approached some years ago by the British newspaper the *News of the World* which wanted to run a feature on the nuns' love lives and sexual regrets.

Not surprisingly, the first impulse was to politely refuse, but someone said, 'Our Lord redeemed the readers of the *News of the World*, the same as He redeemed the readers of *The Times*, didn't he?' And so they allowed a reporter in.

One nun says about the result: 'I regard that experience as one of the great blessings of my life.' Within a fortnight of publication, the nuns had received more than 400 letters from people in terrible distress. 'It was as though the giant agony of the world had been poured over us. It was wonderful.'

(Reported in *The Guardian*, 24 July 1991)

2

Sorting Out the Basics

- You should have full access to people and information, with as much independence as possible.
- Your job is not just to spread favourable news, but to create understanding in good times and bad.
- It is essential to find out what your starting position is – what people think of you.
- You must know what your message is and who you want to tell.
- Have in writing a strategy and press plan.

WHO SHOULD DO THE MEDIA WORK

THERE are no hard and fast rules about who is the best person to be in charge of media relations. It may be a full-time job for one or more people who are in charge of all aspects of public relations and publicity, including press work. Or it may be just a minor part of someone's job, and their main concern is in marketing or sales or even running the whole show.

Whoever this 'press person' is, these considerations should apply:

- The press person should be allowed to know what is going on everywhere in the organisation, however confidential.

10

- He or she should be encouraged to know what is going on, by being invited on to relevant committees, by having a budget that allows visits to far-flung parts of the organisation's empire, and by having access to all sources of knowledge.
- There should be a clear policy of responsibility, with as much independence as possible going to the press person about the sending of releases, making quotable comments, etc. Press work done by committee leads to leaden prose and delay, and is usually bad news in all meanings of the term.
- He or she should have direct access to the chief executive if at all possible.

WHAT IS THE JOB?

The aim of a good press person is not to be a confidence trickster telling endless lies to the media. It is not even to tell only good news, because sometimes there's no avoiding the bad news. A *good press person promotes understanding*.

Your aim is to let the general public, or your specific targets, understand what you are about, in good times and bad. As a result, maybe they will buy your message or your goods; or become your employees rather than someone else's. That, however, is a side effect. You are aiming for understanding, rather than approval. This is sometimes difficult for superiors to appreciate, who think you should be out there beating the drum for greater sales and can only measure your success by such limited targets. But with all advertising or publicity or marketing work, you know that some of what you do is useful and some isn't; the trouble is knowing which is which.

So you do what you can to let people know who you are, what you do or make, and in special circumstances you explain what is going on and why your organisation is following a certain course of action. If you do this well, and if your organisation deserves credit in the first place, you should be rewarded by a better image.

CASE STUDY The Body Shop

Anita Roddick of Body Shop fame is one of the best examples of positive public and media relations. First of all, Body Shop has good products that are value for money and can be bought with a clear conscience. Secondly, Anita Roddick herself is always available for interview; she speaks with enthusiasm, knowledge, and without waffle. Thirdly, the campaigns she associates with (such as preserving the rain forests or promoting membership of Greenpeace) are related to her products and not just a gimmick. She encourages local activities too, such as the Worthing staff providing skin-care help at a hospice.

As a result, Body Shop spends no money at all on advertising; all publicity comes from a winning combination of good product, good employee relations, good image, local involvement, and time and imagination spent promoting all these in the media.

GETTING YOUR JUST DESSERTS

One of many definitions of public relations is that it is 'the planned effort to deserve, acquire, and retain a good reputation'. Another way of looking at it is the old maxim: 'Whitewashing a wall can be done as often as you like; but whitewashing a reputation only works once.'

In the end, better publicity and press relations will only be as successful as your product deserves. If you haven't done the right market research, or if the quality is shoddy, or if you are constantly letting down your employees or customers, then the best media coverage in the world will not help much.

CASE STUDY Henry VIII and His Merry Bed

A couple of craftsmen set up their own company to make four-poster beds. They were reasonably successful, and decided on a gamble: an eight-poster bed, which would be the biggest bed in the world. Other people were brought in to help, such as a seamstress to make the drapes, and a public relations consultant – they agreed to wait for payment till the bed was sold.

A very successful publicity campaign was started, with wide coverage of the bed's launch at Ripley Castle, when photographers and journalists lapped up the 'Tudor' atmosphere of minstrels playing while Henry VIII and his wives romped on the huge mattress.

The bed travelled the country, spent two weeks in Harrods in London, and featured on a popular children's television programme, when 64 children crammed on to it. All this got more coverage.

But the bed remained resolutely unsold, despite letters to the rich and an attempt to auction it for charity. In the end, the bed and sewing businesses both collapsed, saddled with debts. As one of the carpenters commented: 'All the publicity didn't bring us a single extra order.' Those concerned put their time and materials into a project that hadn't been properly researched, and a good publicity campaign could not remedy that.

(Reported in *Financial Times*, 24 November 1990)

So much for the problems of 'acquiring' a reputation. But far worse can be the disaster should you not 'deserve' a good reputation, but go all out for image, not reality.

CASE STUDY Pan Am

The American airline Pan Am saw the number of trans-Atlantic passengers drop after the American bombing of Libya in 1986. Surveys showed that passengers were scared of terrorist retribution, and that they would choose an airline by its security standards. Pan Am therefore decided to beef up their security programme, and made much publicity out of it.

Unfortunately, the much-publicised 'Alert' system was far more froth than substance. For instance, one photocall featured sniffer dogs and armed guards; but the dogs were brought in from kennels and the guns were replicas, because the staff had no fire-arm training or authorisation to carry arms in an airport. The moment the cameras were gone, the props were removed. When the Security Chief pushed for money to be spent on real improvements in staff recruitment and training, and for more screening equipment, he was given the sack. Meantime the PR campaign continued, and Pan Am strove to give the impression that its security measures were second to none. As Dr Jim Swire (UK Families Flight 103) wrote: 'Their intention was to deceive the public that the carrier was doing everything possible to protect them.'

Just before Christmas 1988, it seems a terrorist placed a bomb hidden in a radio cassette recorder on a flight from Malta, which eventually exploded over Scotland in what became known as the Lockerbie disaster. The inquiry slammed Pan Am's slack complacent

> security measures. Not only did Pan Am's passenger figures slump; they also had to pay out millions in compensation to the victims' families.
>
> (As reported in Granada Television's *Why Lockerbie*, transmitted 26 November 1990, and quoted with permission.)

The job of public relations, or publicity, or press work, is never to cover up a mistake or to lie. Most employees may feel it is easier to go with the flow, and to bow to pressure from higher-ups to lie for the good of all. But remember Lockerbie; remember President Nixon and the 'Watergate' affair. The truth has an unfortunate way of coming to light, and if there has been a cover-up, your organisation's position will in the end be far worse.

THE JOB OF A PRESS PERSON

If the job of a press person is not to tell lies, nor necessarily to hard-sell, what will you be doing with your time?

Whether your press person role is part-time or full-time, your aims are to:

- create and foster contacts with relevant media;
- act as a focus for all press contacts, so that enquiries, interviews, comments, etc., are either organised or channelled through the press officer;
- publicise good news and explain bad news;
- plan ahead so as to maximise the chances of publicity;
- monitor results and let others know of coverage.

You might, in the course of a week or day:

- attend executive meetings;
- prepare press releases;
- organise press conferences;
- talk to members or employees of your organisation to foster good relations and keep up to date with what is going on;
- read the key target publications for your sort of news;
- be involved in induction training (to let newcomers know how they can help you and you help them);
- brief senior people before they give interviews or press conferences;
- visit branches and other regions to foster internal contacts;
- update your press lists, using your own contacts or by paying for electronic updates;
- read specialist press such as UK *Press Gazette* or PR *Week*;
- visit and talk to technical specialists in your organisation;

- read, file, and publicise press cuttings;
- do routine admin (labelling envelopes, copying releases, etc);
- chair a quarterly crisis team meeting.

It all seems a lot – it is a lot. So if you are a part-timer, you need to work out which parts of it are the essential ones for you, and that means knowing what you want to achieve and how best you can do it.

WHERE ARE WE NOW?

The basic rule of all marketing, publicity and media work is to know:

- what you want to say
- who you want to say it to.

Unless you know these two things, you will end up wasting time and money, and possibly confusing people. There will probably be an overall idea of what you need to put across, but also for specific occasions you may have a particular message and target. For example,

- Overall message: Our company is caring, friendly, and a good place to work in. (This is targeted at the local community who live near head office, and provide your employees.)
- Specific message: Our new product is cheap, effective, and non-toxic. (Targeted at present and potential customers, and perhaps shareholders who want to know how well the company is doing.)

Therefore you should know what your message is overall, whether you want to promote your product or your image, whether there is a different or extra message in a particular situation, and what you want to say about yourselves.

BUT WHAT IS OUR IMAGE?

If you are not already very clear about your message and targets, then you will have to find them out. Discover your image from as many sources as possible. The easy but expensive way is to commission some market research. This is not necessary if you use your own time and imagination. Go out and ask what people think about your organisation and your products.

Employees Are they happy, or are they bad-mouthing the organisation?

Customers What are your strengths? What are your weaknesses? Why do they use your services or buy your goods or believe your message?

The Community Do they know you exist? If so, are there any strong feelings (in favour of the sponsorship of the music festival: against the lorries going down a narrow street)?

Journalists How do they see you? Do they have a very out-dated image of you and your products (all accountants wear three-piece suits; all factories are noisy, oily pits)?

Schools Are you seen as a good place to apply for a job or a work placement or a project?

Higher education What do students and careers officers feel about your industry in general and you in particular?

And so on, depending on your own cirumstances. The answers will tell you: your strengths; your weaknesses; any threats and looming problems; opportunities for moving forwards.

If you discover there is something wrong with your image, then you are going to have to work on putting it right, whether you are persuading local parents that your delapidated school buildings do not contain equally delapidated teachers and students; or the public that 95% of the money they give to your charity really does go to the cause.

WHO DO YOU WANT TO INFLUENCE?

Who do you want to reach with this message or these messages? The answer may be very specific (e.g. all those people who decide on which software to use for training commercial pilots in aircraft simulators), or it may be very wide (e.g. all animal lovers who might be persuaded to sign a covenant for an animal charity). Usually you will find there will be one or a number of core target groups, but with a particular product or campaign or problem extra targets will appear.

Sometimes you may have to do some very thorough research. For instance, if you are a building firm making roofing tiles, you will need to find out who is choosing your tiles and who is not. Building contractors order and pay for your product so you may at first think that they should be your target. But a closer look shows that, although they generally like your tiles and will order them if given the chance, in many cases they don't get the chance because the architects have already specified exactly what to put on the roof. And the architects remain unconvinced about your product. So *they* are the professionals you have to reach with your publicity.

HOW TO REACH THEM

Once you have identified your target publics, you have to decide how to influence them. It is no good deciding that you want to reach young people with an interest in rock music and then putting out stories that get wonderful coverage in one of the heavier Sunday papers. Or wanting to lobby against a new bypass that will go through an area of unspoilt countryside, and only getting coverage in the local press which influences the people already on your side. So you have to work out which people read which papers or listen to which radio programme. Help on how to do this is in Chapters 5 and 6.

FORMULATING A PRESS PLAN

Once you are clear on your current image, your message and your targets, it is time to work out a press plan and to get it approved by the powers that be. You need to know the policy, the objectives and the strategy.

Overall policy

First, you need to choose the possible options.

WHAT KIND OF COVERAGE

Which of these alternatives do you aim for?
- every bit of publicity you can get;
- hardly any unless it comes knocking on your door;
- something in between: pushing only substantial stories or reacting to dampen bad coverage.

WHO HAS AUTHORITY

How is the chain of command to be organised? These are some options:
- You as the press person issue quotes and comments independently as 'spokesperson'.
- You have full authority to send press releases.
- You can appear on radio and television.
- You don't have authority to do all or any of these things, but you know who does and who carries the can if things go wrong.
- Everything gets passed up for approval – if there's a cumbersome line of people all putting the commas in every press release, then sometimes the press release will miss deadlines, and who will take responsibility?
- There are a number of official spokespersons – try to avoid having just one, because what will happen when that person is sick?
- There are broadcasting spokespersons, who may need special talents and training to come across well on radio or TV.

WHAT HAPPENS IN A CRISIS

Do you have all or any of these arrangements?
- The press person is responsible for crisis management.
- A crisis team is set up to prepare for possible trouble.
- There's a chain of command to make quick decisions in an emergency.

Write your policy down, and then turn to the objectives.

Objectives

It is probably easiest to give imaginary examples as objectives.

For an industrial concern making widgets that are widely used as a basic component for other machinery, the need might be:

1 To raise the profile of one of the largest UK manufacturers of widgets, letting people know its success and diversity. This will be aimed at City and financial circles, the manufacturing industry, and politicians and central civil servants.
2 To sell specific product lines, both well-established ones and any new products. To be aimed at those with authority to buy, both distributors and those needing the widgets.
3 To support existing distributors by creating demand.
4 To improve the image of the northern factory, because local people are very unhappy about industrial noise and smells.

So the overall press strategy could be something like this:

1 Make sure all financial results are publicised.
2 Find and publicise case studies and news of major contracts in business journals and technical press.
3 Organise regional seminars for customers (press invited) to discuss developments in technology or marketplace.
4 To publicise all new products in the technical press.
5 To be ready to offer comments to national and technical press on matters relating to the industry or on any matter in which the company has something interesting to say.
6 To raise the profile of the company chairman by publicising his speeches and opinions in the financial and business press.
7 To use local press to publicise how the company helps the northern factory's local community, and be ready to respond quickly and positively should any specific complaints be made.
8 To set in place a crisis team.

For a run-down inner city school with a falling roll of pupils, the need might be:

1 To promote a sense of pride in the school's achievements among current pupils and parents.
2 To let feeder primary schools know more about the school's strengths.
3 To counter bad publicity lingering in the community about a serious racial incident some years ago.

3

Inside Information — Using Internal Communications

- You need to get the right information at the right time.
- You need co-operation from all your colleagues to give you that information and to help you help journalists.
- Walking the job, visiting other departments and regions, and keeping constant contact is the best way to gather news and remind people of your needs.
- A house journal or newsletter is very useful in keeping up morale and generating stories.
- Keep up the good work by talking about press work in committees, and by having training sessions.
- Monitor your results, and publicise coverage.

FINDING YOUR STORIES

WE'VE all heard of the mushroom style of management – keep your employees in the dark and shovel manure on them. If you are in that unhappy position, then you as press person will be one of the most

4 To influence the local authority in favour of keeping the school open and well funded.
5 To create better morale among present and future teachers.

So the press strategy might be:

1 Publicise all exam results, scholarships, academic achievements.
2 Explain such results in context, e.g. ALL the local schools have done less well in the maths exam this year, or, there may not have been so many grade ones but think of all the less able who have been helped to get grade three.
3 Publicise school activities, such as clubs, sports, interesting projects, involvement in the community.
4 Publicise individual achievements of teachers and pupils, such as the teacher who is a voluntary ambulancewoman at weekends, or the pupil who joins the National Youth Music Theatre.
5 Be more active in joining in with local events, competitions, and using local venues such as the library or town hall for exhibitions.
6 Be prepared to volunteer information on educational matters to the local press, such as government exam proposals, or alterations to the curriculum, or a debate on falling literacy.
7 See if there is any way for a member of staff to become a regular or occasional guest on local radio, offering advice/information/answers to letters/answers to phone-in questions.

There are as many different strategic needs as there are organisations. Make your own list of needs and work out what two or three main strategic needs your organisation has, and how you could meet them through a media campaign.

CASE STUDY Kew Gardens, London

The Royal Botanical Gardens at Kew decided that public money might one day have to be worked for, even fought for. So they decided that they needed to build up support among 'opinion formers' as an insurance against the day when they might have to ask for more funds or face cut-backs.

Research showed that most people associated Kew Gardens with having a pleasant Sunday walk, but knew little of the internationally important scientific research being done. Therefore, those in charge decided that they needed to promote the 'usefulness' of Kew, rather than its beauty; and should try to inform political and official targets, as well as the general public whose support could be vital in a crisis.

As a result, stories were (and are) fed to the press about research projects (such as collecting tropical plants with pharmaceutical possibilities and identifying pollens that cause hay fever). Also publicised is work of international importance (e.g. rain forest preservation) and work of immediate practical use (e.g. finding out from root samples which tree is damaging a house).

The scientists there are available to the press for immediate comment on topical news stories, such as storm damage to trees, so that the public become used to hearing from a 'Kew Gardens expert' whenever anything remotely botanical crops up. And any current story (such as the opening of a new conservatory) has its scientific or practical angle given as much prominence as its effect on visitors to the Gardens.

Lastly, a large amount of TV coverage was sought and found for documentaries on the Gardens at Kew and Wakehurst. This involved the scientists in a lot of 'time-wasting' work helping the programme makers, but it was thought worthwhile in the long term.

WRITING THE PRESS PLAN

Get everything down in writing. A typical press plan might include these sections:

- overall look at what the organisation is and how it is perceived;
- broad press objectives and policy;
- strategy;
- target publics to reach with that strategy;
- which media to aim for;
- how much coverage to aim for;
- lines of responsibility and authority;
- budgets;
- press competitions, sponsorship, awards;
- any research needed;
- any other linked activities (e.g. in-house newsletter, promotional leaflets, etc.);
- important publicity chances in the next year (AGM, product launch, etc.).

Then get it approved and circulated so everyone knows what to expect.

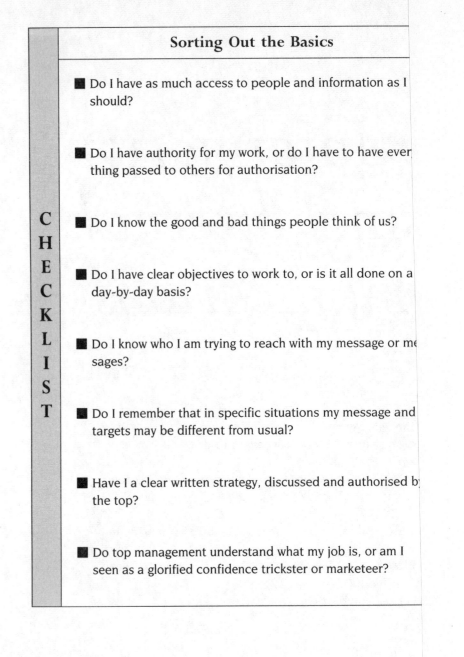

CHECKLIST

Sorting Out the Basics

■ Do I have as much access to people and information as I should?

■ Do I have authority for my work, or do I have to have everything passed to others for authorisation?

■ Do I know the good and bad things people think of us?

■ Do I have clear objectives to work to, or is it all done on a day-by-day basis?

■ Do I know who I am trying to reach with my message or messages?

■ Do I remember that in specific situations my message and targets may be different from usual?

■ Have I a clear written strategy, discussed and authorised by the top?

■ Do top management understand what my job is, or am I seen as a glorified confidence trickster or marketeer?

unfortunate fungi in the cellar. Your specific job is to give out information and you can't do that unless you get it.

Even if you are in an open, well-run, co-operative organisation, you may still appear as a rather alien being without a 'proper' job and it may be that time spent with you is seen as 'wasted' time. Therefore there's a part of the job, seldom talked about, which is:

- getting information in time to be useful;
- getting co-operation and help.

It is important to work out ways in which you can publicise to the rest of your organisation what it is you do, and to get in place as many channels of communication as you can which will let you know what is going on. And you have to find ways to get the news yourself – be your own investigative journalist, in fact. Some of your news is obvious: the updated product, the annual figures, the successful campaign. But what about the marginal stories; the people stories; the small-scale initiative in the building trade that may be just the thing for *Double Glaziers Monthly* but nobody thought to tell you about?

You also need to maximise the help that people will give you internally. After all, one of the chief functions of a press person is to get facts and quotes and interviewees to hand to journalists. Where will those facts and quotes and interviewees come from unless your colleagues are persuaded to put themselves out for you? Why should they be bothered to send you interesting information unless there is something in it for them? At the least, they should know who and what you are, and why you are important.

These are some of the ways in which you can communicate and get feedback:

- walk the job and visit the regions regularly;
- make sure you are on everyone's internal mailing list;
- create a system of 'my own correspondents';
- have a house journal or newsletter;
- always send releases and/or press cuttings to the colleagues concerned;
- set up a press cuttings noticeboard or book;
- monitor your results and circulate them;
- get PR or media relations on to the agendas of committees;
- have mini training sessions.

Everyone in media work will have their own examples of the stories that got away. Everyone will also have examples of being under intensive pressure from a journalist to come back with a fact or statistic or comment NOW, and being unable to come up with anything in time, because colleagues don't phone back.

CASE STUDY The Rower that Got Away

An employee of a Midlands firm was a keen amateur rower. He saw an advertisement for good rowers to take part in an exciting project to re-create a Greek trireme, the latest thing in fighting ships in 300 BC. The ship was being built in Greece with a strong British involvement.

The young man applied and was accepted for the project, which meant a 'holiday' pulling a huge oar in sweltering temperatures to see if the newly built galley was historically correct. He told his manager about it, who was very enthusiastic, arranging extra holiday time and some sponsorship by the firm.

Unfortunately, the manager neglected to tell anyone in Head Office publicity, it never having occurred to him that such a story could be newsworthy. So when the story was picked up by local papers, reporters concentrated on the local rowing club angle, and the help and training the young man was getting from his club. No mention of where he worked, or that his employers were helping too.

The firm had missed a valuable opportunity to tell the local community what good employers they were.

WALKING THE JOB

Ultimately nothing beats going out and finding your own material, because you are the one who has done the research and should be able to recognise the story suitable for any of your media targets. Go out and talk to people round and about; ask them what they're doing at the moment; ask them what the current project is; ask them about the departmental gossip and activities. (It may be wise to have had a bit of consciousness-raising about your job first, or they may think you're the management spy.)

Similarly, you may need to go out to other parts of the empire. Put in your diary or press wall chart regular reminders to visit your regional bases. If you are visiting anyway, in a different capacity, then make sure you leave enough time for doing a bit of story-snooping as well. Even if nothing crops up from any particular visit or chat, you will have reminded people of your existence, and in particular that you are interested in a phone call should something occur to them.

SEND ME THE MINUTES – PLEASE

It seems obvious that you should get all the information necessary to do your job, but check that you are getting everything:

- all important minutes, including those of the research and development department;
- all important reports, especially any which contain market research, surveys, or anything which shows trends and reactions;
- product literature, price lists, technical descriptions;
- up-to-date information on customers, outlets, branches, suppliers, etc.;
- up-to-date information on personnel changes;
- any material relating to industry-wide matters (e.g. trade associations, trades unions, similar campaigners, well-known opponents).

It may be necessary to find out who are the key people who control all these various bits of information. Go and talk to them, explain your needs, and try to get them on your side.

One press person in a merchant bank not only makes sure his office is sited on the same floor as the top brass, but also prefaces all requests for information with 'The Managing Director would like to see …'. He finds the papers come winging along a lot faster.

FIND A STRINGER

It is very useful to have people around the organisation who are your eyes and ears in other departments or regions. From chatting around (or even better, from talent spotting at training sessions) try to identify the people who have a flair for spotting a story.

Give them a target to work for every month – whatever you think is realistic – such as two 'achievement' stories (Packaging's rush order to Paris over the weekend; Class 2B write a song about whales for a national competition); two 'people' stories (profile of the new branch manager; Mrs Brown's amazing stamp collection); two 'human interest' stories (first aider helps at traffic accident); and one feature idea (an interview with the health and safety officer or an in-depth look at the way new European directives will affect the sale of compost). If there is any real 'news', then so much the better.

The obvious place to put their information is in the internal house journal, if you have one, keeping an eye out for stories with outside potential. Don't forget to keep them motivated with plenty of feedback and praise, or even a byline (budding journalists will do anything for a byline, so why not try it with Brown of Accounts too?).

USING THE HOUSE JOURNAL

An in-house journal does not have to be very glossy, although with desktop publishing now available it is relatively easy to put together a good paper.

The primary job of a house journal or newsletter is to work in its own right, to communicate upwards and downwards, and to be an interesting read. However worthy it may be, it is a failure if no one reads it because it is boring or incomprehensible.

Apart from its main purpose, though, you can use the house journal or letter to help with media work in a number of ways:

Generating stories Obviously the in-house publication will print far more stories about your organisation than an outside paper. So people are encouraged to send in ideas because there is a good chance they will be printed. Some of those ideas will be good enough to build on.

Keeping up morale It may happen that a big effort to get media coverage for some achievement or event will fail to get any. If you don't have a back-up, you can end up with a lot of disappointed people who may feel that their efforts were wasted. Thank heavens for the in-house journal! Whatever other coverage you don't get, the story can at least get a big splash there, so you won't get a string of refusals next time you're looking for 35 people to brush their teeth for the camera, or to pad out a large press conference room.

The same goes for VIPs, whether they are inside or outside the organisation. They'll see a few flash bulbs going as they unveil the new lavatory block, and you will have some nice glossy photos to send, as well as the absolutely enormous headline and editorial in the house paper.

'What's My Line?' A useful regular spot in the in-house journal (or video) is an interview or feature about someone's job and/or a personality and interests profile. You or your correspondents can write it, or you can prepare a fixed list of questions to send out to the volunteers, along the lines of 'What do you like best at work?', 'What least?', 'What do you think of your boss?', etc. Be prepared for send-ups! (Not that it matters too much if you are aiming for a jolly read.)

Try to get a good cross-section of people to give credibility. Then file it all away for possible use – Jim Jones is a keen swimmer; Beryl Cannon is a 'natural' for talking about the difficult but hilarious start-up in Scotland; Graham Oliver seems to have a knack for explaining technical processes in layman's terms.

Readers' Letters If people won't write in by themselves, then another job for your stringers is to push them along. (You could even follow the example of certain magazines and write your own, but this is a risky strategy when everyone knows everyone else!). If you can get a lively letters page going, it can be very popular (as in 'real' newspapers); it is also another way of encouraging people to participate and to let you know what they are doing and feeling.

Staff News If there is a regular section on what the staff are doing (promotions, moves to other localities, retirements coming up, marriages, etc.) it helps you keep track too, and perhaps may generate some stories for trade press.

Have you heard this one? Another possibly useful regular feature is a 'Funny or Amazing Story of the Month'. These can often be the sort of story local papers love: 'Cleaner found marriage proposal from 1960 behind filing cabinet', or 'Typing pool nurse injured duck back to health with cheese sandwiches'. If you make it a regular item, then people (and your correspondents) will strive to find something. Even better, offer a prize.

Interviews with management You may be in the unhappy position of being left in the dark most of the time as to board policy, or the latest research projects or what problems may be looming ahead. If so, one way to find out is to keep asking for interviews or material for articles from senior management for the house journal. They can hardly refuse, since communicating downwards *ought* to be one of their priorities.

AND I WOULD LIKE TO SAY THANK YOU TO THE VICAR...

Courtesy is always a good idea. If someone has helped you in any way, don't forget to say thank you. Send the press release with the information or quote to show that you used it. If you didn't, explain why not. Anything that appears in the press should be copied to all relevant people before it appears on the notice-board.

If there are any photos involved, make sure you send copies to all people who appear in them. This is easy if you used your own photographer, but most papers are also very happy to provide large glossy copies of any photos that they print. For special events it can be worth getting a large photo framed and hung in a prominent position. This is especially important if the photo or event in question was seen as a real pain at the time: a permanent record will make it all seem much more fun in retrospect.

BLOWING YOUR OWN TRUMPET

Blow it loud, blow it often. This will help justify your own existence, and also lets everyone know what is going on, which keeps up morale.

The Press Notice-board

Put up cuttings on a notice-board that everyone will see. If you are confident, you can put it in reception, like Unilever do at their headquarters in London. (The press office choose four or five stories each week, and put them on to a large triangular wooden pillar in the lobby.)

There is always a decision to be made here about which stories you put up: all, some, or only positive ones. Whatever you decide, a notice-board will help people realise that stories do get reported, and if you get really positive or extensive coverage of something, morale goes skywards.

The Press Book

Keep press releases in a ring file in plastic envelopes. Keep at least four copies, just in case. List at the front the title, date, and circulation of each (this could be by name of publication, or by category, e.g. 'All local press' or 'All industrial correspondents').

Depending on how much coverage you get, you can also store photocopies or original cuttings of articles with the relevant release. If you get too much coverage for this to be practical, then at least try to cross-reference the cuttings with the press release.

Monitoring results

The normal way to see how you are doing is to count column inches and minutes of air time, by the week or, usually, month. This is, of course, a pretty crude indicator, since 28 inches in some obscure monthly magazine read by no one you are particularly interested in, is actually worth less than 2 inches in the local weekly read by all your employees. But it can be useful to graph the figures over some years, especially if you are at the start of an attempt to up your press profile.

More immediately useful is to break down your results in categories, e.g.: national news sections, national specialised sections, local news, local specialised, trade and technical, national TV and radio, local TV and radio. Then see how particular stories did in each target. If you have the resources, prepare a list every month of all your coverage, under these general headings, and make sure you circulate it.

Another way of evaluating the quality of your coverage (and this can be very useful for keeping an eye on an outside agency if they are preparing press releases for you) is to give a rating for each publication you are trying to place a story in, e.g.

Target	Rating	Coverage
The Barsetshire Bugle	5	6 cm
The County Trumpet	3	8 cm
Corner Storekeeper	2	0 cm
Bun-eaters Quarterly	1	20 cm

There are various ways you can come up with a formula, such as simple multiplication, or a combination of marks for 'appearance at all', plus length of coverage.

GETTING MEDIA ON TO THE AGENDA

Since most people take media coverage for granted, it is a subject that seldom appears on the agendas of meetings except at high level as part of general public relations. But there is no reason why there shouldn't be a 5-minute section of departmental or branch or staff meetings which is all about 'news'. Call it 'Ideas for press coverage', or 'Media work', and encourage people to come with one idea each (you may have to win a few chairpersons over if you aren't present at the meetings yourself).

You can also use that regular agenda item to talk about media coverage, to tell of your achievements, to drum up support for a particular event, or whatever. And you can start mini training sessions.

If you can't justify a separate place on the regular agenda, be ready to jump in at 'Any Other Business' if there is anything interesting to report.

EVERYONE A JOURNALIST

In the search for stories, you want everyone, not just your correspondents, to be aware of what a story is. So you will have to train people to develop a news sense. Either during normal meetings or in special sessions, set up small media training sessions. Another useful place could be on induction courses – catch 'em young.

In 10 minutes, you could quickly cover:

Why Why good media coverage is useful.

Timing An old story is a dead story, so the press person needs to know NOW, not tomorrow, and certainly not next month. Otherwise even a good story won't be picked up by the media. The problem is to persuade your listeners to co-operate when you badger them for help or ask for a quote 'not later than 2.30 please'.

News What your media targets are interested in. Show them sample articles from different papers (e.g. a 'human interest' story from the local rag; a personnel story from the trade weekly; a feature from a glossy monthly).

Press release The basics you need to know (who, when, where, what, and why) to write a release.

Other sessions could cover:

Crisis Explain how your organisation's crisis team is set up. Outline how the press react in a crisis, and therefore the importance of all staff keeping loyal and quiet.

Explain what would happen in a sample crisis, or (which is more fun!) set up a sample crisis. Tell them it is 8.30 a.m. or 5.30 p.m. on a Friday, and a phone call has just come from your lawyers to say that the Chief Executive has been arrested for suspected bigamy. Should your Chief Executive be the sort who objects to his or her name being taken in vain, then something more sober can be substituted. Put the group (who can be at any level of responsibility) into smaller groups of three or four. They can pretend either to be top management or to be themselves, and they have to decide what they are going to do. The fun comes when you inject into the exercise the arrival of a journalist at reception (you don't have to actually do this, of course, just announce it to the group). Has anyone got round to briefing the receptionist yet?

Other items you could add: a phone call from a paper or the radio station (what will you say?; have you appointed a spokesperson yet?); a journalist at the back door (have the rest of the staff been briefed yet?; is he free to roam the building, getting juicy quotes from the tea lady?).

The exercise can be ended by a 'phone call' from the lawyers saying the Chief is now free, because it was all a case of mistaken identity. You can then examine the issues of over-reaction!

A full session like this would take about an hour.

Broadcasting People are always interested in radio and television. If you have been inside a studio or been interviewed on location, tell them about it.

Another exercise that people tend to enjoy and find interesting is the 30-second game (see Chapter 11). You don't have to record the attempts, just time them approximately.

If you have more experience and feel you can handle it, then sample interviews are fun. Even without much broadcasting experience you can organise a question and answer session, where each small group is given a different topic relevant to your organisation (pollution problems; the new gizmo for Christmas; the privatisation of the geriatric ward; the campaign for more playgrounds). They then have to come up with as many questions as they can think of, straightforward ones and controversial ones. Pool the ideas between groups, and then each group thinks about the answers to another group's questions.

If there is time, it is fun to try a few sample questions and answers, timing the results, and see what happens.

If you don't think you have the expertise to handle these more complicated training sessions, then don't forget that many training organisations offer both public and in-house media courses (see Chapter 20) for information on media interviews and crisis training).

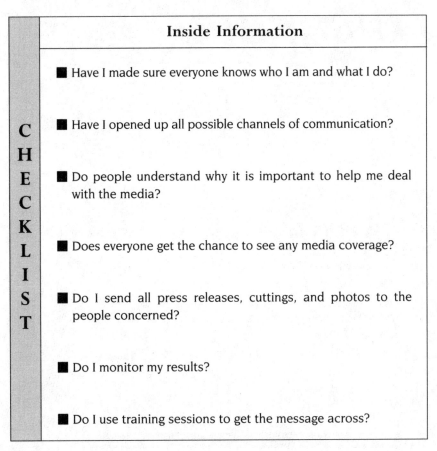

CHECKLIST

Inside Information

■ Have I made sure everyone knows who I am and what I do?

■ Have I opened up all possible channels of communication?

■ Do people understand why it is important to help me deal with the media?

■ Does everyone get the chance to see any media coverage?

■ Do I send all press releases, cuttings, and photos to the people concerned?

■ Do I monitor my results?

■ Do I use training sessions to get the message across?

4

Knowing the Facts

- You need to research your own organisation so that you have all essential information to hand.
- It is also worthwhile knowing as much as you can about your community.
- A fact sheet of basic data is useful.
- An annual planner chart will help you to work ahead and trigger ideas.
- You need to discover which papers, magazines and programmes reach the people you want to talk to.
- Specialist publications list all media and correspondents by region and by subject.

BEING IN THE KNOW

NOW that you know your message and objectives, the temptation is to jump in there and get swimming. But it is best not to plunge too fast. The commonest complaint journalists make about press officers is that they don't know their facts or their organisation. So you need to know your stuff.

Then put that research to work. First, by preparing a fact sheet that can help you find information quickly, and can be sent to any journalist who needs basic facts about your organisation. Secondly, by using your research to shape your press work so that you send out the right signals to the right people at the right time.

It is also very useful to know what's happening elsewhere. What is going on in your community and your field of work? What other people can help or hinder you? What are the hot issues?

Lastly, you'll need to know the facts about the media you might use: which papers, magazines, and programmes reach your targets, and which will be interested in your sort of stories. And who their journalists are, how their deadlines work, and how they present their material.

So you'll have to spend some time researching:

- your own organisation;
- your community, fellow organisations or industries, and competitors;
- the media that you might use.

YOUR OWN ORGANISATION – WHO ARE WE?

HISTORY

Find out as much as you can about your organisation's past. Look through the files and archives; read the books and pamphlets; find the photos and prototypes. At the very least have to hand some basic information:

- when you were started;
- by whom;
- where;
- how many employees there were;
- the basic products or services.

Ideally, get together historical photos or prints, showing the production line in 1911 with everyone in long skirts, or the opening of the office in 1969 by the Earl of Everything. If you can, find examples of early products or campaigns, because you never know when you might be able to add colour to a story with a good historical photo, or flesh out a feature with a 'then and now' comparison between the original Upside-down Pill Dispenser of 1948 and its sleek all-singing all-dancing modern counterpart. Even if your organisation is only ten years old, you can still create a past.

Sometimes knowledge of the archives can help trigger off an idea. Suppose a women's angle is floating around in the news (the anniversary of women's suffrage, say, or a new piece of legislation causing controversy). You vaguely remember something or other in your 'history' box about being the first office in your area to employ a female accountant in 1971, or that you have a photo of the typing pool in 1898. Dig it out – who knows, it could become the focus for a feature in the local paper, or be the added ingredient to an otherwise mundane piece of news about your new Equal Opportunities Policy.

WHO WE ARE

Many organisations answer requests for information on themselves with a copy of the Annual Report. For a journalist this is almost useless, and it will probably be useless to you too in providing vital information quickly.

It is important that you know your basic facts. A paper asks you about your turnover last year, or how many local branches of supporters you have. If you don't know, or even worse give the wrong figure, your credibility is in danger. A press person should either have in his head the basic information, or be able to dig it out within a few seconds.

The vital facts will probably include:

- what you sell/promote/do (and if that is very technical, the expert to consult or pass the question on to);
- where your shops/branches/outlets are;
- turnover and profits for the past few years;
- how many staff;
- who the chairman/president/MD is, with brief biographical details and at least two photos showing different expressions, ready to suit both the announcement of the most successful year ever, and the expression of regret that the Honorary Treasurer has just been revealed as the local peeping Tom;
- profiles and photos of other key personnel;
- who your own useful people are – there will be certain people in your organisation who will be useful to you: the technical person who can deliver instant quotes on Japanese specifications; the person in charge of the school links programme; the excellent amateur photographer, etc. Discover who they are (of course, this will take time), and have to hand their work and home phone numbers so that you can contact them quickly.

Once you have compiled all this information, then put it in a safe and accessible place, and KEEP IT UP TO DATE. There is nothing easier than to regard it as a once-and-for-all task and then to come unstuck a month or year later, because the information has changed. If you have everything to hand, however, you can answer any normal query immediately and correctly, which does wonders for your confidence. More importantly, it gives the journalist confidence in you. A journalist under pressure does not want to hear a lot of umming and ahhing about whether this is the exact figure or not, and whether we could phone you back this afternoon. He or she will expect you to know the basics, and if you do not, you will be bypassed or perhaps never used again.

PREPARING A FACT SHEET

Having done all this work, you might as well use it to the full. It is very useful to have a fact sheet giving the vital basics about products, staff, profits, funding, etc., which you can send to interested journalists or use in a press pack.

A fact sheet does not have to be very glossy, and it certainly should not be long. A single A4 sheet of paper will do, which can be posted or faxed immediately. Once again, keep it up to date, so that you do not waste precious time rewriting it while a journalist is waiting with a deadline looming. Unlike most Annual Reports, it should be short, accessible, and written in non-technical language.

YOUR COMMUNITY – WHO CAN YOU USE?

No business or organisation works in isolation: you have people out there who live near you, provide employees, provide competition, and care about local issues. Even if you are a national presence, such as a campaigning charity, you can identify a community of interest: other similar bodies, government officers who are for or against you, potential sponsors, and so on.

For a 'normal' organisation, working in a region, town, or city area, it is worth being aware of what is going on around you and who could be helpful to you. You may need a quote from a satisfied customer for a feature you are preparing for a trade magazine. Or you need a local sporting celebrity to front a news conference about your latest health campaign. Whatever it is, you need to have a handy list of names. You will gradually build up your own book of contacts and ideas, from:

- Reading the local papers, and noting down relevant people (such as sports stars, councillors, TV celebrities who live locally, the person who runs Age Concern in your area, etc.).
- Meeting people socially and professionally. Keep records of where and when you met the local youth leader, or secondary school head, or the parent at your child's school who is an area manager of a big company.
- Reading and listening at work. Your fellow employees will have their own interests and contacts. Also, note down the professional contacts that your organisation has with suppliers, customers, trade organisations, central bodies, etc.

- Using your library, which can provide information lists and contacts.

Remember, you need to know a name if you can, and where to find that person. Create your own filing and cross-referencing system, so that Mr Brown the local greengrocer appears under 'Customer (retail)' because your company fitted out his new-look shop; under 'Clown' because his spare-time activity is as Mr Jelly the Jolly Juggler; under 'Politics' because he is active in the Conservative Party; and, of course, under 'B' for 'Brown'.

After a few years you should have leads on just about every possible angle. So when you launch your shrimp-flavoured crisps which help prevent gum disease in a bio-degradable pack, you will know just which local dentist is a member of Friends of the Earth and is willing to dress up as a giant-sized crisp packet for a photo. Look out especially for:

- local politicians and councillors;
- heads and staff of schools and colleges;
- local celebrities, such as the home football team, or national celebrities who live locally (they may be useful for press events or photos);
- business people, Rotary members, the Chamber of Commerce;
- the voluntary sector – Citizen's Advice Bureaux, charities, youth groups, the churches;
- leisure and sports groups;
- your friends and your competitors.

It is as well to keep up on local issues, too, such as the mounting concern about the new bypass or the closing down of a secondary school. It may be that you will find useful angles; and in any case, it is rather difficult to show that you are a good member of your community if it is obvious you don't know a thing about it.

USING A PRESS PLANNER CHART

One of the easiest ways to keep control of what is going on is to have a large annual planner on the wall, solely devoted to media work. At the beginning of the year, you write down everything you can think of that could be relevant, and then you continue to add to it as ideas occur to you or events loom up. The sort of things to mark on the planner are:

- *Your organisation's events*
  the AGM
  the Annual Report
  the launch of a new service
  the opening of a new shop
  the appointment of a new director

- *National holidays and festivals*
  Easter
  Ramadan
  Diwaali
  Chinese New Year
  Bank holidays
- *Interesting days*
  Mothers' Day and Fathers' Day
  Valentine's Day
  Red Nose Day
  Budget Day
  the Derby and Grand National
  Shakespeare's birthday
  St Patrick's Day
- *Interesting events*
  the London Marathon
  the Ideal Home Exhibition
  Beaujolais Nouveau race
  Ascot, Wimbledon, Henley
  the Opening of Parliament
- *Local events*
  the County Show
  the Annual Regatta
  the football derby
- *This year's specials*
  Anniversaries (e.g. first powered flight 1903; first motor race 1894; first nuclear power station 1954; the silicon chip invented 1958; end of Second World War 1945; women in Britain got the vote 1921, etc.)
- *Local anniversaries*
  the town got its charter, the bridge was built, the school was founded
- *State visits*
- *One-off exhibitions*
- *Anything affecting your patch*
  Government White Paper
  Ministerial statements
  competitors' product launches
  trade shows
  supplements in papers or magazines on your subject (from their advance editorial list, or publications like *Advance* and PR *Planner*).

Some of this information you will know already, or can find out easily enough. Some of it will become known as the year progresses. Some of it you will find out only if you keep your eyes open: interesting anniversaries, for example, or legislation that affects your business. There is a publication called *Foresight* that lists this sort of information for 15 months ahead. And note that some national papers print anniversaries and national days at the beginning of each year and Sunday papers look at the week ahead. Write it all down. Then you will not plan your new product launch on a day when something else of national importance is happening, or on the same day as a competitor.

Also, you can plan ahead, say, for the Minister of Health's proposal to increase preventive health budgets, so that a draft news release is all ready to put out the moment the speech is made giving the specific figure the Ministry has in mind.

Lastly, national and local anniversaries may just give you the peg you need to create a story.

CASE STUDY: Snack No Longer a Turkey

A snack food manufacturer had a new product that had originally been called 'Turkey Crisps'. The launch did not go well; there was not a lot of interest even in the trade press, therefore few retailers wanted to stock it. Some bright spark decided that, as it was by then July, it would be a great idea to use the twelfth of August, the start of the grouse-shooting season in Britain, as the peg. So Turkey Crisps were relaunched as 'Grouse Chips', and of course given lots of publicity for the week of the Glorious Twelfth.

This time, both the trade press and local newspapers picked up the idea and gave a lot of coverage. (Note that the product still didn't sell – but that wasn't the fault of the publicity person!)

Also on your press plan you will put down the contacts you have with journalists, the press events, perhaps the news releases if you write only a few during a year, the meetings you have with your news gatherers in other regions or branches, and so on. Anything, in fact, that is related to your media work.

WHICH MEDIA TO USE

There is a wealth of information, education, and entertainment media. Not only are there national and local newspapers, radio and television, there are magazines (general and specialist), and trade and technical papers. In theory, you can target your news to any part of the population by choosing your media outlet. (See Chapters 5 and 6 for details.)

You should by now have some idea of your outlets. For many organisations it will be mainly the local press, with perhaps two or three specialist papers or magazines, and an occasional brush with local radio. For some, it will be the national press with local coverage for specific projects. Some organisations are interested only in their specialist press.

But for each message or campaign you should know:

- Who do I want to influence this time?
- Which papers, magazines, or programmes reach those people?

FINDING OUT

The obvious way to find out your target media is to look and listen for yourself. Go to the local newsagents and buy all the local publications; collect the free papers distributed locally; ask colleagues who live in adjacent areas to bring in their local papers. Also, watch out and collect all trade publications in your field, and ask customers, suppliers, managers, etc., which they read. Listen to local radio and television, or ask colleagues and friends to do it for you (more about that in the broadcasting section).

But maybe you are covering a very large region, or you are aiming to use all health correspondents, or your product or message has lots of different angles. Then the task can be too great for individual research and you need specialist publications, such as:

Benn's Media Directory Published in three volumes, UK, Europe, and International. It gives profiles on all media, such as readership numbers, types, and localities.

Willing's Press Guide; Hollis Press and Public Relations Guide These are both similar to *Benn's*.

PIMS Media Directory A comprehensive monthly guide to all media (but can also be bought quarterly and annually).

Publications and broadcasting are listed by place and by subject. So if you make bespoke shoes in Penzance, you can find all papers, radio and TV covering Cornwall; and you can find all national paper correspondents, freelances, and specialised papers interested in shoes, fashion, children, the disabled, small businesses, and any other angle you can think up.

Two-Ten Communications Similar to PIMS, published every two months and annually. Also on database.

Editors Published quarterly in six volumes, it gives all media outlets, plus readership profile and forthcoming special features.

Blue Book of British Broadcasting Gives full information on radio and television programmes, including target, audiences and which regions see which programmes.

PR Planner; Advance Both good for general PR info, and especially to find out what papers and magazines are going to be featuring in the future. All these publications are fairly expensive, but it's really worth finding the budget to buy a comprehensive listing like PIMS or *Two-Ten Communications* at least once a year; and one of the general public relations books like *Benn's* or *Willing's*. (See Chapter 22 for addresses.)

If you don't know which to choose, then find a friend in another organisation who can show you copies. Or you can contact the publishers and ask to see back copies or their sales pack. If you can't afford to buy, many large libraries stock some or all of these publications. If yours doesn't, then try to persuade them to.

With these invaluable reference books in front of you, have a look at what is possible. For instance, this is how *Two-Ten Communications* is organised:

Subject index, e.g.   Armed Forces

Beauty (Cosmetic Trade, Salons, Consumer Magazines)

Education

Gay magazines

Gymnastics

Pension Funds

Selling

Surfing

Tea Drinkers

Trade

Urdu magazines

Etc.

Alphabetic index of all publications

Town by town

Specialist Editors and Correspondents, e.g.

Agriculture

Business

Women

Property

News Media	Nationals
	Agencies
	London correspondents for international press and media
General interest magazines	
TV and radio	
Guildlists, e.g.	Guild of Agricultural Journalists
	Guild of Picture Editors
	Circle of Wine Writers

To show you how useful these reference books can be, here's a case study.

CASE STUDY Designer Tea

One of the leading tea producers installed expensive machinery to foil-wrap their tea. It was state-of-the-art technology but was perhaps unnecessary for their normal line, and was certainly not making a lot of economic sense.

So the idea of a new product, 'fresh' tea, was put forward. The tea leaves would be picked and vacuum packed in foil straight away, preventing them from drying out.

Whether this fresh tea actually tasted better was debatable, but maybe a market niche could be found for gourmet tea drinkers.

Who could be reached with the message via press and broadcasting? There are all sorts of possibilities:

• Potential drinkers (*Target*: style magazines, foodie magazines, in-flight and travellers' magazines. Also food and drink writers in national papers, and radio and TV food programmes. Also 'jolly' TV, such as breakfast shows or afternoon magazines. The story is 'new' tea.)

• Potential high-level employees (*Target*: specialist business and marketing publications with story of innovative management and a product that is ahead of the competition.)

- Investors, shareholders, business community (*Target*: business pages of nationals, business glossies, with story of good management and potential profits.)

- Retailers (*Target*: retail press with story of interesting and possibly successful new product.)

- Restaurants and cafés (*Target*: catering press with story of fashionable specialised product.)

- Employees and community (*Target*: local papers with both heavy and light angle along lines of 'We get it right again!').

Thus one basic story was adapted and angled to many different targets, each reaching a different group. And the media guides were able to provide an instant list of journalists and publications who might be interested in each angle

RESEARCHING PAPERS

Even if you are pretty certain where you want to put your stories, it is worth having a look at everything going first. Go out and buy a copy of every national paper, and all your local and regional papers. Also get copies of all relevant trade publications. Read them, digest them, and make notes on each of them, looking at:

BASICS
- What day is it published, and what is the deadline for copy?
- What area does it cover? And within that ostensible area, what is the core region? A very good story can sometimes fail because you take too literally a paper's proclaimed region; if your story relates to only 3% of the readers, it won't appeal.
- Does it have a particular target group of readers, by age, social class, occupation, or interest?
- How many people read it? (There will be approximately three times as many as the officially proclaimed figures.)

These basic facts will usually be covered in the advertisers' or editorial pack prepared by most publications for those who intend to place advertisements. It is worthwhile asking for one. Also use your eyes: see who is advertising and also look at the job ads, which are a very good indicator of who are the readers.

CONTENT

Let's face it, what makes the front page in one paper may not even make page 7 in another.

Look at *The Independent* on the day a royal birth is announced: their policy is to play down such matters. Compare that with the three- or four-page splash to be found in the tabloids!

The most obvious difference is between the nationals and the locals. As you'd expect, the national press will cover more international news and matters of national importance, while local papers have a local slant. However, some big regional dailies are very complex operations, and even send out their own journalists to cover major international stories.

Even with local papers, though, there will be differences in the kinds of stories they run. Some will see themselves as serious campaigning papers, and be interested in items on local educational standards and the economy and controversy over closing hospital wards. Others will favour the bright and breezy stories about battling grannies and competition winners. They tend to look for the human interest element even in larger stories. And others will relentlessly trivialise every subject.

There may be certain editorial policies in action too.

CASE STUDY Tabloid versus Comprehensive Schools

A headmaster decided he was fed up with the way a certain tabloid newspaper constantly published derogatory stories about comprehensive schools. So he offered to let a reporter stay in his inner-city school all week.

A young journalist, new to the paper, duly arrived and was very impressed during her stay. She wrote her (favourable) piece and even sent a copy to the head before submitting it to her Editor. Alas, the next day she phoned up to say that the piece would never appear: the Editor's only comment was, 'I can't print this – it says comprehensives are all right'.

SPECIAL FEATURES

There are a number of special features to look for:

- The regular articles written by columnists or correspondents. So on Tuesdays there might always be a column by 'The Health Correspondent', or on Fridays a 'Life style' page. Some papers now have complete special supplements every day devoted to Education, Business, Computer, Environment, etc.

- Occasional special supplements. These are add-in looks at 'Banking in the 1990s', or 'The Housing Market'. Local papers do them, too, on 'Training in Northumberland', or 'Agricultural Machinery'. Mostly they are there to attract advertising, but they need stories too.

- What do the 'general' columnists write about? One might have an obsession with cricket, another with local transport, another with social problems or feminist issues. Maybe their prejudices or interests could be put to use.

- Different editions. New technology means that even local dailies can have a number of local editions, so they print a core paper, with one or two pages specially aimed at each small locality.

- Events ahead. Is there a special place for events of interest coming up? It might be useful when you want to publicise in the local press your mass sign-up for smokers giving up; or in the technical press a conference hosted by your president about opportunities for marketing fish fingers in China.

- Special opportunities. Does the paper run competitions, quizzes, sponsored events? Does it like to encourage 'active' readership? If so, there may be chances for you to offer ideas, such as co-sponsoring a poetry or picture competition, or devising your own quiz, or organising a special appeal with the paper's help.

WORDS

How long are news items and feature articles? There is no point in sending press releases of 500 words if no news item is ever more than 70 words.

Count the number of words in a paragraph: a newspaper will normally have very short paragraphs because it is broken into columns. Count the number of words in a sentence: most quality papers aim for an average of 18–22 words per sentence. Generally, what is the language style? Is it bright and popular, sober and dull, full of puns, full of slang? Do they like to use quotes, and how? Some papers tend to start a story with a snappy quote if possible; others leave the quote till half way through, but then use more.

PICTURES

How are photos and graphics used? Some papers seem to use words merely to link together lots of huge photos, so that few stories appear unless they have a photo.

Certainly, many stories run only because there is a good photo. If you can identify any preferences, you have a better chance of placing a photo-linked story. Some papers like arty shots with peculiar angles or settings; some like comic relief; some like children or animals; and let's face it, some like pretty girls.

Let's also face the fact that some papers have abominable photos – the sort where everyone is lined up grinning fixedly at the camera, or some anonymous big-wig is handing a cheque to some other equally uninteresting recipient. Regard this as an opportunity not to be missed. Surely one smidgin of imagination on your part and you can't fail . . .

PEOPLE

Identify the names of journalists useful to you, by looking at the bylines. If you don't take a media directory regularly to update you on who is responsible for what, then you'll have to keep a watch yourself for changes.

Some of the names will be syndicated columnists, that is someone who writes a regular column which is sold to many different papers. Some will be freelances, especially in technical magazines. It can be useful to find good freelances; they make their living by the number of articles they can place, so it is in their interest to find the right angles for as many different publications as they can.

COMPETITORS

What sort of coverage is your competitor getting? How come their boring new ditch digger is getting the full works, while your exciting nuclear powered earth mover never gets a mention? They get headlines when they proclaim their new service for looking after pets when employees are on holiday, and you've been doing it for four years. Their company chairman retires and his entire speech is reproduced; your chairman makes a far more interesting speech to the local Chamber of Commerce and there's not a syllable.

It may be that they thought to contact the paper and you didn't, or that they have been fostering contacts for longer, or that they were just lucky in their timing. Try to learn from the type of stories covered and who is covering them, and tell yourself that if Bunswade and Co. can do it, so can you.

For each paper or magazine, prepare a file detailing all the basic information, and the names of any of their journalists you have dealings with. Also keep any particularly relevant articles.

Contact the editor or advertising manager for a list of forthcoming special editions or supplements, which will help you plan ahead.

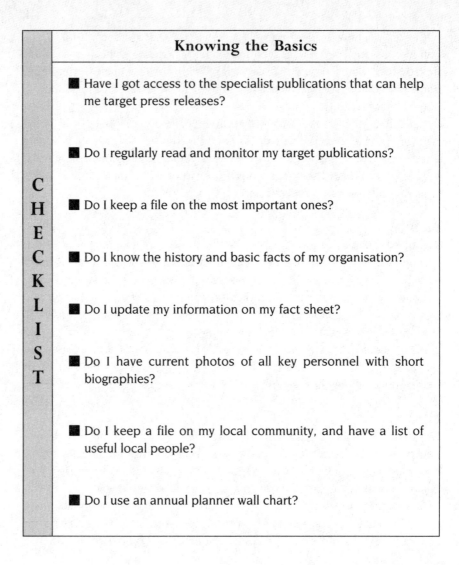

Knowing the Basics

■ Have I got access to the specialist publications that can help me target press releases?

■ Do I regularly read and monitor my target publications?

■ Do I keep a file on the most important ones?

■ Do I know the history and basic facts of my organisation?

■ Do I update my information on my fact sheet?

■ Do I have current photos of all key personnel with short biographies?

■ Do I keep a file on my local community, and have a list of useful local people?

■ Do I use an annual planner wall chart?

C H E C K L I S T

PART TWO
DEALING WITH THE MEDIA

5

The Press

- Newspapers may be national or local, popular or quality, paid-for or free.
- Magazines and trade papers can be divided into professional and trade press (relating to work), and consumer press (relating to interests or hobbies).
- News agencies such as the Press Association are very useful.
- Each publication has its own style and angle; also its own deadline, which may sometimes be way ahead of publication.
- A lot of key information can be found in the editorial or advertising packs which many publications produce.
- There are specialist publications which list titles, addresses, readership figures, and other data, of all publications by region and by subject.

WHY DO WE STILL HAVE NEWSPAPERS?

WHY indeed? Every few years there is a prediction that the end of the printed word is nigh. Either it is prophesied that we are all going to be so glued to the television screen that books and papers will die, or we are all going to be screen freaks receiving instant electronic information telling us which quiche is on offer at the local supermarket, what is happening in Chile, and what time the Steering Group Committee meeting is. According to these predictions we will doubtless be sending love letters by screen too.

Some of this may come true, but so far nothing beats a newspaper for its breadth of coverage, depth of coverage, and its easy accessibility. Even the tabloids have more information in them than any broadcast news programme, and if a quality newspaper were read out on TV or radio it would take 10 hours just to read the news section. Also you can skim and skip; go straight to the sports section; read a bit now and more later; go back and reread something interesting; cut out and keep an article …

As for using nothing but electronic data via a screen, even the most user-friendly system requires a cumbersome working through the menus to find what you want, and in any case, the beauty of a newspaper is that you don't necessarily know what you want until a headline or picture catches your eye. It is difficult to create the element of serendipity (the happy chance finding of something) from a screen because the amount of information it can display at any one time is limited.

For whatever reason, we are still enthusiastic newspaper readers. Britain ranks fifth in newspaper circulation in the world (after the USSR, Japan, the USA, and China, with larger populations). Britain is also very rich in specialist publications: altogether there are roughly 12,000 papers and magazines covering national, regional, and specialist affairs.

AN OVERALL LOOK AT NEWSPAPERS AND MAGAZINES

A newspaper or magazine contains: news, opinion, advice, entertainment, information, and advertising.

In Britain there is a split between national and local papers. The national papers cover national, foreign, and political news; the local papers cover community interests, with town-based evening papers as the most important group. However, some 'regional' papers, such as The Scotsman or The Birmingham Evening Post, are far from regional in their coverage, and will even have their own foreign correspondents reporting on international events.

There is also a split between the popular and quality press. The qualities are strong on political, industrial, and cultural news. They also cover international and financial topics. The readership is usually more 'up-market' and educated; they have large pages (called broadsheet); and the design and layout are relatively traditional and sober. The popular press is tabloid in format – 'tabloid' actually means 'compressed' and is the term used for the size of paper used for these newspapers, i.e. half broadsheet, although it is now commonly used as a generic term for the newspapers that are considered sensationalist, which are printed on this size of paper. Popular papers use big headlines, lots of photos, and a bold layout. They use stories featuring people, which may degenerate into celebrity hounding. Certain papers, like the *Daily Mail*, the *Daily Express*, and *Today* try to hold the middle ground between quality and pop press.

The final split is between the 'general' and 'specialised' papers and magazines. A general paper will be aiming at readers who live in, say, Grimsby, or Devon; or maybe at middle-class Conservatives throughout the country. But a specialised paper will be read only by a limited group of people, with a very particular interest: marketing managers, hairdressers, young girls aged 13–16, electric railway enthusiasts, whatever. Circulation may be small, but the targeting is precise. If you have something of interest to rose gardeners, a piece in two or three of the nationals might reach only 5% or so of them. But a piece in two or three specialised gardening magazines could reach 30% or 40%. It is worth having a browse around railway station or airport news stands, or a large town newsagent, to get a feel for what is on offer and what their different styles are.

THE NATIONAL PRESS

THE DAILIES

Morning daily newspapers are published six times a week. On an average day, two out of three British people over 15 read a national morning paper. Formerly, nearly all British newspapers were produced in and around Fleet Street in London, with possibly a Manchester outpost for northern editions. But new technology has ended the heyday of 'El Vino's' and 'The Street of Shame', so that both editorial and printing facilities are now scattered around London and even around the country. Each paper has a different audience and, of course, size of circulation.

Be careful of circulation figures, though. First of all, actual readership will be roughly three times the circulation figure. Secondly, a quality paper like *The Times* has a large library and reception room readership, so its content lasts a lot longer than a popular daily. Thirdly, not every part of every paper is read by every reader, so that even with a fairly specialised readership the *Financial Times* has more people reading its front page digest of general news than its financial pages.

British national papers can be ranked against social grades (which represent employment rather than income):

A   Business or professional,   *The Times*,
      civil servant, private means.   *Financial Times*
      (About 3% of the population.)

B	Quite senior people, not quite at the top. (About 13% of the population.)	*Daily Telegraph*, *The Guardian*, *The Independent*
C1	Tradesmen, non-manual workers, white-collar workers. (About 32% of the population.)	*Daily Express*, *Daily Mail, Today*
C2	Blue-collar workers, skilled and	*The Sun, Daily Miror*,
D, E	unskilled manual workers, and those on lowest level of income.	*The Star*

Or as a wit once put it, British papers can be roughly ranked:

The Times: read by people who run the country.

Daily Mirror: read by people who think they run the country.

The Guardian: read by people who think they ought to run the country.

Daily Mail: read by the wives of the people who run the country.

Financial Times: read by the people who own the country.

Daily Express: read by people who think the country ought to be run the way it was 40 years ago.

Daily Telegraph: read by people who think the country still is run the way it was 40 years ago.

The Sun and *The Star*: their readers don't care who runs the country as long as she has big tits.

Special points to remember: Daily newspapers

• A story does not necessarily have to be of 'national' interest to be in the national press, though it helps.

• Don't forget all the special sections and columns that appear weekly, which may be interested in quite local stories if they fit into the subject (e.g. education, small businesses, health, environment).

• Monday tends to be thin on news, so a press release or event timed to hit Monday editions can work better than on other days.

• Saturday often has less hard news coverage, but because of the growth in weekend leisure supplements, there may be more column inches. Check on papers' Saturday coverage – it will often be different from that during the week, either in length or content, and many broadsheets sell more copies on Saturday than on weekdays.

• Because a paper's readership is down-market, don't assume its journalists are down-market too. A reporter from the *Daily Mirror* may have just the same background, education, and politics as one from *The Independent*, so don't try to talk down to him. And if you usually have lunch at your local 'good' restaurant, he will not appreciate the cheese and pickle sandwich which you feel appropriate for his readers and thus for him.

THE SUNDAYS

The Sunday papers follow a pattern similar to the dailies, with three out of four British people over the age of 15 reading a Sunday newspaper. The *News of the World* sells five million copies, which makes it the largest Sunday paper in the world. Readership breaks down as follows:

A, B	*Sunday Times, The Observer, Sunday Telegraph, The Independent on Sunday*
C1	*Sunday Express, Mail on Sunday*
C2, D, E	*News of the World, Sunday People, Sunday Mirror*

Most national Sundays publish separate sections and a separate colour supplement or magazine.

Special points to remember: Sunday newspapers
• Sunday papers start to put their editions together on Tuesday or Wednesday. By Friday, things are more or less finalised except for hot news. So a Friday or Saturday press release will probably be too late unless it involves murder, scandal, or a lot of removed clothes (in fact, the stories you *don't* want printed …).
• The Sundays look especially for new angles or in-depth analysis of big stories of the previous week, because they are in competition with the dailies. They also look for 'exclusives'.
• If a story gets covered by a quality Sunday it will probably be covered in greater depth than it would in a daily. On the other hand, fewer stories are printed. So going for a Sunday coverage is something of a gamble.
• A solid topical or controversial story is worth offering to a Sunday on an exclusive basis.
• Most Sunday journalists have Monday off.
• A colour magazine will be in preparation 4 or 5 weeks ahead at least, so if you have a story relating to a particular event you need to give good warning.
• Financial and commercial information is especially interesting to the quality Sundays, since they have heavy business sections looking for news over the weekend that is different in some way from the dailies'.

Some PR firms use what is called the 'Friday night drop' to feed items to financial journalists about their clients after the markets have closed (this may be illegal if it is 'price sensitive' information which could affect share prices). You need not go to such lengths, but the principle is a valid one, especially since businessmen and bankers read the Sunday business sections very thoroughly.

Also a good Sunday story gets picked up by radio and TV from Saturday evening onwards. If it is an important story it will generate Sunday lunch-time 'reaction' comments, and may be used for 'follow-ups' by the Monday papers, especially if nothing much has happened over the weekend.

But if your information isn't given much prominence in the Sunday papers, it will probably be ignored by everyone else.

CASE STUDY Use of the Sundays

Half-way through the British miners' strike of 1983, once miners were beginning to drift back to work, the National Coal Board (NCB) wanted to influence more to go back each Monday morning.

So they decided to concentrate on the Sunday papers, which have a larger readership than all the national dailies put together. Only the Sunday papers were invited to send reporters to the Friday and Saturday NCB press conferences, so they carried the story first. But the other papers and broadcasting services always followed it up, adding to the impact. So on a Sunday the papers and radio and the television were all giving coverage to the management line, which would be influencing not just wavering miners but also their families. And on Monday morning, as they faced the decision whether to go in to work, their Monday paper would be presenting management's case too.

THE LOCAL PRESS

For most organisations, large and small, commercial, charitable or educational, the local press will be the main target of stories. Three out of four adults regularly read a regional or local paper, and some provincial evening papers have very large circulations (e.g. *Manchester Evening News* with over 290,000). Certain regional papers (such as *The Scotsman*) are more like nationals in both their coverage and range of readership.

There are roughly 90 morning and evening dailies, and 430 paid-for weeklies. These are dwarfed by around 950 freesheets, which are mostly weekly and financed by advertising. The first free newspaper, called the *Daily News*, was launched in Birmingham in 1984, and in the early 1990s the total circulation for free papers is over 40 million and rising.

It was the local press, rather than Fleet Street, which was the pioneer of modern newspaper technology. Journalists key in their own stories direct, and the old-fashioned compositing room has given way to phototypesetting, so local papers can be very flexible and individual. Many dailies and weeklies print several editions, changing either whole pages, individual news items, or advertisements for the different places they cover.

The regional and local press cover an amazing diversity of news. Whether you have a new product or service, an angle on a local issue, a message to plug, an effort for charity, or something to boast about, there is room for you.

MORNING DAILIES

The big morning regional papers tend to cover a mixture of national news and major items from around the region. They are read by 5.7 million people, and some of them have circulations approaching 100,000. They tend to have a middle-class or business readership.

EVENING DAILIES

They are usually more parochial in their coverage, although they will still cover national stories. Although called 'evening' the first edition will often be in the morning with further editions through the day and the main edition timed to catch people on their way home from work. Circulations can be large, mostly in the 20,000–100,000 range, though some reach 200,000 plus. The largest is the London-based *Evening Standard* with a readership of just under 500,000.

The content of an evening paper is being decided the afternoon and evening before, with only urgent or exciting new stories getting in on the day, so if you want to place something in an evening paper you may have to gamble. If you send a release to arrive on Wednesday morning, then it will probably be too late for the Wednesday evening paper. If it is picked up by a daily for Thursday, the Thursday evening paper won't want to run it unless there is some new development or angle. So if you particularly want a story in your evening paper, you may have to send a release on Tuesday evening to catch the Wednesday paper, remembering that the daily won't want it for Thursday if it has already appeared on Wednesday!

Similarly, timing a press event can be a headache if you want coverage from both dailies and evenings. Before 11.00 and the daily journalists won't want to come; after 11.00 and you're unlikely to get evening journalists unless it is a very exciting story.

WEEKLIES

Weeklies will almost exclusively cover local news and business. Their circulations tend to be small, between 5,000 and 60,000, with most about 16,000. Most towns have their own weekly, and the big cities have suburban papers, with around 430 titles in all. Many of them are published by large groups with a number of papers under their wing, both paid-for and free.

FREE NEWSPAPERS

Most homes in Britain now have one or more freesheets, or free newspapers as they prefer to be called, thudding through the letter box once a week. Some are little more than a glorified sheet of classified ads, but some are reputable papers in their own right.

For advertisers (and for you trying to get maximum coverage in your local community), they have the advantage of getting into every single house in a given area. Also, research shows that – although you might not have thought so – they are read quite thoroughly. Do a straw poll of colleagues and see how many of them at least skim through their free newspapers to see if anything interesting catches their attention – you might be surprised. So don't despise the free papers. You may get more glory from a story in *The Times*, but remember that the purpose of the exercise is to reach particular targets rather than your chairman.

Many free newspapers are very short-staffed, so they are an excellent target for a press release written in their house style, especially if there is a good photo too. The editor just does not have enough reporters or photographers to go out seeking stories, so can be very grateful if anything like a decent story comes along all ready to use.

THE LOCAL GLOSSIES

A fairly new development is that of the free glossy magazine, covering a county or large region. As with free papers, they depend on advertising to survive, though some also aim at bulk purchases to golf clubs and country hotels and the like. Their content is mostly of the huntin', shootin', and fishin' kind, aimed at the Country Set, a sort of '*Tatler* for Tyneside' feel. They do cover the business scene, need all the help they can get with material, and are a good way to reach the wealthier sections of your area.

Special points to remember: Local newspapers
• The local press want local news – whether on local issues or local people.
• They also like a local angle on a national topic, so if government legislation will affect dairy farmers, they will want to hear from local dairy farmers, not a London spokesperson.
• Many a story that ends up as a national 'exclusive' began life in a local paper.
• Local papers have a strong business element, and figures show that local businesses and traders read them carefully.
• Young people are also strong buyers of weeklies (presumably to check out on films, clubs, etc.) and the less well-off may not buy another paper.
• Many local papers use syndicated material bought from big national newspaper groups, so a regular column bylined 'By our City editor' or

'From our motoring correspondent' may well come from London and the paper doesn't have a financial or motoring correspondent at all. So it is worth checking out the specialised jobs.

• A good idea for a special supplement will often be welcomed, as these bring in the advertising revenue. One community health group proposed an article near Christmas about the various health hazards posed by frozen turkeys if not properly cooked; they gave graphic details of the effects of salmonella poisoning and stories of people whose Christmas had been ruined by frozen turkeys. This was printed flanked by advertisements for same frozen turkeys placed by all the butchers in the locality!

TRADE, TECHNICAL AND SPECIALIST PROFESSIONAL PRESS

You name it, there is a trade paper that covers it. Whether you need a publication for doctors, fish friers, apple growers, reflexologists, or nannies, don't worry because there will be one. Sometimes more than one – there are five different magazines for British undertakers, for example.

The trade press ranges in style from cheaply produced newsheets to glossy professional monthlies full of stylish photos. Strictly speaking, the trade press is read by the trade (retailers, agents, brokers); technical journals are read by technicians (electricians, builders, engineers); professional magazines are read by professionals (lawyers, doctors, architects, teachers). But generally the term 'trade press' covers all publications specially aimed at people in a particular job.

One useful distinction is between a 'vertical' and 'horizontal' publication. A vertical publication will be for all those in a particular industry – grocers, teachers, computer programmers. A horizontal publication will be for types of reader – company directors, sales people, in-house journalists – who may be working in very different industries.

Some have subscribers, which may mean their readership is not large; some have a controlled circulation, which means they are sent free to selected readers; while some are sent to members of an organisation, which ensures regular distribution but which is dependent on the size of the membership.

Many of them have very long lead times, especially the monthlies and quarterlies, so if you have an idea for a feature or an item relating to a trade exhibition or a particular season of the year, you must plan well ahead. Christmas issues tend to get planned in July, for instance, so it is no good telling *Corner Shop Quarterly* in November about your special holly-decorated buckets for the housewife with everything, because by then they'll be planning for Mother's Day, and thinking daffodils.

If in any doubt as to whom a trade publication reaches, remember the ways to find out:

- specialised publications (like *Hollis Press and Public Relations Annual*, *Benn's Media Directory*, or *Advertisers Annual*);
- the paper's advertisers' pack (sometimes called the editorial pack);
- the jobs that are advertised;
- the goods and services advertised.

SPECIALIST MAGAZINES

Once again, there are so many titles it is bewildering. Look in *Two-Ten Communications* or *Advertisers Annual* and you will find thousands of titles appealing to every segment of society: hobbyists, women, pensioners, computer freaks, athletes, airline travellers … They are sold by newsagents and bought by the general public. Many are printed in colour and use a lot of photos.

For publicity purposes they can be invaluable, because if you can hit the right angle, your news can be irresistible. They tend not to have large staffs and any one journalist will probably cover a number of fields. Also, they use freelances a lot, so you may see the same writer crop up in a number of similar magazines.

Two particular areas to remember in this category are, firstly, the women's magazines, which cover an enormous range of material from family and children's affairs to the environment and international news. And secondly, in-flight magazines, which are read by a wide range of people, especially business people.

Special points to remember: Trade press and specialist magazines
• They tend to look for:
 – news and new products;
 – informed comment on news, important topics, etc.;
 – features.
• There is great scope to become 'rent-a-pundit' (i.e. become the person journalists ask for comment on a particular subject) if you can be a source of good quotes or technical information (or at least, if you know who in your organisation can be). Let the relevant press know that you are always happy to find someone to act as spokesperson for 'Midlands solicitors' or 'Inner City primary schools' or 'Small independent dog kennels'.
• Most journalists are a pretty ill-informed lot; the exceptions tend to be found in the specialist press. A specialist reporter may actually know how a computer works, or what are the implications of the latest fall in coffee prices. So they can be great allies.

• However, because the journalist understands the technical language, don't fall into the trap of couching your release in total technical gobbledygook, leaving it to him or her to translate for the reader. So you must still angle and write any releases in a way that is suitable for the *readers*, not the specialist journalists.

• The trade press and specialist magazines are looking out for features from insiders, e.g. your woman in Prague who has made the break-through in marketing food mixers there could write an article of interest to marketing publications, white goods and electronics publications, general business magazines, etc., as well as possibly featuring in business pages of the ordinary press. (See Chapter 9 for more about organising and writing a feature article.)

• Remember the deadlines – magazines plan way ahead. Make sure you get a features and special supplement list from all the publications you might be interested in (or subscribe to PR *Planner* or *Advance*, which will list them all for you).

EXAMPLE A Typical Editorial Pack

Works Management is a monthly magazine sent free to 22,000 managers in British manufacturing industry. They have an editorial programme folder which lays out the circulation by industry, and by job title (so that one can work out that a 'typical' reader would be a works manager in electronic or mechanical engineering), but it also reaches many managing directors and is interested in food, textiles, chemicals, and many other industries.

The programme gives advertising rates and deadline for copy (one month before the publication date for ads; at least two months for editorial).

The two vital sections are:

1 The layout showing special features for the year ahead. In June 1992, for instance, the special articles were on dust and fume extraction, training MBAs, computerised maintenance, and a special report on quality. Other features and special reports during the year included: shutdown planning, health and safety training, forklifts, distance learning, flooring, roofing, and energy.

2 A section called 'The Editorial Opportunities' in which the editor positively encourages people to get in touch:

'We take considerable time and trouble to find interesting case histories which illustrate, in managerial language, the quantifiable benefits of particular techniques, products and services.'

You can capitalise on these editorial opportunities by suggesting story themes, supplying relevant application stories and acting as a source of expert quotes.

So there it is – an editor of a publication actually begging for you to tell him about your wonderful doings. There are many other publications who are equally keen to hear from you, if your story or service is at all relevant to their readers.

THE NEWS AGENCIES

There are very few newspapers that do not use news agencies for at least some of their material, especially international news. The Big Four western-based agencies (Associated Press, United Press International, Agence France Presse, and Reuters) collect news from all over the world and distribute it to newspapers, broadcast media, government agencies, and embassies. Their services reach a world total circulation of 450 million, and Reuters alone processes up to five million words a day of news-related text through London.

Within Britain, however, there is also a national news agency called the 'Press Association' (PA) which was set up by regional and local papers to act as a service for them. The PA supplies UK press with home news 'down the wire' and they have their own network of journalists and specialist correspondents.

The system works in two ways. Firstly, someone in the regions picks up an interesting or urgent news story and sends it back to London from where it is sent to other national and regional papers. So it is worth discovering who is your local PA person, because he or she can gain you wider coverage.

Secondly, PA will cover national stories or specialist stories from London, and either inject a local angle (in covering a conference, for instance, giving both the general story and a selection of quotes from people of interest to different regions) or leave it to the local papers to find their own local angle.

They run a big office in Fleet Street, with news reporters, a City Desk, and all the normal selection of specialised correspondents.

There are also other smaller or local news agencies, which you will find in publications like *Hollis* or *Benn's* or in your local Thomson phone directory.

THE DAILY ROUTINE

For a daily morning paper, the normal routine goes like this:

9.30 a.m.   Copy tasters and the news editor start to look at the news that has come through overnight. They take phone calls from correspondents, and skim press handouts, eliminating most of them. The night duty editor will brief them on anything of interest and tell them if any reporters on the night team have been sent off to cover stories.

10.30 a.m.   The morning editorial conference is held. The editor meets all the section heads to decide which stories are going to be covered and how. They work from the diary, which lists all events happening that day; from wire sources; from radio and television; and from their correspondents. Each editor outlines the main plans for the day, and probable lead stories are decided on. Reporters and photographers are then allocated tasks.

11.00 a.m.   The reporters are getting briefed on the angles and probable length of the stories they have been given. Then they might do some background research or phone calls, before leaving the office to go and visit sources or events.

12.30 p.m.   Most reporters are out, but there are people around to continually monitor news coming in, and to receive phoned-in copy. Specialist correspondents will be filing their reports, as well as feature writers, reviewers, etc. The sub-editors will be working on wire reports, and any copy as it is received.

3.30 p.m.   Many of the journalists will be back, checking out facts or waiting for sources to send them comments or quotes. In most modern newspaper offices, each journalist will have his or her own computer terminal so that copy can be sent directly to the graphics workstation to be set up for the actual page. The graphics team will have been preparing maps and diagrams, as well as preparing the overall layout.

4.00 p.m.   The pictures editor is deciding on which photos to use, and how to crop or enlarge them. As well as traditional methods, photowire transmitters can be used to receive photos down telephone lines from anywhere in the world.

5.00 p.m.   The final editorial conference meets, to decide which stories will make the front page. This conference is larger than the morning one, since by now the final shape of the paper, including advertising, leaders, features, photos, letters, and news, is getting fixed. But there is always room for last-minute changes if something more important happens.

6.30 p.m.   All copy is filed. The sub-editors are checking, editing, shortening or lengthening. They are also writing the headlines. They work with the photos and typefaces, to create the most attractive layout. This is mostly done electronically nowadays.

7.00 p.m.   Computer printouts present columns of copy. Pictures and advertisements are cut out manually and the whole page is pasted up. Whole pages will be transmitted to the printer, often electronically. Printing may take place in another city, or even another country.

10.30 p.m.   The paper goes to bed, but the night editor has his team on hand to watch for any changes in the news, and will if necessary completely revamp the front page for the later editions. He or she will also monitor other rival papers, ready to brief the editor next morning.

THE ROUTINE OF EVENING AND WEEKLY PAPERS

All papers follow a similar routine to the morning dailies, but with a different schedule. The so-called evening papers in fact have their first editions coming out mid-morning, so their daily cycle runs from mid-afternoon for the first editorial conference, through till about 10.00 next morning for the final one. Most of their news will have been decided upon by late evening, though of course they remain flexible for big stories, and update their editions, until the final one timed to catch people on the way home from work.

A weekly usually publishes on Thursday or Friday, so they are setting outlines for features and 'soft' stories on Friday or Monday, and working frenetically on Wednesday or Thursday.

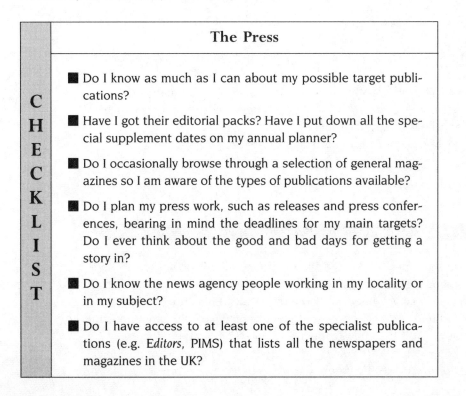

The Press

CHECKLIST

■ Do I know as much as I can about my possible target publications?

■ Have I got their editorial packs? Have I put down all the special supplement dates on my annual planner?

■ Do I occasionally browse through a selection of general magazines so I am aware of the types of publications available?

■ Do I plan my press work, such as releases and press conferences, bearing in mind the deadlines for my main targets? Do I ever think about the good and bad days for getting a story in?

■ Do I know the news agency people working in my locality or in my subject?

■ Do I have access to at least one of the specialist publications (e.g. *Editors*, PIMS) that lists all the newspapers and magazines in the UK?

6

Radio and Television

- Just like newspapers, radio and television programmes have their own style and audiences.
- Stories may be either national or local, hard news or soft features.
- The most useful contact for radio programmes is the producer or the reporter (who is often a freelance).
- The most likely contact for television is a researcher.

THE ELECTRONIC AGE

HOW do most people get their information? Like it or not, more and more people get their news from television and radio rather than anywhere else. In a survey undertaken by the Health Education Authority in 1991, for instance, 40% of people said they got medical information mostly from television, 30% from newspapers, and only 8% from their doctors.

The average adult watches 25 hours' television a week, and listens to the radio for 20 hours a week. Certain programmes, such as Britain's

Independent Television News (ITN) *News at Ten* and BBC Radio 4's *Today*, attract huge audiences, so that if you are lucky (or unlucky) enough to get on the evening news programmes, at least half the population will have heard of your success or ghastly failure.

Yet many people looking for publicity seem to regard broadcasting as the icing on the cake. This may be just fear or it may be that getting a story on TV or radio seems to be so difficult compared to getting one in the press.

DEALING WITH A DIFFERENT ANIMAL?

You're not really dealing with a different animal once you meet broadcasters. Their main needs are the same as newspapers and magazine journalists' needs: exciting, lively, relevant news that will make people listen or watch the programme, rather than go off to make a cup of tea or change channels.

The main differences between the broadcasters and the press are:

- **Actuality** – the sense of 'being there'. At its most dramatic it is a live report from a war zone; at its dullest it is the thousandth political report from Downing Street with a shot of Number 10 in the background.
- **Immediacy** – getting the news first. Even an evening paper with three or four editions has some time-lag between an event and its reportage. But a radio reporter can telephone through a description that could be on air at once, and an ENG (Electronic News Gathering) camera crew can set up a live television link. Even overseas news can be reported as it happens, now that portable satellite dishes can be set up anywhere, even in the Arabian desert or Afghan mountains.
- **Pace** – the snappiness, the punch, of broadcasting. The average news item on television is 30–90 seconds; on radio, 10–25 seconds. A so-called 'depth' interview will be a maximum of three minutes. So you won't get time for a detailed analysis of your arguments, or a list of the attractions of your product: if you get on at all, you'll be off again before you realise it.

However, just as there are different styles of newspaper and magazine, there are different styles of radio and television. A common fallacy is to think 'A radio interview!' without remembering that it's one thing to be door-stepped by a radio news reporter wanting a quick incisive comment on a potential strike, and another to be in a studio engaged in a jolly chat (sandwiched by pop records) about finding out your family history.

This chapter deals specifically with British broadcasting, but the types of programme will be the same in most other countries.

ANALYSING BROADCASTING

Whether radio or TV, most programming is organised into units, each one completely self-sufficient: news and current affairs, science and features, music and arts, documentaries and features, light entertainment, sport, drama. Of course, local radio won't have the same commitment to drama as BBC Radio 4, but you'll find at least a nod in all those directions in most broadcasting organisations.

For publicity purposes, however, it is really more useful to cut things up in a different way: national versus local; hard news versus features and music.

That's because you have to remember your target. First, that means knowing whether what you want to say is of local or national interest. If it's local, then plug the local for all its worth; if national, go for the national statistics and importance.

Second, is the news hard or soft? Hard news is topical, dramatic, maybe controversial; it will go on news bulletins, current affairs programmes, sports magazines. Soft news is general, often non-topical, personal; it will appear on chat shows, magazine programmes, specialist programmes.

NATIONAL AND LOCAL TELEVISION

NATIONAL TELEVISION

This is BBC 1 and 2; Channel 4 (composed of input from the regional companies and from independent producers); and the ITV companies (who share a core of programmes, but also have their own local programming). There is also breakfast television. Lastly, there is satellite and cable television.

LOCAL TELEVISION

This comprises the regional ITV (Independent Television) companies doing their own regional thing, especially with news magazine programmes; and the BBC with its rather sparse local news bulletins in each of its regions. Most local news is between 5 and 10 minutes long daily, with perhaps half an hour a week for a more 'local current affairs' format.

There are also the more specialist local programmes, which might, for example, have a youth and entertainment angle giving a 'what's on' guide and introducing local bands.

This breakdown illuminates why it is difficult to get on television: there's very little space for local comment and views, and even the commercial stations with a supposedly local base have their eyes all the time on the main scheduling which brings in the big advertising. So if you have a news story, it will probably have to be quite big to make it. And if it's a soft story, you're competing nationwide.

NATIONAL AND LOCAL RADIO

NATIONAL RADIO

In the early 1990s this means BBC Radios 1 to 5, though national commercial radio is on its way, with Classic FM for starters. As you'd expect, they aim to reach a national audience, and therefore look for items, stories, and documentaries that will be relevant, or at least interesting, to everyone. But there are the specialist programmes, of which more below.

LOCAL RADIO

These can be BBC or commercial. Also there are the community stations, which are growing, and hospital and student radio stations.

There are roughly 38 local BBC stations and 100 commercial stations in the early 1990s. Each local station has a core region in which is concentrated the bulk of its listeners. You can find out where it is from *The Blue Book of British Broadcasting*, or if you are listening to a commercial station note the geography of the advertisements.

The geographical heartland is local radio's main interest, and it is bad luck if you are situated on the margins – your story will have to be very good to be used. But if you are usefully situated, then your local story – whether an export success or an interesting anniversary or a controversial campaign – will be what they want.

Also, local radio stations have a legal duty to broadcast both local and youth-oriented material, as a certain percentage of their output.

Community radio generally has a much smaller target audience – not just a particular geographical area, but a particular sort of person in mind. Listeners may be a particular ethnic group or lovers of 'easy-listening' music or a particular age. This can be very useful if you have a particular group you want to reach, such as Afro-Caribbeans or traditional jazz fans.

Similarly, many hospitals have their own radio stations. These are mostly filled by record requests from or for patients, but they also do interviews and have guests. And large campuses will have a student radio station. If you're lucky, would-be journalists anxious to practise their reporting skills before applying to the BBC will be running the campus radio at the time you need it. But don't forget, the personnel will change from year to year.

REACHING ABROAD BY RADIO

There are three useful outlets if you have stories that you want to promote outside Britain:
- BBC External Services;
- The COI (Central Office of Information);
- British Forces Broadcasting Service (BFBS).

BBC WORLD SERVICE

The best-known radio service in the world is the BBC External Services which operates out of Bush House in London. It includes the World Service which broadcasts in English 24 hours a day, and the particular regional and foreign language sections (from Arabic to Urdu) which generally broadcast for a number of hours only.

It is funded by the Foreign and Commonwealth Office, so has a brief to present Britain to the world. Thus it has programmes that act as a show-case for British technology or business. However, the glowing reputation of the BBC around the globe is based on the other facet of the External Service; its balanced and impartial presentation of news and current affairs. This was really laid down during the Second World War, when the BBC (unlike the Axis broadcasting services) reported the Allies' losses and set-backs as well as their successes. People believed the BBC, and the ethos and the reputation has continued.

Listening to the World Service news can be a salutary experience: Britain's affairs will often come very low down in importance, and we get a global assessment of world events rather than a British or even European one.

Bush House broadcasts drama, sport, music, and speech programmes. The World Service looks for items that will both interest British expatriates (so they can be quite parochially 'British') or be of world interest, such as international organisations or research. The specialist departments, such as the African Service or the language services, obviously look for material relevant to their particular audience who will usually be non-British.

THE CENTRAL OFFICE OF INFORMATION (COI)

The COI is another government department. Its main job is to promote official information and liaise with other government departments on how to get messages across. So it will be in charge of anti-litter campaigns or safety-belt films in the cinema.

Of particular interest, though, is the Overseas Radio department. Their job is to make radio interviews and programmes which go mostly to liaison officers in British embassies around the world, who then try to place them in local radio stations. So any export success, or new technology, or research relevant to another country is of interest to them. They empha-sise the positive, so an interview with someone from the COI will never be a frightening experience.

BRITISH FORCES BROADCASTING SERVICE (BFBS)

The BFBS exists for the British forces and their families overseas. They have stations located abroad (especially in Germany and Cyprus) and also a central focus in London where tapes are prepared and sent abroad to be broadcast locally.

Their atmosphere is Radio 2-ish, with lots of music, record requests and jolly chat. But they do interviews of all sorts, about anything that might interest men, women, and children in the Forces, which could include books, education, sport, new consumer items, environmental campaigns, etc. Obviously anything with a military angle will go down well, too.

REACHING ABROAD BY TELEVISION

With the advent of satellite television, all sorts of new possibilities exist to get your message abroad. In the early 1990s these are the main British outlets:

- BBC World Service News
- British Satellite News
- Visnews
- Worldwide Television News (WTN).

BBC WORLD SERVICE NEWS

Since 1992 the BBC has broadcast a television news service which is similar in style to World Service radio, with bulletins every hour. It is beamed out by satellite to subscribing television stations. The main concern is news that will be interesting world-wide, so it has to be a pretty big story.

BRITISH SATELLITE NEWS

This is run by the Foreign and Commonwealth Office (FCO) and has a remit to promote 'positive' British news (superseding what used to be done by the Central Office of Information TV and Films Division). The material is prepared in London and sent by satellite to be broadcast on foreign television stations.

The FCO also runs a features section (UK *Today*), which looks for success or technology stories that will be interesting to foreign television (and can be fairly local for one particular place).

VISNEWS AND WTN

These two organisations are news agencies, selling news and sport material to over 600 broadcasting stations around the world. Visnews began in 1957 and is owned by Reuters, the BBC and several Commonwealth broadcasting organisations. WTN began in 1967 and is owned by ITN, ABC (American Broadcasting Company), and the Nine Network of Australia.

Both Visnews and WTN also act as sources for background information, such as library pictures of a town before an earthquake destroyed it.

TYPES OF RADIO PROGRAMME

Just as you need to research newspapers and magazines, you need to listen to programmes. They have their own style and content.

The hard news programmes are looking for immediacy and general interest and often controversy. If they want something, they'll usually want it NOW, and once the particular day or week has passed, the story will be dead.

Soft news programmes are interested in specialist items, or jolly up-lifting interviews, or advice that can be vaguely linked to a topical event. They want something relevant to their particular audience, whether it is middle-aged housewives or professionals in community health.

Here are the common types of radio programme which are of particular interest to someone seeking publicity.

NEWS

A typical radio bulletin will last around 2–4 minutes, with each item lasting about 15 seconds. Most radio news will be presented by the newsreader, but important items will usually have a 'soundbite', either a reporter on the spot telling us what has happened or a very short quote (10–15 seconds) from an appropriate person. The reporter will phone in a report or send it down the internal lines from one studio to another. Important ongoing stories (a big fire, or an industrial dispute) are covered by a radio car which is a direct mini-studio.

The BBC have their own internal news agency called the General News Service, for both radio and TV, which relays important news to 200 teleprinters and a computerised system.

A service called Rip 'n' Read makes complete summaries of national and international news for immediate broadcast. Commercial radio uses IRN (Independent Radio News) for news reports. IRN works from a central base in London, with many stringers and freelances working for them.

CURRENT AFFAIRS

A wide variety of programmes come under this heading, from Radio 4's *Today* every weekday morning, to local affairs round-ups on local radio. Such programmes usually look at news in more depth, which in radio terms means interviews or panel confrontations. They will be looking for topicality, i.e. some news peg that they can hang an interesting item on to, but not necessarily always 'serious' stuff. In fact, sometimes a light-hearted item jollies things up.

MAGAZINE

These range from the news end of the spectrum (*Financial World Tonight*) to the soft feature (BBC World Service's *Outlook*). Magazine programmes like this tend to have a presenter linking items, who may perhaps do studio interviews as well, which will be relatively long (2–4 minutes). The rest of the programme will be either location interviews or 'featurettes' (a mini-report with at least two interviewees and a linking commentary, lasting about 2–5 minutes). The outside recordings will often be done by free-lances, either from their own ideas or commissioned by the producer.

SPECIALIST

If you are working in a particular field then these will be of interest. They are magazine programmes generally, but with a specific audience in mind: anglers, parents with schoolchildren, the disabled, business people.

STRIP SHOW

Less exciting than they sound! The classic strip show is *The Jimmy Young Programme* on Radio 2. Records are broken up by studio guests, weather reports, recipes, anecdotes, etc. The format is usually quite light, though that doesn't mean serious topics won't appear.

Strip shows are fairly cheap, and can be a great way to promote something, since an interviewee will usually get at least 3 or 4 minutes to say his or her bit, and with any luck, maybe even more after the next record . . . The presenters on strip shows are usually DJs rather than journalists, so questions tend to be pretty obvious and down-market. They won't often have time to do any research before the programme, so questions will come off the top of their heads.

This doesn't mean interviewees can relax totally, however. The questions will tend to be of the 'I'm just a simple sort of bloke, but . . .' variety, which can sometimes be the hardest to answer.

The vital thing in a strip show is to keep it lively and jargon-free. Someone interesting will be given the mike; someone who drones will be continually interrupted since the presenter will be anxious to keep things pacey.

One rather disconcerting aspect of a one-man or one-woman radio programme (especially in local radio) is that the interviewer will be setting up the next record, writing the intro for the next guest, stacking the commercials, and making the coffee, at the same time as interviewing. It can be very disconcerting to talk to someone's back.

PHONE-INS

The cheapest form of broadcasting: one presenter, a couple of telephone lines, and that's it. Many phone-ins like to have a studio 'expert' to field the answers. The format is then an introductory chat between presenter and guest ('Explain to me, Cynthia, exactly what being a school nurse is like') for anything up to 20 minutes, followed by questions from callers

('What should I do about my son's head lice?'). The style is relaxed, helpful, and usually the guest will be protected from time wasters or arguers by the presenter, who tactfully steps in if necessary.

As with a strip show the 'expert' has to have the knack of putting things simply but not patronisingly. It is wise to have a pad of paper handy to write down names of callers and the outline of their question or problem. Refer to them by name as the question is answered, and later too ('Your difficulty with the rottweiler, Mrs Smith, has a solution similar to Mr Gaslop's problem a few minutes ago . . .').

DOCUMENTARIES

A documentary programme will be a one-off or part of a series. They usually last either 15 or 30 minutes. The commonest format is to link up snippets of interviews done on location with a commentary in the studio. Sometimes the interviewees will get quite a long time (one minute or so) before the presenter continues from the studio; more often, however, the pace is kept up with short links and short clips (15–30 seconds). Sometimes the studio is not used at all, but everything is done on location without linking commentary, and the audience makes the connections.

Those taking part in a documentary are usually approached by the producer or interviewer because they fit the bill (a local women's group; an oil company; leader of the Campaign to Save the Natterjack Toad).

TYPES OF TELEVISION PROGRAMME

Television is complicated by the need to provide pictures as well as words. Everything is far more cumbersome and expensive. A radio reporter can interview, edit, and even broadcast all by him or herself; a TV interview requires at least three people to take the pictures, plus a specialist videotape or film editor, a sound mixer, and a whole team of production people to get it on air.

Like radio, there are different types of programme of particular interest to press people.

NEWS

Television news usually lasts between 5 and 30 minutes, although the Channel 4 News on weekend evenings luxuriates in nearly an hour. Some are national bulletins; others are regional news. They will have one or two presenters, with general reporters and specialist correspondents doing location work.

BBC TV News is serviced by the same internal agency as radio news – the General News Service. In addition, each BBC region has its own newsroom, which is responsible for the local news bulletins.

ITN is an autonomous news service, feeding news to ITV regions. They have teams in the North and Midlands, but mostly operate from London, sending out teams and equipment to the story wherever it is.

Like any news operation, television news works to a very tight schedule. Once a story is identified as being potentially interesting, not just a reporter has to be assigned to it, but also a film crew. This takes organisation, so when the news editor makes a plan, everyone knows it may be scrapped, since it is easier to call off coverage than to lay it on at the last moment.

The criteria are: importance, credibility, and actuality. A really important story will be broadcast without any sound or visual element, though the news team will try desperately to provide it, even if it is only library footage. But most stories, especially for television news, will stand or fall by their actuality: is there an eye-witness? Is there film of the defendants being bundled into court? Is there a spokesperson who can sum up the message in 15 seconds? The better the picture, the more likely that the story will end up on air.

As sound or picture tape comes in to the newsroom, stories move up and down the running order. The final order will not be decided until a few minutes before broadcast, and sometimes things will even be changed during the programme. So when a news broadcaster says 'I need it NOW', it may well be the truth.

CURRENT AFFAIRS

The flagship current affairs programmes like BBC 2's *Newsnight* or ITV's *World in Action* are similar to a news programme. They react to whatever is topical that day, but examine the news in depth with 'experts' of various sorts giving their opinion. Such programmes will be under time pressure; they will also look for the controversial or even confrontative angle. Other current affairs programmes, like BBC 1's *Breakfast Time* are much more relaxed about their 'newsiness', and are quite happy either to interview a politician on the latest legislation or an actress about her kiss 'n' tell book.

SPECIALIST

There are plenty of specialist television programmes: for black people, young people, anglers, gardeners, parents, financiers, etc. They will normally look for a combination of the topical ('What's new at the Caravanning Exhibition?') and the soft ('An interesting nursery which specialises in herb gardens . . .').

Items will normally be quite long (2–6 minutes) with actuality footage important. They often don't like too much studio time.

DOCUMENTARIES

As with radio documentaries, the content of most television documentaries is determined by the production team. If the programme is looking at, say, the tobacco industry, the team will decide on the overall shape and angle of the programme, and then go out to get interviews that will fit (a community health doctor to talk about drug effects; an advertising agency to reveal how smoking ads prop up most glossy magazines; a political lobbyist). They will choose interviewees by reputation, recommendation, or because they have used them before.

However, if the idea comes from a particular source (a local zoo manages to interest regional television in a behind-the-scenes documentary) there's obviously a better chance that the source can influence things.

HOW BROADCASTING IS ORGANISED

In one way it is easier to deal with radio and television than a big newspaper, because you can find out who is responsible for which programme. There's no overall editor as on a newspaper, just individual editors or producers in charge of particular slots. Even the newsroom tends to be a more compact group; though there will be a news editor, the team will often be smaller and more recognisable than a newspaper's newsroom.

The way it is organised is like this:

Heads of departments Glorified beings, their job is to oversee the strategy, create schedules, and hire and fire staff.

Commissioning editors and senior producers They have overall responsibility for a series, such as BBC 1's *Panorama* or Radio 4's *Woman's Hour*. They agree outlines, budgets, staffing, and forward planning.

Producers and editors They are the key people in actually making a programme. They choose the team, identify the main ideas, edit, and get the programme on air. They are important, but also very busy, so it can be difficult to make contact with them.

Directors They organise filming, being in charge of location or studio work, and the video or film editing process. A director will usually be an aspirant producer, unless it is a drama production, in which case the director is the more important person since he or she is in charge of the whole artistic side.

Reporters and presenters Contrary to popular belief, presenters, however well known their faces, usually have very little power over whether a story goes on air. They tend to sit in the studio being fed scripts or interviewees, and can make only minor changes.

Reporters have a lot more power. They work with researchers or directly with the producer to cover a story, deciding on the news angle and who to go and interview. The specialist correspondents are very experienced journalists, and well worth cultivating if you can.

Researchers They really only exist in television, but are the single most important people to identify if you want TV publicity. They do all the donkey-work in identifying interviewees, finding locations, getting the briefings, checking the facts, and generally getting together all the information needed by producers, directors, and reporters. They are vital links, since if the producer decides he wants an interview with a local employer about whether local 17-year-olds can read and write properly, he will tell the researcher to find the right person. The researcher then recommends someone. The more newsy the programme, the more pressure the researcher will be under.

Production assistants In television, production assistants (PAs) are usually female, and aspiring to greater things. Meantime, she is dogsbody – typist, organiser, timing film shoots, booking hotels . . . In radio, the term PA can be used instead of 'studio manager', who is in charge of studio recording and broadcasting. They are an important part of the programme and often move on to become producers.

HOW A RADIO PROGRAMME IS PUT TOGETHER

Let's take a daily programme like BBC Radio 4's *Today*. There is an overall editor, and a team of 'editors of the day', who are responsible on any particular day for the programme. Each editor will have a certain number of items which can be prepared in advance for his or her programme. These are taken 'from the diary', and may be about a big sporting event or the launch of a campaign or a response to a ministerial speech.

Staff reporters or freelances are sent to cover these stories in advance, either doing one-to-one interviews or featurettes (mini documentaries). This material is timed and an introduction is written for each. Other diary stories are set up, arranging for studio interviewees to come on the morning of broadcast.

In the 24 hours before broadcast, the editor of the day is on constant alert for news stories that can be used. Radio and television is monitored; news services like Reuters and Press Association are scanned; and specialist correspondents will phone in with any hot tips. Reporters are on shift to go and cover any late-breaking story, or to do quick research on who would be the right person to bring in to the studio to do live interviews about something that has happened. They may be phoning hotels to find where a visiting dignitary is staying; or phoning hospitals to track down a salmonella expert willing to talk.

By around 10.00 p.m. a running-order has been organised, with a provisional list of items and live interviews. This will change during the night if necessary. Even during the programme things may change, should a studio guest not appear, or an interview runs over or under its expected time.

The presenters will appear two hours before the programme goes out, to look over the items, rewrite the links, and prepare for the live interviews. *Today*'s presenters are experienced, influential journalists in their own right, and make suggestions about the content and style of the programme.

Once *Today* is on the air, the editor may change or revamp things, either talking through headphones to the presenters, or passing them the typed introduction to a just-arrived item.

Guests are ushered in during the pre-recorded items, and may or may not have time to chat to the presenter before going live. Everything is carefully estimated to the last second, and even as the programme is going out the editor will be deciding which items to shorten or cut altogether in favour of something more interesting. Finally, it all comes to a close, there's a sigh of relief, and a 'Thank you, everyone'.

HOW A TELEVISION PROGRAMME IS PUT TOGETHER

A news or current affairs programme for television will not be so very different from the *Today* programme described above, though it will be more complicated. There will have to be more pre-selection of items, since a camera crew is far more expensive than a radio reporter with a tape recorder. Also library footage has to be found, satellite time booked, and rehearsals are more fraught because words and pictures have to match perfectly.

So let's look instead at a documentary series for prospective students on how to choose a subject, apply for a university or polytechnic place, find accommodation, etc.

The idea will first be mooted at a departmental meeting, and a producer assigned. He or she will have a team of one or two researchers, a production assistant, and maybe a director. The outline for each programme is decided, and the researchers start to look for people and locations. They phone up any contacts they have in the appropriate area and talk to them about the facts. They get names of other people with expertise who might be good on camera. If an interview seems likely, they visit the location and decide on where to film. Finally, they look at library footage and stills to fill in visual gaps.

The producer and researcher together write a shooting script. This includes anything the presenter will say to camera on location, and the particular shots that the film crew are expected to get (such as a scene of milling freshers arriving at the station on the first day of term). They prepare a timetable and the filming and interviewing is done.

The film and interviews are edited, any commentary that goes with a film segment is recorded, and then it is all put together into a final script. Everything that will be said is on the right-hand side; everything that will be seen is on the left.

Everything moves into a proper studio, probably for a whole day. In the morning, the presenter rehearses the lines and moves, the camera operators rehearse their shots, and the production team rehearse the mixing together of the pre-packaged bits with the studio bits. In the afternoon, everything is recorded, without stopping if possible, on to a final master tape including the opening and closing credits. Any audience or guest participation will be timed to fit in with the already prepared segments, and the presenter will be expected to keep to the exact second.

The programme is then stored until broadcast.

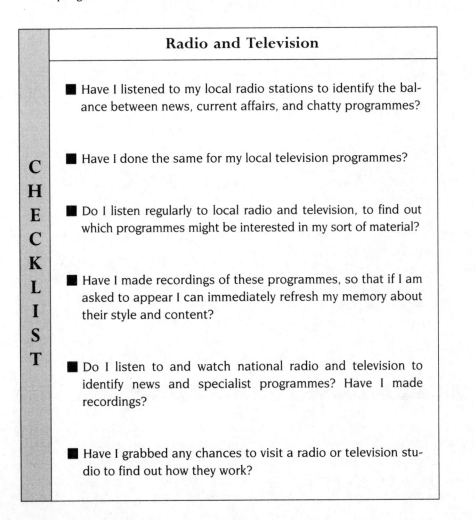

Radio and Television

CHECKLIST

■ Have I listened to my local radio stations to identify the balance between news, current affairs, and chatty programmes?

■ Have I done the same for my local television programmes?

■ Do I listen regularly to local radio and television, to find out which programmes might be interested in my sort of material?

■ Have I made recordings of these programmes, so that if I am asked to appear I can immediately refresh my memory about their style and content?

■ Do I listen to and watch national radio and television to identify news and specialist programmes? Have I made recordings?

■ Have I grabbed any chances to visit a radio or television studio to find out how they work?

7

Getting to know Journalists

- Journalists are human, too; they include the good, the bad, and the ugly.
- They have a job to do, and most of the time their interests will coincide with yours.
- They are looking for 'newsworthy', topical, and attributable stories, preferably with an individual touch.
- They are under pressure of tight deadlines.
- They need you as a source as much as you need them for publicity.
- Find the journalists most involved with your sort of story, and talk to them.
- Keep up regular contact, and say thank you whenever you can.

WHAT MAKES A JOURNALIST TICK

THESE are some of the words that people use to describe journalists: unreliable, pushy, callous, trivialising, sensationalist, cynical, unreasonable about deadlines, antagonistic. Yet journalists have friends and families, so they can't really be the complete monsters that this list evokes. So what is it about them or their job that gives this impression?

First of all, journalists – contrary to popular opinion – are human, too. They have their ups and downs, good days and bad days, and will react to being criticised or being praised like everyone else. Having said that, there may be a certain sort of person who is attracted to journalism as a career. Most of us are aware that journalists are busy, rushed, on the move, and have no time for the niceties. Of course, it suits journalists to say the job makes them that way, but people who want to work in newspapers (new reporters especially) are not usually anglers in their spare time.

They tend to be people who were good at exams at school because they work better under pressure (often last-minute swots, because they only concentrate when there is a deadline looming). They will be wonderful at assimilating things quickly, but less good at the long-haul effort; interested in lots of things, but perhaps with no time for a hobby of their own. They will rush to buy a newspaper on holiday, in case some story is breaking. The rationale for this is 'I must keep up so I will be able to pick up immediately once I get back', but it is really a need for a news fix. The result of all this is that many journalists take a pride in being under pressure, and in some instances manufacture it because otherwise they just can't get the adrenalin going. There are very, very few who will sit down and write a feature article today if their deadline is next week.

The other thing about journalists that outsiders tend to find alien, is the angle with which they view the world. Events are evaluated for 'interest' rather than worthiness, and if a journalist is fed up with a story because he or she has heard it twice before, then the assumption is that the general public is fed up with it too.

Life tends to be lived at an intense pace, with enormous saturation in something for a day or two, but then that topic is dropped completely. So it can sometimes be difficult for someone in journalism to make connection with a person or an organisation which works slowly, steadily, 'boringly' towards one goal. Hence an obsession with the 'new'. And with 'newsworthiness', that can come across as callousness, so that a 'good' day is one with a really horrendous disaster. The Gulf War in 1991 was a 'superb' war, because it increased the sale of papers and the viewing figures, and gave lots of scope for all the things reporters like: action and people and maps and pictures and human interest.

Of course, not all journalists fit this description, but there do tend to be traits in common. They also have things in common with people in other jobs: they don't like getting told off or being criticised or being led astray. They also respond well to praise or thanks or genuine helpfulness or just seeing a face they know at an event. If a journalist likes somebody then he or she will often be more considerate and helpful than towards someone who is arrogant, rude, or a lying toad. In fact, to reiterate, journalists are people, too.

HOW A JOURNALIST SEES THE JOB

A journalist has a job to do, and an editor carefully watching to see that the job is done. The main concerns are:

1 **To get the same story as everyone else** Editors monitor other similar papers and publications, and they want to know why a particular story has appeared elsewhere and not in their paper. A journalist who files a story, and then discovers a missed vital fact or has failed to get a quote which someone else has got, is told off.

So journalists are keen to get the same facts, quotes, and handle to a story as the opposition. This is one reason they move in packs, to keep an eye on everyone else. You will also often see a little huddle after a press conference, when the reporters get together and agree on the main significance of what they have just heard. (This is done in a fairly joking and informal way, but it is done all the same.)

CASE STUDY Getting the Story

During a big strike in the 1980s, there was a succession of meetings between the industry's management and the trade unions. There was tremendous competition to get the latest comment, and reporters and broadcast crews would be sent to the locations even before the meetings began, to nobble those arriving.

After a time, both sides in the dispute agreed to hold secret talks to keep the press at bay. This ploy was only moderately successful, because motorbike despatch riders were used to discover the venues, and the news pack would also watch each other's movements. As the meetings finished, there would be a desperate scramble to get comment – a number of times people got pushed, tables were turned over – until finally someone broke an arm.

Charges of press 'harassment' were made; but in the end, those involved in the talks gave in to the realities, and organised proper press conferences after each day's talks. This did not totally stop the doorstep gang, but eased the pressure, since the journalists involved knew they would at least get the same story as everyone else, whereas before their fear had been that they would have to return with nothing.

---

2 **To get a different story from everyone else** The ultimate different story is A Scoop, which all cub reporters dream of. Oh, to be the one who

reveals the scandal in the Town Hall, or the marriage plans of the current pop star! Usually it is more a matter of getting an extra angle on a current story, or a different quote, or a better photo; something to add individuality to the basic facts.

3 **To file the story in time** The most wonderful article is no good if it is delivered after the deadline. Yesterday's story is dead today, because other papers will have already used it.

Deadlines have a reality to a newspaper, which is governed by that daily or weekly or monthly cycle. Of course, if something amazing happens after the normal deadline, the deadline will be moved to accommodate it, but the call to 'Hold the front page!' happens a lot less than 1940s' movies might lead you to believe. For a journalist writing up a story, it is just no good to be told that you 'may' come back with a quote or fact this afternoon. Either you will or you won't, and if you promise to phone back and then you don't, you will not be asked again.

But why do journalists ring you up at 4.30 demanding a comment by 4.45? Why don't they give you reasonable warning? It may be that someone above decided that there was extra space to fill, or that the story warranted padding out a bit, or another story failed to materialise. Or it may be that someone else has let the journalist down, so you are number two or even number five on the list. Whatever the reason, you can decide either to go with it and make the best use of the opportunity, or to turn it down as 'unreasonable' and lose the chance. The choice is yours, but you won't change the journalists' behaviour, because it is dictated not by their inefficiency but by the pattern of their day.

4 **To have ready access to the right people** All journalists would rather sell their grannies than lose their contacts books. In it are all the useful people he or she could possibly need. It will be a lengthy and varied list, such as: the councillor on the financial committee, the mother of the local lad turned football star, someone in a local travel agents/building society/bank /estate agents who will give an instant assessment, an old school friend who works for the biggest local employer, various public relations people, voluntary organisations who don't mind providing a 'case' to fit a story, e.g. a pregnant schoolgirl, or a reformed alcoholic, or a cardboard box dweller, a doctor who can provide background on health issues. And so on – every name and phone number of people heard of, or known, who might be called upon for briefing or a quote or an instant human interest angle.

A contacts book means speedy access. If a story breaks to do with a food poisoning scare, or a financial scandal in a local firm, then there may be only a few hours at most to put together a piece. There is no time to be searching around for the right person to talk to, so the journalist relies on the people already known to be reliable and willing.

5 **To get attributable facts and quotes** News editors do not look kindly at stories which have no firm facts in them. Facts, in this context, mean times, dates, names, and quotes that can be attributed to actual traceable people. Hence the obsession with people's names and ages and descriptions, and getting them to say something, however banal, that can be put in quotation marks. 'John Brown, aged 84, wearing tartan trousers, said afterwards, "I've never seen anyone looking so unamused".' We are probably supremely uninterested in John Brown and his trousers, but the description and quote add 'life' to the incident.

CASE STUDY The Junkie Who Never Was

In the 1980s, a young American woman reporter won the Pulitzer Prize for her account of young junkies in New York. In particular she profiled an 8-year-old boy who was a heroin addict.

There was a terrific brouhaha when it was discovered that the young boy did not exist, but was a composite portrait of a number of young people she had come across. No one disputed the basic facts of her article, and that the dreadful lives she described were real, but she had sinned against one of the basic rules: your story stands or falls by traceable attribution.

She lost her prize and her job.

---

6 **To write something that readers can relate to** Another of the basic rules drummed into cub reporters is that 'news is people'. It is not statistics, technological description, or chemical formulae (although there may be a place for all those in technical publications).

It is no surprise that a story about teacher shortages will concentrate on little Emily who can't go to school for the fourth week this term because she has no teacher (with heart-rending picture of said little moppet outside the school gates). Rightly or wrongly, this is seen as more interesting than a break-down by Local Education Authority across the country of which areas have what percentage of what type of teacher missing over the last six months compared to the same time last year. To non-journalists, this can be seen as trivialising: to journalists it is seen as humanising.

7 **To get 'news'** No journalist wants to be a pipeline for company puffs, but will be willing to be used if the product or campaign or event is made to sound 'newsworthy' (see Chapter 9).

Each journalist will have an idea of what his or her own editor will want, and there is no point in over-selling an idea or story. Many a journalist has fallen for a cry of 'Wolf!' once, but if the promised wolf turns out to be merely an escaped poodle, he won't come running next time, however big, bad, and hairy the wolf is made out to be.

8 **To get the truth** Not all journalists see themselves as investigative newshounds, out to expose corruption and wrong-doing. But a certain amount of cynicism goes with the job, and no one wants to be manipulated by a smooth PR operation into publishing facts that are shown to be absolute nonsense a month later.

So a journalist will ask awkward questions, will watch for a flicker in the eyes that indicates evasion, will not automatically take your word for it. There is also the tendency, in the interests of 'balance', to put the opposing view in. This can often be annoying, especially if you don't particularly respect your opposition.

CASE STUDY Not Seeing the Trees for the Forest

A local health education authority was involved in events to publicise the annual No Smoking Day. They put a huge amount of effort into organising a photo call of 200 people breaking out of an enormous cigarette packet 15 feet tall, and invited the local press and television along.

The only fear was that the event might be disrupted in some way by Forest, the pro-smoking group largely funded by the tobacco industry. In previous years, Forest activists had come along to similar events and stolen the headlines by spoiling them.

This year all went well, and the organisers sighed with relief when things went off smoothly and the press vanished without any sign of Forest presenting a spoiling argument.

Imagine the health people's disgust, however, when they opened the papers to discover that Forest's point of view had got coverage after all: when Forest didn't turn up on the day, the reporters had specifically phoned them up, asked for their comments, and printed them alongside the anti-smoking messages.

9 **To write clearly and attractively** One person's clear language is another person's over-simplification. A journalist will keep away from jargon and technical language, and try to present the story in an accessible way. But if you are an expert in the subject, this approach is infuriatingly patronising and ignores all the important subtleties in favour of gross generalisations.

Rightly or wrongly, newspaper people believe that the general public is turned off by hedging, complex argument, and too many shades of grey. Therefore they will concentrate on the memorable image or the immediately understandable single fact. Thus: 'AIDS will kill 30 million by 2008' becomes the story, ignoring the complexities that may make this a huge overestimate. As far as a general paper is concerned, this would just clog up the story and spoil a good headline.

Thus, while the 'experts' can and should continue to try to educate the journalists into the complexities, it is also wise to try to anticipate how your story might be treated. If only one over-simplified aspect of your message is going to be printed, then isn't it better that you should choose which one, than that some ignorant journalist should make the choice (and may well choose something either silly or minor)?

MAKING CONTACT WITH JOURNALISTS

It is worth identifying the key journalists who are likely to be covering your stories, and then make contact with them to introduce yourself. There is no need to be shy: all journalists live or die by their little black book of contact names and phone numbers. You may be a very useful source of stories and information, so they need you as much as you need them. Here is the basic procedure:

1 **Identify the right person** Don't assume that the right person is the editor. In a busy daily or weekly, the editor is too far removed from the actual stories. If your sort of material is likely to be 'newsy', you might want to contact the news editor, but usually it is better to find the correspondent or reporter who deals with your sort of subject (health, business, education, consumer, etc.). For smaller-staffed publications, like specialist magazines, it may be the editor or the deputy editor.

2 **Pick up the phone** Phone at the right time. That usually means 10.30 to 11.00 a.m. for a morning paper; mid-afternoon for an evening paper; and either Monday or Friday for a weekly.

3 **Arrange a meeting** Contrary to popular opinion, you do not need to stuff a journalist full of caviare and tournedos. A simple lunch, or even sandwiches in a pub, is perfectly adequate. Some journalists even prefer a quick coffee where they can get the business done without hours spent

stuffing themselves. Explain who you are, and say that you'd like to meet.

4 **Get a briefing** Find out from the journalist what sort of stories will interest him or her, and the publication in general. Ask how you can help, what are the good days to phone or send releases, what are the deadlines, and for any information that will help you to help the journalist. Also ask if there is anyone else he or she thinks might want to meet you.

It is wise to give some impression of having read the journalist's publication. Even better, comment on some recent article he or she has written!

5 **Give a briefing** You don't necessarily have to have a hot story to promote at this stage, though if there is something coming up you can use it as a starting point. It is useful, however, to remember your initial research into why you are seeking publicity in the first place. Are you an important employer locally? Are you an interesting charity with a message and lots of community involvement? Do you feel there is a credibility gap between your organisation's real identity and how other people see you? Whatever it is, fill in who you are, what successes or problems you are addressing, and what sort of stories you might be able to provide.

Give him or her your prepared fact sheet about your organisation, and any other useful material to fill in the background.

6 **Offer to be rent-a-pundit** As well as discussing what sort of stories you might be winging in the journalist's direction, also offer yourself to be an instant source should he or she need someone in your line. You may not have the authority to be a 'spokesperson from the industry' yourself, but at least offer to find someone who could give quick background briefing or an instant quote, should the journalist need it. (A word of caution – don't offer to do this unless you are sure you can deliver the goods.)

7 **Discuss forthcoming stories or events** If anything is coming up, or you have some vague ideas for features or events, then trail them to see if you are on the right track.

Another way to make contact with journalists, both those you know and those you don't, is to invite a group along to lunch or to visit. This may be a group with similar interests, such as 'industrial correspondents' or 'fashion editors', or editors and news editors of local papers. Or it may be a mixed group, such as one or two news people from local papers, one or two specialist writers from the appropriate technical press, and some freelances working in your area. It depends on the aim. If you are wanting to provide a general introduction to who you are, or clear up some common misconceptions, then you might as well invite a number of journalists in the same line to all come together.

But if it is a more general approach – a new campaign with lots of possible angles, or a new production unit that will provide more jobs, with new technology, special provision for the disabled, and a Japanese garden at the back created by the landscape design students of the local polytechnic, you can invite along a motley crew who will not be competing with each other because each will be looking for a very different angle. There are various ways to lure a group:

- **A lunch with your top people** Get together some or all of your top people, and invite the journalists along to have lunch with them. The ideal numbers are approximately four or five journalists to three or four of your people. On a grander scale, some organisations invite along 20 or 30 journalists to mix with nine or ten top people, but at this scale it becomes more of an 'event' than an informal getting-to-know-you affair.

  Make sure you brief your people to be informative but not foolish in what they say. No 'off-the-record' comments.

- **A facility visit** Invite along a group to see your factory/school/shop/sorting office in action. This is especially useful if you are normally rather inaccessible, either because of security reasons or just that you are a long way away. If the latter, arrange a minibus to leave from a central location, and use the travelling time to brief them.

  The normal structure is a short (not more than 20 minutes) introduction, then a guided walkabout, then an opportunity for each journalist to pursue their own line, for example to go back and interview an operative or talk to the financial manager in depth.

  Don't let them run free, though. Have enough staff on hand to allocate one minder to each journalist. If that is not possible, or the logistics don't allow the journalists to follow up straight away, then make sure you offer them the chance to come back again at another time, should they want to.

- **A junket** Organisations with big budgets can provide anything from a day at the races to a weekend in the Seychelles. Car manufacturers are particularly adept at arranging 'test drives' in the Atlas Mountains or Provence or some such location that just happens to also be sunny and beautiful and expensive.

  Junkets tend to attract a lot of takers; the danger is that they may not be very cost-effective.

CASE STUDY Games and Shows

The manufacturers of a fairly well-known family game employed a public relations firm to promote it. One of the ideas was to have an international competition for players of the game (which involved logical thinking rather than luck or word skill). So this was organised, and the finals took place in a hotel near Stratford-on-Avon over a weekend. About 40 journalists were invited too, with their partners, and as an extra incentive were offered seats for a Saturday night performance at The Royal Shakespeare Theatre. About 30 journalists took up the offer, and there was a good amount of coverage, ranging from TV items to colour sections of Sunday papers.

The cost, however, was phenomenal, so the next year the manufacturers had to cut back the budget. The competition was still held, but in London, and journalists were merely invited along to watch, with no offer of free hotel or theatre tickets. The interesting result was that coverage only dropped by about 20%, while the cost was more than halved.

KEEPING UP CONTACTS

Once you have made the initial contacts, then don't let them drop again. Make a note on your annual planner of when you have spoken to or met someone, and then put down on it a reminder to call that person again in 3 or 6 months' time. If you have in the meantime been in touch about a particular story, then you need not bother. But if you haven't, then try to find some angle or potential story that might interest that particular person, and contact him or her again. It is useful to keep a file of 'soft' stories or possible features that can be used on these occasions.

Every so often you might have a story which you think will get better coverage if it is given an 'exclusive' tag. Try it first with the publication you think most likely to use it, or to a journalist you want to cultivate. If it is refused, then offer it to someone else. Never offer the same 'exclusive' to two publications at once, because if they both take it up you are in big trouble.

It is also worth keeping a file on each journalist you have contact with. Keep a record of:
- the paper or papers (especially if a freelance);
- job title or responsibilities;
- phone number (home too, if you can get it);

- preferred time or days on which to call;
- cuttings of articles about you which he or she has written;
- personal details, such as hobbies, background, family, etc.

The last point is so that you can give the impression of actually caring about the journalist as a person, not just as someone to be exploited. After all, aren't you pleased if someone you met 5 months ago remembers that you are passionately keen on birds, or that your eldest child was about to take her A Levels?

PRAISING AND THANKING

Journalists get very fed up with people who continually phone them up to complain, but never to say thank you. It is worth phoning or writing to thank someone who writes a piece about you. You may sometimes have to grit your teeth to do it, manfully ignoring the misspelling of your chairman's name, and the omission of one of the most vital points you had wanted to get across. But unless the whole article is really atrocious, it is better to say an unqualified thank you, rather than harp on the inaccuracies. Just be pleased that most of it was all right.

Praise is useful for two reasons: first, the journalist will probably nearly fall off the chair with amazement that anyone took the bother, and should think more kindly of you as a result; secondly, if you do ever need to complain about something that has really misrepresented your position, then you are more likely to be listened to.

CASE STUDY Received With Thanks

The press officer of a big oil company attended a training course where she was told to thank journalists. Somewhat sceptically she tried it out and sent a fax to a trade magazine which had published an article about her company's management reorganisation.

Within three hours she had a return fax, thanking her for her thanks, and offering to do a profile of the chief executive officer.

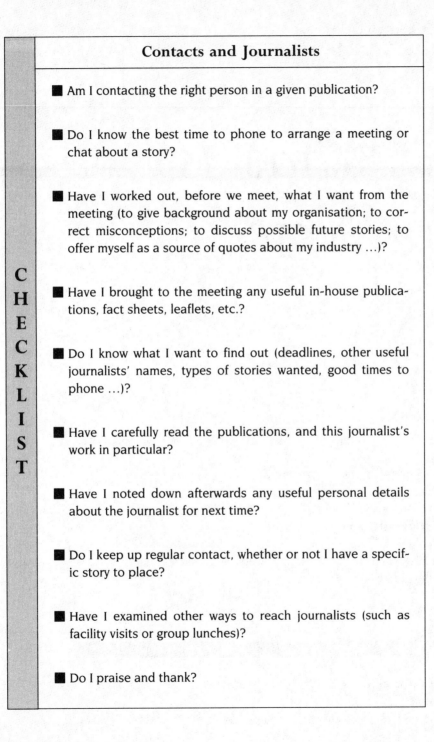

Contacts and Journalists

■ Am I contacting the right person in a given publication?

■ Do I know the best time to phone to arrange a meeting or chat about a story?

■ Have I worked out, before we meet, what I want from the meeting (to give background about my organisation; to correct misconceptions; to discuss possible future stories; to offer myself as a source of quotes about my industry …)?

■ Have I brought to the meeting any useful in-house publications, fact sheets, leaflets, etc.?

■ Do I know what I want to find out (deadlines, other useful journalists' names, types of stories wanted, good times to phone …)?

■ Have I carefully read the publications, and this journalist's work in particular?

■ Have I noted down afterwards any useful personal details about the journalist for next time?

■ Do I keep up regular contact, whether or not I have a specific story to place?

■ Have I examined other ways to reach journalists (such as facility visits or group lunches)?

■ Do I praise and thank?

C H E C K L I S T

8
What is News?

- It is important to find out what makes you different from others in your line.
- When looking for stories, or briefing others to look, work through a list of possible topics.
- People are always top interest.
- New ideas are interesting, too, and any successes.
- Research done into your history and your community should provide lots of ideas on historical links, anniversaries, and connections with other groups or events.

A DEFINITION

THERE are as many definitions of 'news' as there are journalists:

'News is what makes someone sit up and go "Gee whizz!"' (a US television presenter).
'News is people and local news is local people' (anon.).

'News is what someone somewhere doesn't want you to print' (William Randolph Hearst).

'News is what a chap who doesn't care much about anything wants to read' (Evelyn Waugh).

So news has to be new and relevant and interesting; being worthy is not enough. If it is vibrant and startling and different, then so much the better. The editor of *The Sun* said that the ideal story would be WIN FREE SEX!

Even the staider newspapers have played that game. As a spoof some years ago one of the broadsheets created SEX-CHANGE BISHOP IN MERCY DASH TO PALACE, as the news story with everything. Most of the time, you'll have to aspire to more mundane material.

FINDING A STORY

There are some stories that write themselves. Should your factory burn down, with 49 firemen in attendance performing heroic deeds; or should the research and development department come up with a working model of a time machine; then you are likely to get all the press coverage you could possibly cope with.

Alas, in the real world most stories are 'soft'. You have a new improved gizmo that is not so very different from last year's model, or you want to publicise the summer fair. Such news is important to you and to your potential customers or clients, but is in competition with other similar stories to get coverage in the press or media.

The first thing to do is to DISCOVER THE DIFFERENCE. What is it about you that makes you different from others in your field? Let's say you make chocolates; how are you different from other chocolate manufacturers?

- The chocolates are handmade;
- They are machine-made with the very latest and best equipment.
- The fillings are based on traditional recipes handed down for four generations.
- You began last year in your kitchen and now employ ten people.
- You gift wrap for no extra cost.
- You gift wrap very elaborately.
- The chocolate is extra-good quality.
- The premises used to be a church.
- Three generations of family have been members of the firm.
- Your twenty-fifth anniversary is coming up.
- You make special seasonal chocolates like Valentine hearts and reindeer.

- The shop has just had a face lift.
- You are a husband and wife team.
- You have got your first order to supply a local department store.
- You are about to sell your one hundredth giant Easter Bunny/your one thousandth bumper box/your one millionth peppermint crisp.
- You donate reject chocolates to the local orphanage.
- You sell reject chocolates at a discount and give proceeds to charity.
- One of your employees is a spare-time hot-air balloonist.

And so on. Make a list of all the things that make you different from other people. Look at your product; your process; your customers; your people; your history; your outside activities.

SOME IDEAS FOR POSSIBLE STORIES

If you work your way through this list (and keep it in mind as you do your walkabouts and story-searches, as described in Chapter 3) you are almost certain to find something that is going to make a story.

PEOPLE
Since people are always interesting, let's look at them first:
- Has a staff member won anything?
- Or radically changed career (from actor to chicken sexer)?
- Has anyone invented something or come up with a bright idea?
- Has anyone an unusual hobby or interest?
- Or does something interesting or worthy in the community?
- Has anyone met or worked with or had an association with someone famous?
- Had an unusual holiday or trip?
- Is anyone battling against the odds (been ill but now returned; disabled but plays hockey; deaf but plays the trumpet)?
- Has anyone a long family connection (second or third generation to work here)?
- Has anyone been a hero?
- Is anyone a member of a local sports team?
- Or a member of a well-known local family? Or a twin?

What about organisation and employment of people:

- Are you a family operation changing to non-family?
- Do you employ more young people than average?
- Do you employ more old people than average?
- Do you employ more women or ethnic minorities than average?
- Do you operate an Equal Opportunities Policy?
- Do you have any 'first ever' people? (First woman director; youngest manager; oldest employee; first black MBA to be hired.)
- Do you have any interesting personnel developments (a crèche, a variant on flexitime, a special kind of bonus scheme)?
- Are you involved in special training schemes?
- Do you have any interesting overseas links (e.g. with academic institutions or with overseas managers on training courses)?
- Do you have links with local schools or colleges?

Other personnel stories could be interesting:

- Who is being promoted?
- Who is retiring?
- Do you offer retirement training/help/unusual pension package?
- If you are planning an expansion, how many new jobs or new chances or new promotions?
- Are any staff taking leave to do study or go to the Third World with your support?
- Do staff go on any unusual training schemes (e.g. the Outward Bound sort)?
- Do you have a uniform? Does it have a tradition? Are you planning to update it?
- Do you have any unusual rules (like banning all reports longer than one page)?
- Do you have a no smoking policy?
- Do you have a staff day out?
- Do you have a special Christmas party?

And the community in which you work:

- Do you contribute time or materials or people to your community in any way? (If not, why not?)
- Do you have links with local schools and colleges?
- Do you offer materials to local schools, playgroups, etc.?
- Are you specially helpful with young trainees on government schemes?
- Do you have a good record of placements?

PRODUCT

Whether it is something that people use or a service they buy or a message that you want to promote, there may be a special newsworthy element:

- Is it for a particular group (children, left-handers, secretaries)?
- Does it meet any special need?
- Do you use odd materials or production methods?
- Where did the idea come from?
- Are there any inducements to buy or participate?
- Is there any special way of selling or promoting (e.g. product parties)?
- Do you have a special way of attracting members?
- Do you have members or outlets in interesting places (the Orkneys, in a prison, in an Oxford college)?
- Do you have a special way of campaigning (e.g. Lord's Taverners use celebrities willing to play charity cricket matches)?
- Are you very seasonal (swimsuits or Christmas or winter sports)?
- Do you have any problem with the weather (frost/heat/rain)?
- Are you especially 'natural'?
- Are you particularly 'green'?
- Are you especially 'traditional' or local?
- Do you have a particular philosophy (avoiding testing on animals/buying only British/not using additives)?
- Do you have any special export successes?
- Do you export to anywhere different (e.g. sleeping-bags to Iceland or sheep dip to the Falklands)?

METHOD OF PRODUCTION

- Is there anything special about your equipment?
- Are you re-equipping?
- Do you do your own research and development?
- Do you meet especially high standards (not just EC but US too)?
- Are there any users of your products who are particularly well known (individuals or companies)?
- Do you have any special accolade from a customer (e.g. they waive their own quality checks and allow you to supply direct to the retail customer)?
- Do you ever have shortages of a raw material that lead to 'just in time' dramas?

- Are you doing an environmental audit?
- Do you have particular hazards in your production? (Build up credit by emphasising that you exceed all the required safety standards and have an excellent record. Make sure this is true!)

PLACES

- Are you located in an historical or interesting or peculiar place?
- Are there any famous names associated with your building?
- Are you in a brand new building?
- Are you restoring an old building?
- Do you have an especially attractive garden or setting?
- Are the public allowed in ever?
- Are you specially sympathetic to disabled customers or visitors?
- Are you installing a lift/a ramp for wheelchairs and push-chairs?
- Have you got a ghost?
- Are you renovating? Moving from small premises to bigger or better?
- Are you extending?
- Are you using solar power? Heat pumps? Special recycling equipment?
- Are you fighting bureaucracy to make some improvement?
- Are you fighting bureaucracy against some rule that is, in your opinion, hazardous or stupid (e.g. a regulation against putting up anti-theft shutters, or not allowing you to put up an easily read notice to indicate where you can be found)?

MONEY

- When is the AGM or Annual Report?
- Is your turnover going up? Your profits?
- Are they going down? (In which case anticipate the way you are going to stress the positive.)
- Is your chief executive getting a big pay rise? (You'd better start anticipating the questions again.)
- Do you have an interesting bonus scheme?
- Is one part of the business doing especially well?
- Are you going to take over, or be taken over, or be involved in a management buy-out?
- Are you expanding or diversifying?

- Are you going to go public?
- Are you struggling along on a shoe-string?
- Are you launching an appeal?
- Are you raising funds in an interesting way?
- Do you have one big sponsor?
- Do you have potentially interesting donors (e.g. half your money is raised by children)?

HISTORY

- Have you any anniversaries coming up (5 years in Luton; 50 years in existence; 20 years since mechanisation introduced; 100 years since women were first employed)?
- Have you any association with historical figures?
- Do any of them have anniversaries coming up?
- Was your founder/first director general/chairperson interesting?
- Are there any general anniversaries that could be linked to you (e.g. you have a photo of the factory celebration of VE Day in 1945)?
- Have you ever had a disaster that was overcome?
- Have you ever been the forerunners of something?
- Were you the first to invent or introduce or sell something?
- Do you have interesting pictures/models/samples of past products or people?

Keep this list of possible ideas in mind as you do your walkabouts and chats to people, or look at the written information that comes your way. You can also brief your 'correspondents' (see Chapter 3) on what to look out for.

Sometimes you will want to use a story straight away, like a visit to your headquarters by a Japanese delegation; but sometimes you might want to file it away for the future. For example, a possible anniversary date for two years' time; or a job shadowing scheme with the local sixth form college that might be a feature article. Then you can bring it out in good time, or use it as bait for meeting a journalist. For instance, you might have a friendly reporter whom you haven't seen for some time; you don't have any 'hot' news suitable, so you fish out one of your 'anytime' ideas and use that as the initial talking point at the meeting. It may be that it won't be used, but at least you've re-established contact.

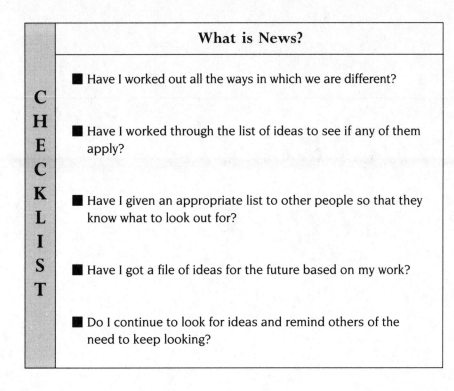

What is News?

■ Have I worked out all the ways in which we are different?

■ Have I worked through the list of ideas to see if any of them apply?

■ Have I given an appropriate list to other people so that they know what to look out for?

■ Have I got a file of ideas for the future based on my work?

■ Do I continue to look for ideas and remind others of the need to keep looking?

**C
H
E
C
K
L
I
S
T**

9

Finding the Angles

- You can develop a news sense by analysing angles and keeping a list.
- Every possible variant on every possible story has been done before.
- A brainstorm session will help you to think of all the possible angles you could use or create for a particular story.
- When inspiration fails, you can work through a list of angles and try to find at least one that will liven up your news.

WHAT ABOUT THE BORING BITS?

THE lists given in the previous chapter should provide lots of ideas for possible stories arising from your work and people.

The next problem is the routine stuff; the 'same old story' that you want to plug, like the presentation of a cheque to a voluntary organisation, or the giving of long-service awards to four employees, or the bring-and-buy sale. The trick here is to find the angle or news peg that will make your rather routine story into something a bit more special. And that requires a bit of imagination and research. Undoubtedly some people have a special flair, but don't despair because you think you haven't: even the most famous journalists had to learn.

CASE STUDY Scoop? What Scoop?

A certain reporter began her career in a local radio station. In her first few months she arranged a routine interview with a local important personage, and because he was very busy he asked her to come round early to his house the next day to do the recording.

She arrived, rang the bell, and was met by a policeman. 'You can't do an interview,' he told her, 'Mr So-and-So is dead.' 'He can't be,' she replied, 'I only spoke to him yesterday.' 'That is as may be, Miss, he's dead now.'

So off she went back to the editor to say that she hadn't got the planned interview because Mr So-and-So was dead. 'Dead?' he queried. 'How did he die?' She replied, 'I don't know, the policeman didn't tell me.' The editor's voice went up a tone or two. 'Policeman? What was a policeman doing there?'

A somewhat shame-faced Kate Adie was sent off forthwith to discover the facts about the mysterious and sudden death of the prominent businessman, to get a scoop in spite of herself.

So if even top reporter Kate Adie has to start somewhere, don't feel you can't do it because you are not a natural. Anyone can develop a news nose with a bit of research.

There is no such thing as a new angle. It has all been done before, so if you want to get ideas just keep looking at what other people are doing to get coverage. Then plagiarise. Look at your competitors and see what coverage they are getting and which angles work. Look at the way that competitions are run by newspapers and adapt the idea for your product. Listen to local radio phone-in quizzes and see if you can get a similar plug.

CASE STUDY Golf into Greyhounds

A betting shop manager wanted to get more publicity about a fairly big annual greyhound meeting in his area. He happened to be listening to the local radio station and heard a competition which was being sponsored by a local golf shop. Three contestants were lined up on the phone, and the first had to choose a 'hole'. The appropriate question was asked, and if he got a 'hole in one', he got a big prize. If he didn't get it right, then the hole passed to the next person, and then to the next. More clues would be given each time, as the 'ball' got closer to the hole, but the prize got smaller. Finally, if none of the original three had got the answer, it would be thrown open to all listeners who would phone in.

The betting shop manager decided to adapt the idea. He contacted the other radio station operating locally, and put forward a proposal for a quiz with questions about horse and greyhound racing, with contestants opting for 'runners', with shortening odds as more clues were given, and so on. This was taken up and got him a week's daily plug for minimal cost.

So don't try to re-invent the wheel: it is quite sufficient to change its colour or size!

HOW TO USE ANGLES

One way to start is to look at your answers to the questions in the previous chapter and see if you can bring any of those angles into play. For example, if you have a bring-and-buy sale that vaguely coincides with your founder's birthday, then give the sale a theme to pick up on it and promote it as 'Founder's Day': 'All the stallholders will be wearing kilts to celebrate the 120th birthday of Angus McLeod, founder of the Young Waifs and Strays Home. And there will be an exhibition about him in the foyer. The prize in the raffle will be a huge bottle of whisky, and to complete the Scottish theme, the Dagenham Girl Pipers will start everything off.'

If that doesn't work, then have a look at the angles listed below. If necessary, work through the list, jotting down ideas – however crazy. Even better, invite a group of colleagues to a brainstorming meeting to inspire each other.

Some ideas can be rejected straight away; some might need research (e.g. can you find a director willing to pose in a gorilla suit? Does Doris the retiring tea lady have any good anecdotes about what it was like to work in the firm 40 years ago? Can you rustle up the funds to provide a reasonable prize for a limerick competition?). Eventually you will come up with one or more angles that can give this particular story extra appeal. Then choose one angle, or possibly a number of different angles that will appeal to different targets.

IRRESISTIBLE ANGLES

Some stories will bring a gleam to a news editor's eye and will be all but irresistible. Practically every story printed or broadcast will have one of these elements:

- sex and scandal;
- human interest;
- children and babies;
- animals;
- the common touch;
- surveys and reports;
- local angle;
- make 'em laugh;
- flavour of the month;
- charity;
- controversy and conflict;
- anniversaries and special dates;
- good heavens!;
- new and novel;
- first ever, last ever;
- winners and losers;
- green;
- the figures game;
- celebrities and royalty;
- a good photo (or good actuality for broadcasting).

That makes 20 irresistible angles. Any one of them greatly increases the chance of your story making it into print or on to the air; if you can combine two or three, success is almost certain.

There are also a few extra quirks for broadcasting, on top of the basic 20.

Let's look at each in more detail, with examples from various local papers (mostly just the first paragraph or two, to give the idea).

SEX, SCANDAL, AND SHOCK HORROR

Generally, these are the stories you particularly *don't* want publicised about yourself (but enjoy reading when they are about someone else).

There are certain papers which take pride in digging the dirt on those in high places. There are also papers who boost circulations by reporting of the 'Naughty Vicar Who Liked Knickers' variety. However, even the so-called quality press is not immune. Page 3 of the *Daily Telegraph*, for instance, will often report lurid sex cases under the guise of 'Court Reports', and they tend to give rather greater length of coverage to the salacious evidence than to the eventual verdict.

For most organisations the fear is not so much that your chief executive will be found to have run off to the Caymans with the cash, but that your product or campaign will be attacked. See Chapter 18 about crises, but remember that, like it or not, your bad news is someone else's hot story.

And if you think that that proves that the press and media are irresponsible muck-rakers, just watch people reading newspapers and see which articles are most avidly read.

EXAMPLE Don't Buy This Product

(Names are changed)

ALERT OVER LETHAL SHOWER CUBICLES

Up to 200 shower cubicles in Bamsworth swimming baths are to be replaced after the discovery of a potentially lethal hazard.

The danger was uncovered earlier this year when a Pellham youngster was injured when the door of a shower cubicle at Pellham Leisure Centre exploded without warning. The little boy was badly cut when he was showered with razor sharp glass fragments.

EXAMPLE Shock Horror

OLD PEOPLE'S HOMES SHOCK

None of Bustingham City Council's 47 homes for elderly people meets fire safety regulations, says a secret report.

HUMAN INTEREST

One of the most common ways to bring a story to life is to add what is called 'human interest'. All that this means is that a dry statistic or a generalised story is made 'human' by adding a real person to it. For example, rather than talk about '16 redundancies', the story will feature one of the people losing his or her job, so that readers will be able to identify with the issues and emotions. So personalising a story will pay off. Try to find a person who exemplifies your story, or shows how well you are doing because an employee is now able to buy a better flat, or can be linked with you to add a human dimension, as in this example:

EXAMPLE Personalising a Course

A local adult education centre wanted to publicise their courses in a more imaginative way. One story they got published was this:

JOE TAKES THE PLUNGE

After 7 years learning French, 74-year-old Joe Crowther has finally made the grade. He has moved up, on the recommendation of his teacher, Madame Paulet, from the Intermediate to the Advanced Class.

'When I retired,' said Joe, 'I thought I'd keep my mind active by joining some classes at the local adult education centre. I'd done some French at school but not enough to really talk on holiday, so I joined the intermediate class.'

Seven years on, Joe has enough confidence to go up a grade. 'I know it seems a long time,' he laughed, 'so I don't suppose I'm a model student. But I really enjoy the classes, and now I can order a drink in French or do some shopping.

'Maybe in another seven years I'll be able to chat up some girls!'

Imagine what coverage, if any, this would have had without the personal element: 'Learning French is interesting' – not much mileage there!

YOUNG AND OLD

Age makes news. There is mileage to be had if you can bring the very young or very old into your story. Maybe it is because both these groups seem vulnerable; maybe it is because they appeal to an 'oooh-aaah' instinct.

So can you find angles relating to the 'oldest ever' person to be taking part in a sponsored walk? Or the 82-year-old buying a mountain bike from your shop? Or passing an Honours degree in Fine Arts? Similarly, it is always good news to get children into the story, or even better, into the picture. A child achieving something (winning a competition; joining Mensa; writing a poem; meeting a star; gaining a GCSE aged nine; taking part in a sponsored row) will be more newsworthy than a 30-year-old doing the same thing. And as for babies ...

EXAMPLE Baby Power

A Health Education group wanted no-smoking publicity. They printed a number of tiny T-shirts with the message 'I'm a born non-smoker'. These were given to all babies (parents willing) born on No Smoking Day.

The prospect of being able to photograph five or six new-borns swathed in identical T-shirts proved quite irresistible to the press. And when the idea was shared with other groups around the country, many used it the next year with equal success in their own regions.

EXAMPLE Which Health Cut Will Wound Deepest?

A Health Cut which may mean 'Disaster'

Two thousand Leamington pensioners will be denied vital health care at home because of lack of money. Doctors have warned that it could spell disaster for many frail elderly people – forcing more on to hospital wards – when their community nurse is taken away on 1 May. From next week she will be moved to other duties within the health service because of the health service cuts. Dr Michael Ashmore said the decision was a nonsense. 'It's a false economy which will increase hospital admission rates. It's the inarticulate and frail, who haven't got a voice, who will suffer.'

(*Leamington Spa Courier*, 26 April 1991)

Undoubtedly, in this last story the 'frail and elderly' *will* suffer but, one wonders, was it just coincidence that this particular example of the health cuts in action was chosen by whoever gave the information to the paper?

ANIMALS

Animals are just as newsworthy as children, whether as performing pets or ravening monsters. Most summers you will find that stories about animals suddenly emerge to fill pages empty of political news. They are usually of the ravening monster sort: giant cockroaches that live in the sewers; super-rats which gobble up poison with the same effect as spinach on Popeye; or a ferocious breed of dog that is about to roam our streets attacking everyone on sight.

The rest of the year we tend to read about cuddlier creatures that do clever things, or save their owners from a fire, or look interesting.

EXAMPLE Goats with the Most

MO-HAIRY TIME FOR GOATS

More than 30,000 knitting enthusiasts flooded into Esher's Sandown Park where the only livestock on show was a pair of mohair goats!

The animals formed the centrepiece of a display showing the story of mohair from start to finish at the sixth Knitting Needlecraft and Design Exhibition.

As well as the goats, there were fashion shows and a variety of workshops and demonstrations. And there were manufacturers and traders from all over the country selling everything the hand and machine knitter could possibly desire.

(*Surrey Comet*, 25 January 1991)

The interesting thing with this story is that the only display in the exhibition which would not help you to knit better was the aspect which got the big coverage (and of course the picture).

THE COMMON TOUCH

Under this heading comes anything that is going to affect a lot of people. It may be job gains or losses, local politics, health, education, new bus routes, the weather, police, and so on. In a local context this will also include lots of general information on shops, restaurants, sports clubs, and even jumble sales, exhibitions, and lectures.

Almost every local paper will run a column or more called something like Community News, or Events Coming Up, or Looking Ahead, which will include this sort of public information. And the news pages will be stuffed full of any development which affects jobs or services in the area. There are plenty of negative examples, so let's concentrate on a positive one.

EXAMPLE Mundane but Solid

OPEN DAY AT UNIVERSITY

Would-be university students can get a glimpse of academic life today at the sixth open day of University College of Wales.

Visitors will see displays, demonstrations, and exhibitions by all the departments of the College. And six lucky visitors will receive a free T-shirt sporting the distinctive logo if they find a winning card in their visitor's pack.

SURVEYS AND REPORTS

Papers love a story that can contain: '… claims a report published this week', or '… according to a survey of local young people'. It must be something to do with the faith accorded to hard figures and statistics, or maybe it allows a 'feature-style' story (eating habits, or what men think of women, or the state of public lavatories) to be paraded as middling-hot 'news'.

So if you have done some research that shows something interesting about your type of product or your customers or what parents feel about maths teaching in your school, then let it be known. Similarly, if you want to publicise something, see if you can get the information packaged into the form of a survey or independent report. It doesn't have to be an expensive market research project: it could be accosting everyone in the shopping precinct on one Saturday afternoon with a set of questions.

EXAMPLE Reach for the Sky

SMALL IS NOT SO BEAUTIFUL

More than 80% of small women have to try on at least ten garments before they can find one that fits. A survey commissioned by a mail order firm 'Pocket Venus' shows that small women have a tough time of it to find clothes that fit.

'There are more small women out there than the major manufacturers seem to realise,' said Liz Morton the managing director. 'They have to go round shop after shop trying things on, before they finally buy something they may not like the best but which doesn't make them look like Orphan Annie.'

Liz, herself a pocket venus at 5 feet 1 inch, used to resort to children's clothes. But she hopes her mail order catalogue will fill the gap for 'small women who want to be elegant and professional'.

'My aim is to help that 80% get a bit more pleasure out of fashion.'

THE LOCAL ANGLE

This is one of the biggest categories. There are various twists to it:

People: local person makes good; local person wins regional/national award or competition; famous person lives here; famous person used to live here; famous person's ancestors used to live here.

We're the best!: local business wins a contract; our schools/companies/ hospitals perform better than national average; we are greener/cleaner/ pleasanter than average.

Oh no, we're the worst!: our exam results/politeness/pollution are worst in the country.

Success: local branch gets more members/money/sponsors; local product does well; local something goes national.

Local angle to national story: how we compare to national trend; something national happening here; local response to national event.

CASE STUDY Promoting Successful Locals

The Industrial Society and National Westminster Bank launched School European Societies and decided on a national competition a few months later to publicise them.

Once the finalists in the competition to find the best society were announced, separate press releases were sent to the various regions where the four schools were located. All the local papers gave good coverage to 'their' finalists, along the lines of 'Pupils from such-and-such School are hoping to win a trip to Paris on Concorde after reaching the finals of a top European competition'.

There was then further coverage once the winners were announced: 'Pupils of Such-and-such School won £1,000 as third prize in a competition to find the best School European Society. These Societies aim to prepare school children for the single European market by undertaking project work', etc., etc.

MAKE 'EM LAUGH

Anything with an element of the odd or the amusing or the different is valuable: a picture of someone wearing a silly costume or a story with a punchline. Particularly irresistible is the sight of someone in authority (the headteacher or the managing director or the local MP) making a fool of him or herself.

EXAMPLE Creased with Laughter

An enterprising small firm set up an ironing service in the City of London, promoting it as ironing-while-you-wait.

They then organised a line of 'City gents', all trouserless, apparently waiting for their ironing to be done.

Nearly half the national papers carried the story because of the humour of the photo.

FLAVOUR OF THE MONTH

Suddenly something will become fashionable and then fade away again. While it is in fashion, the subject will be done to death; once it is out of fashion, no one will touch it for another two or three years. The topic may be a very serious one, like sexual abuse, which comes into the news because of a particular event or legal case. Often it is relatively trivial, like 'dangerous pets' (a favourite most summers) or a new food fad.

The problem with a 'flavour of the month' angle is to pick the right moment, before it becomes stale. But it is worth trying to spot trends to see if you can find some twist in your own activities that would fit them. A good example was the rush of European enthusiasm linked to the creation of the single European market; many companies managed to link their European activities or plans to that particular peg.

If you are 'lucky' enough to be at the centre of a hot story (e.g. you are a primary school and there is suddenly a lot of concern over reading standards), then react fast and strong with your side of it. If you do, you can set the agenda and get excellent coverage.

But it is a mixed blessing, especially for voluntary organisations who, through no fault of their own, suddenly find themselves last month's flavour, unable to place any story at all.

EXAMPLE The Greenhouse Effect

For about six months in 1990, everyone was writing about the greenhouse effect. Here are some of the different angles on the topic:

- hot weather: speculations on effect on crops, tourism, housing;

- turbulent weather: so speculations ditto;

- rising sea levels: effects on coastline, cities, tourism, infrastructure, construction;

- ozone: investigations of skin cancers, tanning preparations, sun-blocks, tourism trends, fashions for white skin and cover-up clothes. Also product changes, to aerosols, fridges, etc.

CHARITY

Although being worthy is not a guarantee of coverage, it can often help. Things that people do to help charities or individuals are often more likely to be covered than things they do to help themselves. So if you raise £100,000 which will go to a local voluntary organisation, it is more likely to get publicised than if you raised it to renovate the canteen.

If you are at either the giving or receiving end of 'charity', then don't forget the other partner. Get together and see if you can maximise coverage by joint effort. Best of all, try to find a link between the donor and the voluntary organisation.

EXAMPLE Milk with a Heart

A low fat milk powder manufacturer sponsors the British Heart Foundation. Together they organise sponsored slims each year with money going into heart disease research for each pound in weight lost.

Winners get a free holiday, and there are link-ups with local businesses in each region. For instance, a clothes store might donate vouchers to those who slim by a certain amount, so they can buy new clothes to fit their new figure.

Everyone concerned benefits from the publicity.

CONTROVERSY AND CONFLICT

Issues that raise emotions are always in the news. It may be a strike, or a war, or protests over the new bypass. If it generates heat, then it is in.

So don't be surprised if the only time you catch sight of a reporter is when you have industrial action brewing. 'Where were you when we were proclaiming our successes?', you may moan; but it is human nature to eavesdrop on a couple who are quarrelling rather than discussing the price of potatoes.

EXAMPLE Book Burning

One of the many sad aspects of the Salman Rushdie affair (over the publication of *The Satanic Verses* in 1990) was that moderate Muslims found it difficult to publicise their feelings about the book when it was first published.

None of the media was interested in hearing about Islamic objections to a novel, and some months went by with religious groups feeling increasingly frustrated.

Eventually, therefore, certain Bradford Muslims decided on what was basically a publicity stunt. They organised a march that featured the public burning of *The Satanic Verses*.

Sure enough, this did the trick. The echoes of Nazi book burning and the apparent blow to a free press brought the journalists running, and the anti-Rushdie campaign was up and away.

Many moderate Muslims regretted the incident later, since the story was hi-jacked by intemperates of all sides, taking their cue from the sensationalist incident. But at the time, it seemed the only way to make their voice heard at all.

ANNIVERSARIES AND SPECIAL DAYS

These might be your anniversaries, or they might be more general anniversaries. Whether general or particular, see if you can create a story on the back of an anniversary. Watch out for them and plan ahead. Good standby stunts include:

- dressing up in costume of the period;
- serving food/selling products at price of the time;
- exhibition of photos and products of the time;
- 'What we at Bloggin's Pork Pies did to help women get the

vote/to celebrate the end of World War Two/to improve on the original recipe …'.

Also keep a watch for special days during the year (and chart them on your annual planner – see Chapter 3). Days like Valentine's Day, Mothers' Day, Derby Day, Budget Day, Comic Relief Day, and so on, can be useful pegs for stories. Either you can use the theme for some rather mundane event, like opening a new shop outlet, which can be engineered to happen on a special day ('All those engaged on Valentine's Day will get a free bottle of champagne at our new wine store'), or you can create stories to fit the topicality ('Heart-shaped buns to be baked specially for Valentine's Day by Jones the Baker'). You can even create an emotional link ('"Think of those who can't find their Mum to say they love her," says group working to make it easier for adopted children to contact their biological parents').

You will need to keep your eyes open to find out anniversaries and special days. Read national and local papers carefully; look at reference books such as *Writers and Artists Yearbook*, PR *Planner*, *Conference and Exhibitions Monthly* and UK *Press Gazette*, which all feature diary pages of events. *Foresight* has a whole anniversaries section for 15 months ahead. Also browse through books with titles like *Great Events in History* or *Famous Inventions* or books about your local history, and jot down possible useful dates for future reference.

EXAMPLE The Beaujolais Milk Float

A Kent local dairy decided to use the Beaujolais Nouveau race for its own ends.

They contacted a local wine shop and arranged that part of the 'race' should happen on one of their milk floats, delivering the first cases of that year's vintage to the shop door.

The angle of 'milko delivers vino' was very successful.

GOOD HEAVENS!

This is the 'gee whizz' factor, the sort of story you just have to read out at the breakfast table. *The Sunday Sport* makes them a speciality ('B52 Bomber found on the Moon'), but even serious papers will give room to amazing stories, if they sound respectable (like the cold fusion experiments, which held out the hope of nuclear fusion in a test tube).

> ## EXAMPLE Yuck!
>
> ### LEECHES GET TO GRIPS WITH A HEALTHY PROFIT
>
> A mainstay of medieval medicine – the leech – is making a comeback as an aid in the modern technique of micro-surgery.
>
> A South Wales company, Biopharm, which supplies leeches to 150 British hospitals, has announced a sales increase of 150 per cent over the past year.
>
> The leeches feed on the surgical site for about 20 minutes, injecting anti-coagulant to keep the blood flowing, and then drop off.
>
> (*The Guardian*, 10 December 1991)

NEW AND NOVEL

Almost by definition, anything that is new is 'news': a new product, new campaign, new discovery, even a new managing director. Things that are novel include strange haircuts or the latest fashion or a dancing flower.

> ## EXAMPLE Dog's Toothpaste
>
> ### DOGS GET RING OF CONFIDENCE
>
> Dogs were given a chance to give bad breath the brush-off today with the launch of a new canine toothpaste. The makers are convinced it could make millions of our four-legged friends easier to live with.

FIRST EVER/LAST EVER/THE ONE AND ONLY

It may be the first time a poodle has climbed Mount Everest, or a Briton has gone in space, or that the new bestseller has been stocked in Bricktown or that a local person has raised over £500 at a bring-and-buy.

Last evers are usually sentimental: the last time a boat will sail; the last time old technology will be used; the last time a pupil will walk out of the old school gate.

One and only: the stuff of the *Guinness Book of Records*.

EXAMPLE Black Mentors and Students

HIGH FLIERS LEND A HAND

The UK's first mentor scheme is enabling successful black entrepreneurs and professionals to partner young black students.

Dr Ken Ife, 34, is managing director of a highly successful company. Priscilla Chin, 17, is on a business studies course at Islington Sixth Form College.

The two were brought together last year by the Islington based Mentor Scheme, which partners young black or ethnic minority students with successful black professional and business people, who act as role models.

It is the first of its kind in Britain …

(*The Guardian*, date unknown)

The total article was about 2,000 words long.

WINNERS AND LOSERS

Everyone loves a competition. However ridiculous the award may be (Miss Toothy Smile Receptionist of the Month) it will often get covered. If you work things right, you can even get three pieces: announcement of competition; names of finalists (with a separate press release to the local paper/s of each person); presentation of prize to winner.

It is worth trying to get a paper interested in sponsoring some competitions. They specially like anything (like a quiz) that can be run over a number of days or weeks, because it bolsters circulation.

EXAMPLE The Landmark Trust

The Landmark Trust is an organisation that buys and restores old, interesting properties, and rents them out as holiday lets.

They used the occasion of their twenty-fifth anniversary to organise an architectural competition in *The Observer* colour magazine. It ran over three weeks, had at least two pages devoted to it each week, and featured the twelve Landmark properties which would be offered to the winners for a week's holiday (off-season, so it wouldn't

> actually cost the Trust very much).
>
> It was a classy competition, fitting *The Observer'* s image; allowed for good colour photos, so was good for the magazine section; and ran over three editions.

Another sort of winner story is if someone makes good after a long time or lots of tries (twenty-four attempts at a driving test).

Don't forget losers either. Eddie the Eagle made his name by continually being last in ski-jumping competitions; so much so, that it was also news when he finally wasn't last! So don't forget heroic failure stories too.

GREEN

Once upon a time green was a flavour-of-the-month topic. Now it has a place all of its own. Many papers not only have an environment correspondent but also a green page or section, and stories with a green angle surface even in the business pages.

So if you are doing something interesting with an environmental angle, let them know: clearing up a waste area, creating a wild habitat garden, changing your production process to make less pollution. Be careful, however. The public and journalists are now rather cynical about 'greener-than-thou' claims. So don't make any announcements until you are sure you are not vulnerable to investigations. It is no good proclaiming how wonderful you are in improving your packaging so it is bio-degradable, if you are still pouring chemicals into the local river during your manufacturing process.

EXAMPLE Rats!

RENTOKIL TRIES TO KICK THE POISON HABIT

Rentokil, the company which makes money by blasting vermin with poisons, turned over a new leaf yesterday. Rather like a bank robber who loses his zeal for theft, Rentokil announced that it was trying to kick chemical pesticides.

Instead a mouse will be tracked by infra-red surveillance, captured alive, and taken discreetly away to meet its maker.

(*The Independent*, 24 September 1991)

THE FIGURES GAME

This is a stand-by stunt to add excitement to a routine event. Find some impressive-sounding number and make an event of it: the millionth customer, the hundredth Porsche sold, the thousandth pupil to get a university place.

Another way to play the figures game is to add up numbers. You find the combined ages of the people concerned ('One hundred and nineteen years of experience between them') or the product ('Doris has poured out 23,000 cups of tea in her time as tea lady') and dress that up as the story. It is a last resort sort of ploy, but can work well.

EXAMPLE Using a Coincidence

SEASIDE TOTS

Women regulars at a seaside pub are steering clear of their favourite bar stool after a mini baby boom. No fewer than eight have ended up in the labour ward within the last six months.

The women are all regulars and darts players at the Hanover, Harwich, Essex.

(*Morning Advertiser*, 6 May 1989)

EXAMPLE Long Service Awards

124 YEARS OF SERVICE

Five employees of the Royal Mail were last night awarded medals and cheques for a total of 124 years of service between them.

CELEBRITY AND ROYALTY

One of the great angles! Anything a real celebrity does can be news, as they know to their cost when even a speeding offence committed by a soap star will get reported.

If you can get the Queen, then you are made. Most of the time you'll have to aim lower, but don't despise the appeal of the Mayor or the Senior Vice President from Head Office.

Keep an eye out in the local media for celebrities who live locally and keep them on file.

A word of caution – there is always a danger that a celebrity will take over, especially if you are unlucky enough to invite someone whose marriage breaks up the day before your event. Journalists will be far more interested in his or her personal life than in your campaign for better sports facilities. Try to get someone 'safe' and, if possible, someone with a reasonable link to your message.

There is more information about finding and dealing with VIPs in Chapter 12.

EXAMPLE Tenuous Connection

LAST PORTRAIT OF BALLERINA

A Devon artist and lifelong fan of Dame Margot Fonteyn completed the last portrait of the great ballerina days before she died.

Sally Porch, of the Porch Gallery in Dawlish, was commissioned by a London businessman to paint Dame Margot.

The massive 30-square-feet work was finished days before the Royal Ballet's Prima Ballerina Assoluta died.

(*Western Morning News*, 23 February 1991)

PHOTOS AND ACTUALITY

A good photo will often carry a story. Each paper has its own preference, but if you can provide either a good picture or an opportunity for a good picture, you should at least double your chances.

What will often happen is that the picture 'becomes' the story, with just 30 to 40 words beside it to explain. Never mind, people will notice photos and are very likely to read the caption. See Chapter 13 for more about photographs and photographers.

'Actuality' is the word used by broadcasters to describe the atmosphere of an event. It may be the sound or sight of children in a playground as a backing to an interview about a school closure, or the echo in a swimming pool when talking about water polo.

Most broadcasters like something that gives a specific atmosphere rather than just a neutral interview.

Radio will also be especially interested in things like music, rap sessions, or strong voices with a good regional accent.

STORIES WITH EVERYTHING

The aim is to get at least one, and if possible, two or three elements of the irresistible in a story. If you look at the examples above, many of them have more than one angle. And here is a story that has about six.

EXAMPLE Count the Angles

MARTIN'S GOT DESIGNS ON CHRISTMAS!

Phew! It's almost Christmas time again. And little Martin Hedley is doing his best to get you in the right mood to deck the halls with holly, and tuck into the turkey and the plum pud.

Martin, six-and-a-half, from Peterhead, won the competition to design the 1990 TV-am Christmas card. And yesterday he was in London to get a silver salver from *After 9* presenter Kathy Tayler.

Martin beat off 500 other entries in the competition for disabled schools all over the country.

Said Kathy: 'The designs were so good I wish they all could have won, but Martin's was a particular favourite of mine.'

[Plus photo, of course.]

(*Daily Record*, 25 July 1990)

Just to show how it can be done, here's a spoof story, the winner of a competition in *The Independent Magazine* to write a news story from a non-event. It was published in June 1990 when Mrs Thatcher was still Prime Minister.

EXAMPLE Count the Angles – Tenuous Connections Part 2

MAGGIE'S LIMO IN NEAR MISS

George Turkington, 42, a driver for the Government, surveyed the wreckage strewn across the A1 yesterday. It was a result of a pile-up only 30 miles from the Prime Minister's birthplace at Grantham, Lincolnshire. One of the two drivers involved, 22-year-old student Debbie Rovers ('As far as I know, I'm not connected to the Prime Minister,' she told our reporter), escaped unhurt …

The Government car, a Rover, arrived 20 minutes after the accident and was delayed for half an hour. Mrs Thatcher, who Turkington believes twice used the car in 1986, was spending the day in Truro.

(*The Independent*, 2 June 1990)

The frightening thing is that it sounds just like a genuine press story …

SPECIAL ANGLES FOR BROADCASTING

The main angles will be just the same for broadcasters. They look for human interest, for local angles, etc., just as the press do. But there are extra quirks.

ATMOSPHERE

Editors look for something that gives authenticity or colour to a piece. It may be children playing in the background for a report by the education correspondent about rising or falling school rolls. It may be a brass band at the fête, or a flight of hot-air balloons, or a radio interview done inside a real tennis court to give the right acoustics. So if you have something to offer that will make a good sound or a good moving picture, then tell them so. Or you may have to create the effect, by thinking of a good acoustic or visual background.

CASE STUDY Blowing up a Story

The Industrial Society was launching a national campaign called 'Industry matters'. This began with a huge gathering of sixth formers at a conference in London to be addressed by – amongst others – Prince Charles.

He wasn't likely to say anything controversial, so there was no angle there for television. And hundreds of sixth formers listening to speeches wasn't too exciting either.

So thousands of balloons, printed with the slogan, were ordered, to be sent off 'to spread the message'. With the promise that Prince Charles would send off his balloon too, Thames Television were bombarded with phone calls. They came, filmed, and that evening led their local news round-up with a shot of the balloons floating off into the London skyline. This was then followed later in the programme with a 90-second piece on the conference, including Prince Charles letting off his balloon in the company of photogenic schoolgirls, and – hooray – a clip of his speech promoting the actual message of the campaign. It was as usual a combination of angles that worked: royalty plus a good visual effect.

TALKING HEADS

It is rare for a broadcast report not to include at least one person being interviewed. It may be an eyewitness to a crime or an environmental spokesperson or a local councillor; but most editors dislike reports that are just 'voice pieces', i.e. a straight talk by a reporter giving the news.

For some broadcasting, talking heads are practically the only thing to be heard. Local radio survives on a diet of music, interviews and phone-ins. Often a studio guest is expected to sit in the hot seat for up to half an hour, expounding her all on the joys of pig-rearing in a back yard.

So watch out in your perambulations for people who would be good speakers about facts or issues, whom you could offer to radio or television as instant pundits. This could be for simple chat shows or phone-ins, or in response to some topical item for the news.

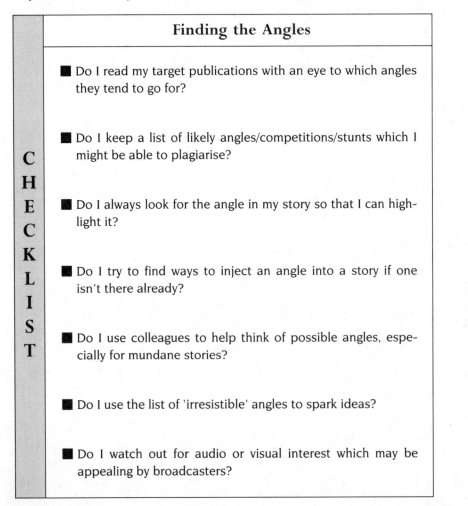

C H E C K L I S T

Finding the Angles

■ Do I read my target publications with an eye to which angles they tend to go for?

■ Do I keep a list of likely angles/competitions/stunts which I might be able to plagiarise?

■ Do I always look for the angle in my story so that I can highlight it?

■ Do I try to find ways to inject an angle into a story if one isn't there already?

■ Do I use colleagues to help think of possible angles, especially for mundane stories?

■ Do I use the list of 'irresistible' angles to spark ideas?

■ Do I watch out for audio or visual interest which may be appealing by broadcasters?

PART THREE
GETTING YOUR MESSAGE ACROSS

10

Writing a Press Release

- A good press release saves time and effort.
- If well written, it will keep you in control of the message and the language.
- All essential facts should be there (especially the five Ws – who, what, when, where and why), structured and expressed in newspaper style.
- The first paragraph is the most important part.
- If necessary you should write more than one release, using different angles for different targets.

WHAT TO CALL IT

WHAT should you call your written information to a journalist? Some people say that broadcasters get shirty when they receive something entitled 'Press release', so you should call it a 'News release'. But you may not be telling 'news'; you may be giving a reaction to someone else's initiative, or giving background information of some sort. Americans use the term 'Communiqué', but that sounds a bit pretentious on this side of the Atlantic, though it may catch on. You could try 'Media release', and be different; or stick to the safe option, which remains 'Press release'. Broadcasters aren't totally daft.

WHAT A PRESS RELEASE IS FOR

Up to a quarter of all press and media stories come from press releases. How else do you think journalists get to know about the latest survey or product or what the Single Parents Support Group thinks about today's Government initiative?

A good press release will:

- give new information;
- spark off ideas;
- save the journalist time by providing quotes, facts, and background;
- be written clearly and concisely so that it can be used without drastic rewriting;
- give contact names and phone numbers for more information.

In writing a press release you will often be doing the journalist's job. If you do it right, then your words will end up in print, and your message will come through loud and clear.

If you get it wrong, either your release will end up in a bin along with the other 80% of all those received; or it will appear in a very different form. If the information in your press releases doesn't get used at all, then it means you are either trying to push non-stories (to please the chairman?) or are not finding the right publication.

If the information is used but your words always get drastically rewritten, then it means you are having the right ideas, but you are not fitting your writing to newspaper style. So it will be worth going back to research the language and length of articles of your chosen targets.

HOW TO WRITE A PROFESSIONAL PRESS RELEASE

There are simple general rules on how to structure and write an effective press release. If you keep to them, you shouldn't go far wrong.

OVERALL IMPRESSION

You don't have to spend a fortune, but a good-looking release gives a professional first impression. That means a logo if possible; a big heading saying 'Press release' (see above); and possibly coloured paper to make it catch the eye.

Some public relations firms make a point of their ability to dress up releases. Sending a release as a spoof telegram or as a crossword puzzle may attract attention, but can be counter-productive because most journalists start to wonder whether the story is any good if it has to be dressed up so elaborately. It is more important that it is businesslike, well laid out, and *short*.

TYPING

Use double spacing when typing your release and leave wide margins on both sides. Use A4 paper and type on one side only. This looks good, and also allows subs to edit and put in their printing instructions.

DATE

Date it at the top. Then put 'FOR IMMEDIATE RELEASE', or embargo it with a formula like 'NOT TO BE USED BEFORE 11.00 HOURS, 5TH MAY' or 'EMBARGOED TILL 01.00 HOURS, 12TH DECEMBER'.

It is usually best not to embargo unless you have to. It is appropriate for financial figures which will be made public at a set time; or if you are giving the text of a speech which someone is going to deliver (in which case, state 'Check against delivery', just in case the speaker falls under a bus on her way to the event or decides to change the speech at the last minute).

The other time when an embargo can be used is if you particularly want the trade and technical press (who generally have much longer lead-in times for publication) to be publishing your news at the same time as the weeklies or dailies.

Otherwise an embargo is regarded as an annoyance by journalists.

HEADING

Some people spend more time creating a wonderful headline than on writing the release. This is wasted effort. The subs on a paper are paid large sums of money to think up succinct or witty headlines, and as a matter of principle won't use yours, however good it is. That doesn't mean, however, that you should stop bothering with the headline: if it's long and dreary, the copy taster (who screens out all releases sent to the newsdesk) will be inclined to bin your release straight away. So keep the heading short (6–10 words) and interesting. Put in the gist of your story, so that (as with most newspaper headlines) someone can read just those seven or eight words and have some idea of what you are actually saying. If you can make it bright and witty as well, so much to the good, but don't spend hours over it.

Not: 'THE INDUSTRIAL SOCIETY ANNOUNCES THE 1992 ANNUAL CATERING SURVEY OF BRITISH COMPANIES'.

That headline tells you what the release is about, but not what the story is.

Instead: 'LEANER FITTER STAFF ON THE MENU, CATERING STUDY SHOWS'.

Now we know the general drift – it is to do with employees eating better. Note the amount of detail given. Don't bother with specific names and places, unless it is a very significant part of the news.

Other pieces of advice about headlines handed out to subs, which are applicable to you too:

- keep punctuation to a minimum;
- try to use an active verb;
- don't cram in too much information;
- don't ask questions;
- avoid abbreviations unless they are an essential element (such as ICI, GCSE);
- avoid stale jargon words.

THE VITAL FIRST PARAGRAPH

Your release will stand or fall by its first paragraph. 'Who the hell ever reads the second paragraph?' said the editor in the wonderful newspaper play and film *The Front Page*. He was thinking of newspaper readers, but it is the same for press releases. If a journalist is faced with a daily pile, there is no time to read them all right through to the end. Most will be glanced at and discarded after the first few sentences.

Tips for getting a perfect first paragraph

It must attract interest It must reveal the main news or your chosen irresistible angle. If you have decided that your main angle is going to be a celebrity link (see Chapter 8), then there is no point in revealing it in paragraph four. Put it up front.

It mustn't get bogged down in detail Figures should be rounded up or down, titles and descriptions should be kept short, the main statement should be delivered as a punchy summary.

It should stand on its own Read it to yourself (or better still, to someone else) and check whether someone could make sense of it without reading any further. Could the first paragraph be printed as it stands and still get across the message?

It must be short It should not be more than 40 words, and probably no more than two sentences.

The five Ws

Like a journalist covering a story, you must include the five Ws in your press release:

- **Who?** Margaret McArdle, a leading authority on industrial catering.
- **What?** Food at work is becoming healthier.
- **Where?** In a survey of British catering operations and staff dining rooms.

- **When?** Published today.
- **Why?** Mirrors High Street trends, but also employers benefit from healthier, fitter staff.

Depending on the story, you might also add

- **How?** Questionnaire sent out annually since mid 1960s.

If you are going for a human interest angle, or profiling a new appointee, then it is essential you include (either in your story or in background notes) lots of *Who* details like age, place of residence, family, and so on. *Private Eye* mocks this journalistic habit of printing irrelevant private details, but some papers deem it necessary and get cross if you don't tell them.

Give the full title and first name of anyone mentioned: 'Mrs Jackie Newcombe, Personnel Manager at Middleton International Mousetraps Co, said ...', not 'J. Newcombe of MIMC said ...'.

STRUCTURE AND SHAPE

A newspaper story has a structure all of its own. Ignore all memories of school essays, where you first looked at the background, then at the evidence, then at the analysis, and finally came to a balanced conclusion. A newspaper story, and hence your release, has a spiral shape like this:

Headline – very short summary.
First paragraph – 20–40 word summary of the essential facts.
Next 2–3 paras – repeats story in more detail.
Final Paras – gives background, quotes, and general info.

So you often end up reading the same story at least three times, each time in greater depth.

As Keith Waterhouse points out, many stories, especially those with a human interest angle, read like the game 'Consequences':

What resulted	'Tears all round'
When	'on Monday morning'
Adjectives and names	'gobsmacked tea ladies Millie and Mary'
Event	'saw vending machine'
Where	'in corridor of their office building'
Why	'Tea ladies being phased out'
And the world said ...	Quotes from Millie and Mary, the other staff, and management.

(Based on Keith Waterhouse, *Waterhouse on Newspaper Style*, Viking, London, 1989.)

A sub using your story without rewriting will edit *from the bottom up*. So you have to imagine what would happen if you lost the last two paras –

would some vital piece of information be lost? If so, your structure is wrong. In fact, you should try to write it so that it could be cut down to just the first one or two paragraphs, and still get across your main point.

It is true that some newspaper stories have a 'pay-off line' at the end, which is like the punchline in a joke. But your release shouldn't.

THE KISS PRINCIPLE

Most releases should be one page of A4 only; two at the absolute maximum. If longer, you are probably cramming in too many facts or angles; concentrate on the ones you think are the most attractive. *Keep it short and simple* (KISS). If it is a wonderful story, then they will come back to you should they want more detail.

Paragraphs should also be kept short. A newspaper column is usually only four or five words across, which means that paragraphs are only 40 or 50 words long. Keep your paragraphs to the point.

SIGNPOSTING

If you do have to stretch to two sides, then put 'More follows' or 'cont. on page 2' at the bottom of the first page. When you have finished, then write 'End' or 'Ends'. This is to make sure that if the pages get detached from each other the journalist knows to look for the second page.

NOTES TO THE EDITOR

If you have lots of technical detail to impart, or extra quotes, or background information about the project or the organisation, then don't put it in your main release. Keep that short, but have a separate sheet with its own heading such as 'Further information' or 'Notes to editor' which the journalist can use for reference. Don't forget to cross-reference it to your release, in case it gets separated (and state on the release that there is another sheet with further details).

TARGETING

Another common reason for writing a long release is that you are trying to satisfy too many different styles of publication. You may find yourself struggling to get all the vital information into two pages, let alone one. If so, that's probably an indication that you should be splitting up your information into different releases.

If you have a story that has two or three aspects to it – a children's art book written by an Afro-Caribbean woman who lives in Birmingham – then you'll do better by writing a number of versions of your release which will be sent to different targets (local press, ethnic press, women's pages, and education correspondents).

Even a less obviously complex story could be divided up:

- local press: angles about jobs, success, local people;
- trade press: factual, sobre, technical aspects;
- consumer press, upbeat local radio, free papers, etc.: wacky, jolly, human interest, informal.

You will undoubtedly say you don't have time to write more than one release; but you will get better coverage if you do.

USE QUOTES

A good quote adds life and colour to a story, as well as pinning it to a named person. The danger is that a quote from the chief executive will be so bland or so obviously a puff that it is useless. Try to encourage people to be themselves; it's usually better to get them to speak a quote than to send it to you in a memo. Your aim is to get a quote that is reasonably short (no more than three sentences usually) and that sounds as if someone actually spoke it.

It has been known for a suitable quote to be manufactured on behalf of someone. If you do exercise creativity in this way, make sure you tell the person concerned before a journalist gets on the phone directly to him or her.

See if you can spot in newspapers what the *New Yorker* calls 'Quotes we doubt ever got quoted', since journalists resort to doctored speech too. Here is one from the *San Francisco Chronicle*, which allegedly quotes an English couple in a story about a ferry strike:

'This is a lousy break for us, because we're here from England and we were told the ferry was a great treat. It's just too bad because we're headed for Los Angeles this afternoon and I guess we won't have a chance to ride the boat.' (Quoted in *Waterhouse on Newspaper Style* by Keith Waterhouse, Viking, London, 1989.)

CONTACTS

After 'Ends', give at least one person who the journalist can contact for further information. There should be both a work and home telephone number, so that if the journalist needs to get in touch at 6.30 p.m. (or 6.30 a.m. for an evening paper) the contact can be found. Very, very seldom does a reporter abuse a home phone number. If there is any doubt about whether someone will always be around to answer those phones, then give back-up names and numbers. Those people whose names appear at the bottom of a press release should make sure to have with them any information they might need at home as well as at work, just in case.

WATCH YOUR LANGUAGE

The previous points look at the content of your release. Now let's look at the language. You are not aiming to be a columnist yourself, so don't worry too much about style. Your words should clothe the facts clearly and simply; if there is a need for more, the journalist will do it. There are simple rules to remember, however, to help you communicate:

Watch the hype Curb your natural tendency to be over-enthusiastic about your event or product. Use with care words like 'unique', 'a giant step forward', 'amazing advance'. What might be fine in an ad will look just silly to a cynical reporter.

No jargon please Even a technical publication tries to avoid too much jargon. In general, stick to common language and explain technical terms. No one will be enthused by 'A breakthrough in the design of menu-driven end-user interfaces', or 'The new pharmaceutical preparation which eliminates the necessity of surgical intervention'. As Harold Evans (former editor of *The Times*) said, 'Sentences should be full of bricks, beds, houses, cars, cows, men and women.'

Compare 'All children upon attaining the age of five years must be paid for at the appropriate rate', with 'All children over five must be paid for'. Even technology can be made understandable. The Director-General of the Health and Safety Executive spoke at a conference making a plea for simpler language in documents intended for the press or public. He quoted this example from an HSE report about Bradwell nuclear power station: 'Irradiation induces slow changes in the physical properties of graphite components, the accumulation of Wigner energy and changes in the air reactivity properties', which he translated to 'Irradiated graphite catches fire on contact with air'.

Short words and phrases Where there is an alternative, use the shorter form:

near	not	adjacent to
because	not	as a consequence
now	not	at this moment in time
although	not	despite the fact that
make	not	manufacture
about	not	approximately

Also use the more everyday form of language, even if it may mean two words rather than one:

take part	not	participate
meeting	not	rendezvous

| set up | not | establish |
| best | not | optimal |

But don't take this to extremes by falling into tabloidese. The popular papers have a style of their own which is shorter and catchier but also often stronger in meaning:

about to	becomes	poised
disagreement	becomes	clash
rise	becomes	soar
controversy	becomes	row
vital	becomes	key
reduce	becomes	cut
encourage	becomes	boost

Watch that you don't become a tabloid parody.

Avoid excessive adverbs and adjectives

completely untrue	frank and full discussions
strange phenomenon	deep blue sea
mutual agreement	complete and thorough research
major nuclear disaster	

See how many you can take out without altering the meaning.

Beware of jargon Because you understand it, that's no guarantee that anyone else will! If you use your own jargon and technical words you will either fog the readers or bore them.

Sometimes totally meaningless phrases get used: 'This partnership gives us visibility at a strategic level,' says Joyce Flam, 3rd Party Marketing Manager. Sometimes it is just too technical: 'The case study shows that 52.3% of participating patients taking 325 mg of aspirin on a daily basis significantly decreased their relative risk of suffering a re-infarction during the study period.' or 'The improved process extrudes a length of 10.5 cm diameter rounds of HDPE, each measuring 25 cm.'

Translate and give word pictures. So the above examples could read: 'More than half the people taking an aspirin a day (52.3%) greatly reduced their chances of a second heart attack.' and 'The improved machine is like a sausage-maker. It makes a line of sausage shaped pieces of plastic, 10.5 cm across and 25 cm long, using High Density Polyethelyne (HDPE).'

During the Gulf War a press release about the bombardment of Kuwait from the USS *Missouri* used the expression: 'Massive shells each weighing more than a VW Beetle.' This is far more immediate than saying 'weighing 1264 pounds'.

Beware of initials If you do need to use initials, then explain them first, and if necessary explain what it all means: 'The International Monetary Fund (IMF), set up as the guardian of the free world's monetary system, will be challenged by the new world order ...' Avoid at all cost more than one set of initials in any sentence (unless your company name is one of them).

Give facts not generalisations Don't talk about a 'lot of jobs' or an 'increase in turnover' or 'many people came to the fête'. Journalists will want the hard facts, so give figures.

But don't clog things up too much either. Choose two or three key figures and leave it at that. Any more detail should go in a 'Notes to editors' page. Similarly, don't say 'Many customers claim that our service is the best in the area'. Far better to get one authenticated quote with a name attached to it.

Use newspaper conventions Here are some conventions of newspaper style:
- Initials do not have full stops after them (BBC, IBM, GATT).
- Numbers up to ten should be written as words; 11 and on as figures (unless you are talking of 'hundreds of people' or 'thousands of millions')
- Never underline anything in a release, because that is a printer's instruction to set italic type.
- Don't overuse capital letters except for proper names and titles; nor quote marks round words, except for quotes: The wonderful new 'device' for peeling grapes is a breakthrough in fruit technology. There shouldn't be quote marks around 'device'. But in the next example the quote marks indicate a direct quote: Described by M. Escoffier Junior as a 'wonderful new device', it is a breakthrough in fruit technology.

EXAMPLE 1

PROMINENT BUSINESSMAN UNHAPPY ABOUT BUSINESS RATES[1]

At the Newtown Chamber of Commerce[2] yesterday, a spokesman[3] for Gobble Yoghurts gave astounding[4] evidence to 45 fellow businesmen about the dire and disastrous[5] effect of rate increases on small shops, saying 'Many local retail outlets[6] are struggling already in the present downturn of the economic situation[7]. The all too real threat is that another financial burden in the shape of huge rate increases will send them under, and then all of us will find fewer point-of-sale opportunities.'[8]

The MD of Gobble Yoghurts, Mr J. Gantham, further stated that at least 24% of his wholesale customers in the area have already intimated to him that they could foresee closure in the next six months.[9] 'What will come in their place?' asked Mr Gantham. 'What will the local community do when the local food retailers shut?'

He called for concerted and immediate action on the part of the Newtown business community, suggesting that they only pay their rate bill under sufferance, forcing the local authority to threaten legal action.[10] 'If we only pay at the very last moment, this will bring home how unhappy we are, especially if we all write an accompanying letter to explain our actions.'

1   Hardly a gripping headline, though it does give an idea of the story.
2   Unnecessary detail at this stage. In the first paragraph only give the place if it is vital to the story.
3   Who is this spokesman? Give his name and title.
4   Let's hope the evidence *is* astounding.
5   Don't pile on the adjectives.
6   Most people would use the word 'shop'.
7   The spokesman sounds more pompous by the second.
8   Altogether far too long, too wordy, and lacks focus. We don't yet really know what this story is about. So far it sounds like a pompous speech by some bod or other saying that high business rates are a Bad Thing; to the bin with it!
9   Unnecessary extra bit to the story that doesn't really add to it.
10   Ah, at last we come to some meat. This angle should be right at the beginning, to inject a bit of controversy and action.

RE-WRITE 1

BUSINESSMAN WARNS COUNCIL TO WATCH OUT FOR HATE MAIL

Jerry Gantham, MD of Gobble Yoghurts, called yesterday for all Newtown businesses to unite against higher business rates by 'paying to rule'.

He told a meeting of the Chamber of Commerce: 'Local shops are going to close and that will affect us all. We can show our digust by being as slow as possible in paying our rates, and let the authorities know we are doing this for a reason.' Adopting the 'work to rule' tactic used in industrial disputes, he called it 'pay to rule'. Mr Gantham suggested that all 45 of his listeners should force the local authority to threaten legal action before they pay their bills, and warned the Council to expect lots of hate mail: 'We should all write an accompanying letter to explain our actions.' ·

Research by Gobble Yoghurts shows that one in four corner shops expect to close in the next six months, unable to cope with the huge increase in business rates on top of the recession.

This release now starts with a headline that promises controversy; the first paragraph has the 'pay to rule' angle; the language is much punchier; and the detail comes at the end.

Here are some headlines and first paragraphs:

EXAMPLE 2

SURVEY SHOWS BEAUTIFUL COUNTRYSIDE LOST

A 34-page survey published today by the Southern region of the Save Britain Trust and the West Devon County Council shows that 500 square miles of beautiful countryside have disappeared under inappropriate development and road building during the last decade.

Try this instead, with less detail and more direct language:

RE-WRITE 2

COUNTRYSIDE DISAPPEARING UNDER ROADS AND HOUSES

Beautiful countryside is vanishing forever under concrete at a shocking rate, a survey published today shows. An area of fields, trees and flowers the size of Greater London has disappeared in the last ten years. In its place are roads, houses, and unnecessary farm developments.

Here is another one.

EXAMPLE 3

HEAD OF MARRIAGE GUIDANCE GROUP SPEAKS OUT

Mrs Teresa Bowman, Chairwoman of the Catholic Centre for Marital Counselling, spoke to the East Grimsdyke Women's Institute last Wednesday about changing attitudes to sexuality and the effect on marital problems.

We know lots about who spoke and who heard it, but nothing about what she actually had to say. (And why 'last Wednesday'? Someone hasn't got their act together.) It is vital to get the message into the beginning: what was her interesting angle about the subject?

RE-WRITE 3

CATHOLIC MARITAL COUNSELLOR CALLS FOR SEXUALITY NOT PORNOGRAPHY

Mrs Teresa Bowman, head of the Catholic Centre for Marital Counselling, believes that the modern world's obsession with sex and sexuality 'can be a very positive help to a marriage'. She told a meeting of the East Grimsdyke's Women's Institute yesterday (4th June) that there was a difference between sexuality and pornography. 'Sexuality is one aspect of our loving nature and should be part of a good marriage; pornography exploits our base instincts and is usually destructive,' Mrs Bowman said.

HOW TO SEND IT

The most important factor in sending a release is to send it to a named person if at all possible. Check that the person whose name you have used is still there. Second best option is to address the envelope to 'The health correspondent' or 'The sports page'. If it is a genuine news story, then send it to the News Editor. If you are in doubt about who to send it to, by all means send two (one to news, one to the specialist) but it may be wise to say so on each.

Once you have a good relationship with some journalists, it is useful to send the straightforward release to everyone, and then phone up individually any journalist for whom you have a special angle. Don't overdo the 'Did you get my press release?' phone calls, unless you have something else to say. The point of a release is to save time, not lead to endless follow-up calls.

Unless there is some special time factor involved it is usually not advisable to use fax for your releases, because you can't be sure that your message will get to the right desk.

Another option is sending by courier: this is expensive but efficient.

PREPARING FOR A RESPONSE

Once a release arrives, any of these things can happen:
- it gets put in the bin;
- it gets put in the files for future reference;
- it is used straight away, either in full or part, using your words or rewritten in some way;
- it is incorporated into a larger story (e.g. local reaction to the plan to build a hypermarket);
- it is followed up for further detail.

You have to be ready for a follow-up. It may be a very simple matter of a few additional facts; it may be that your original idea is going to become a feature which requires an interview, photos, and any suggestions you can make on other companies or organisations with something to say on the subject.

There is more about preparing for interviews in the next chapter, but basic rules of response are:
- Make sure all named contacts are briefed and available for at least three or four days after the release is issued. They should have all basic information with them at work and at home.
- Named contacts should be at the end of a phone or be able to phone back quickly (within 20 minutes). It is no good having essential meetings going on the day after you issue a hot press release. So plan ahead.
- Send a copy of the release to anyone in the organisation

who is involved in the particular issue or event. Then if a journalist does want a quick response from someone in Research or from a particular branch, that person will already know what it is all about.

- If you think there is going to be a big response, brief the switchboard where to put press calls.
- If the matter is controversial, make sure that everyone who might be approached knows what to say and who is the official spokesperson. A cunning journalist may try to bypass official channels and go straight to some innocent employee for uncensored comment.

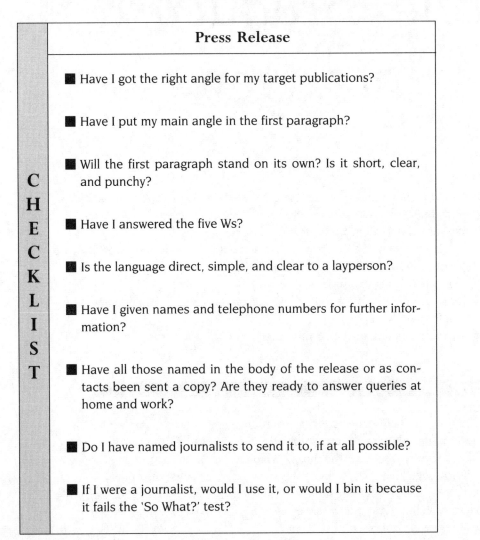

Press Release

C
H
E
C
K
L
I
S
T

■ Have I got the right angle for my target publications?

■ Have I put my main angle in the first paragraph?

■ Will the first paragraph stand on its own? Is it short, clear, and punchy?

■ Have I answered the five Ws?

■ Is the language direct, simple, and clear to a layperson?

■ Have I given names and telephone numbers for further information?

■ Have all those named in the body of the release or as contacts been sent a copy? Are they ready to answer queries at home and work?

■ Do I have named journalists to send it to, if at all possible?

■ If I were a journalist, would I use it, or would I bin it because it fails the 'So What?' test?

11

Preparing for Press and Broadcast Interviews

- You should be in control from the start by calmly refusing to answer any questions until you are ready.
- The message should be simple, clear, and direct.
- You stay in control by actively turning each question into an opportunity to say what you want to say.
- Good examples bring your points alive.
- You can prevent misunderstanding by keeping answers short, and summarising frequently.
- Only go 'off the record' when you know precisely what you want to achieve.

RESPONDING

IT'S best to regard all requests for information as 'interviews', whether it's the local paper phoning up for clarification of a press release, or a half-hour documentary profiling the boss. Whatever it is, someone has to respond to questions posed by a reporter. Those questions may be informed, sensible, helpful questions; or they may be silly, biased, hostile, or irrelevant. Either way, the interviewee wants to make the interview a success.

A successful interview depends on: *thorough preparation* and *enthusiastic performance*. A third element could be added: *keeping control*. You have only yourself to blame if you allow yourself to be rushed into comment, or if you say the 'wrong' things.

Whether you are going to be interviewed for your local paper or for *News at Ten*, the same basic principles apply:

- ask questions beforehand from whoever is setting up the interview;
- do your own research on the programme or publication, and if you can, the interviewer;
- work out what *you* want to say;
- think of all the ways you can get that message across, with loads of examples, stories, gripping statistics, and personalised comment;
- practise answering every question, nice or nasty, that could come your way;
- on the day, be friendly and relaxed, but watch for the traps;
- at the end, sum up your main point so that it sticks in the mind – the mind of the interviewer or the mind of the listener.

HAVE I GOT EGG ON MY FACE?

Many people walk into an interview in the same frame of mind as the scantily clad girl in a knife-throwing act. She has to stand there, unable to control the flashing blades, hoping that the knife thrower will be competent, sober and favourably disposed towards her. If he gets it wrong, all she can do (once out of hospital) is resolve never to appear in that act again.

For some people an interview is like that. They sit and hope that the 'right' questions will come their way; they feel they can't control the proceedings; and if things go disastrously wrong then their only response is to refuse to talk to any journalist ever again.

But in how many other aspects of their work do they have that attitude? Do they go to a meeting with a client and hope that somehow the right arguments and selling points will just magic themselves into their mind? Of course not; they prepare beforehand.

So how do you measure success in an interview? Is it: 'Phew, well I didn't make an absolute mess of it!' Or: 'I got my two main points across and I was able to tell my best anecdote even though the questions were a bit irrelevant.'

Success shouldn't be measured by how little egg you got on your face; any interview should be seen as a chance to get across your message whatever the questions and however nasty or incompetent the interviewer may be. *Failure to prepare is to prepare for failure.*

DELAYING TACTICS

One vital way of keeping control is to refuse to be hassled into answering any questions until you are good and ready to do so. A journalist will phone and imply he just 'wants something cleared up'. Before you know where you are, you're answering in-depth questions on company policy without any preparation or clearance. And once in the middle of that situation it is almost impossible to extricate yourself.

The only answer is not to get there in the first place. If a journalist phones up out of the blue, go through this procedure:

- Calmly and politely fob off all his questions, however cunningly and perserveringly he asks them.
- Ask for his name and publication.
- Find out what it is all about (see the questions below).
- If it is absolutely routine or in response to your press release (in which case you should already be prepared) then answer. If it is more than checking a fact, then give yourself a chance to do some thinking, even if it is only five minutes' worth.
- Find out the deadline and show you are willing to co-operate. (A journalist may try to rush you by telling you it has to be *now* – you will have to judge whether this is true or not; it is more likely to be within the next half hour than the next minute.)
- Ask him to phone back after a reasonable amount of time, or offer to phone back yourself by a set time.
- Use whatever time you have got to work out your main message and examples, and anticipate any trouble.
- If you are in any doubt, check him out (note that a freelance may be unknown to the switchboard, so ask if he is on the staff or freelance; if the latter, who is his contact?)

No journalist has the right to hustle answers out of you, even if she has a microphone in her hand. You always have the right to prepare.

IT'S RESEARCH TIME AGAIN!

If you don't already know about the publication or programme, find out:

What is their target audience or readers? Which of them fit into your target publics? (Note that some programmes, for example breakfast television, have different audiences at different times.) What kind of information is of interest to them, therefore what aspects of the topic are likely to come up?

How do they approach stories? Sensationalist, jolly, combative, serious? For a broadcast interview, what you hear is what you'll get, so you should know whether you'll be facing someone relentlessly mid-Atlantic and upbeat, or a hard and unforgiving journalist. For print journalism, things are more complicated, since an apparently serious reporter could go away and write a very silly piece. Therefore ask which section of the paper your interview is aimed at (a diary piece will have a very different flavour from the business section).

How long are their articles or interviews? Get a copy of the publication and read it; listen to the radio programme and time the interviews (it may range from 12 seconds to 6 minutes, depending on the programme). Prepare your material with the correct length in mind. You'll need to do more homework the longer it is.

If you can't see or listen to a live broadcast before you are interviewed, then ask for a cassette to be sent to you. If this doesn't work, Tellex Monitors (address in Chapter 22) can send copies of most programmes – at a price.

Particular questions to ask your contact are:

What is the general theme? They won't tell you specific questions, because this closes off opportunities to improvise; also you would probably arrive with a ten-page list of answers that are approved by the board: safe, and extremely boring. But various codes of conduct do lay down that a journalist should indicate the general line (and stick by it).

Why are you approaching us? If you've just issued a press release, then the answer is obvious. But if an interview request comes out of the blue, it is worth getting an answer. For instance, is it to present a typical employer's reactions to new bylaws? Or to provide an opposing point of view to someone else? Or to be part of a feature on inner city schools (and if so, are we illustrating 'good' aspects or lousy ones!)

Why now? Is there some element of topicality involved? If so, you should thoroughly familiarise yourself with it (e.g. new legislation being discussed).

How much do you want? How long will it take? Broadcasters especially may be cagey about this one. Which researcher or producer would willingly admit that their two hours on your premises will result in a maximum of thirty seconds on air? Keep pushing until you get an answer, and then decide whether it is going to be worth it for you.

Who else are you talking to? This will prepare you for the type of questions that may come your way, and also some of the arguments you might want to use. If your sworn enemies are also being approached, you will have to prepare your debating points.

SPECIAL QUESTIONS FOR BROADCASTS

Who will be the interviewer? Listen to them beforehand, if you can: some interviewers specialise in the softening-up approach with an absolute stinker kept for the last question; others may ramble and waffle so that you have to fight for your own air time. It may be hard to listen to work by some radio interviewers, who are often freelance, but at least you can discover how the presenter of the programme introduces and winds up pre-recorded material.

One to one, or as a panel? Particularly watch this if you are dealing with a controversial topic. Are you going to be set up in an eyeball-to-eyeball confrontation, and if so, are you happy about it? If your interview is part of a longer programme, then are your opponents also appearing, and if so, before or after you? (If possible, of course, get your bit in after the opposition's.)

Any film or other sort of introduction? Serious programmes will often preface an interview with a film introduction, or a round-up by another reporter. If so, make arrangements to see or listen to it before the actual broadcast, even if it is only minutes before.

Live or pre-recorded? Studio or on location? Is there a choice? More about the respective merits of live/pre-recorded and studio/location in Chapter 15.

WHAT DO I WANT TO SAY?

Before an interview, sit down and write out a list of ten or so points you want to get across. They might be general points ('Very few black Africans are pot-bellied refugees despite the impression you might get from the media') and also specific ones for now ('We need old blankets and clothes for the Bamango flood victims').

Look at your points and choose the three or four that best fit this particular interview topic and these particular readers or listeners. Be single-minded in then discarding the other points. It is far better to put across a few points well, than to attempt to say everything sketchily.

One reason for this is that you want to keep control of the interview. If you can actively shape all your answers towards your three or four points, then irrelevancies are less likely to creep in.

The other reason is that people (and that includes journalists) don't retain your pearls of wisdom in the way you'd like them to. In fact, the more you tell them, the less they retain, because the brain seems to operate on a 'One out, all out' basis. Give it two or three new facts and it is quite happy to put them on file. Give it ten or twelve and it goes into a spin and ditches the lot.

CASE STUDY

A senior manager in a Northern health region gave an interview to a big local paper about the implications of the Government's plans for reorganising the NHS. During the 30-minute conversation he spent three-quarters of his time talking seriously about the subject in response to the reporter's serious questions.

But when the questions shifted to speculation on how privatisation might work, he innocently continued to respond, and talked of 'possible' contracts, hotel-style food, water-beds on demand, etc. As far as he was concerned, this part of the interview was just a jolly chat.

On publication, at least 90% of the article was this peripheral speculation and he was very embarrassed by the quotes put to his name. He could not deny having said them, but readers would not know that most of what he said was far more substantial.

In this example, the mistake was to relax once the main points were said. 'I've got my points across,' he thought, and stopped working at it. You must never relax! Every question, every answer, must be treated the same – as an opportunity to seize control and say what *you* want to say about your two or three main points. Resist all temptation to start to talk about *anything* else.

That means that even after half an hour, you should still be just as anxious to fit your answer to your message as you were at the beginning. (See below for a way to practise this.)

GETTING THE MATERIAL

Once you know your main points, you need to work out how best to put them across. Put yourself in the journalist's shoes. What sort of material does he want? What will make a lively and interesting broadcast or article from her point of view? Then look for ways to provide the goods. For each main point:

1 Identify case studies or anecdotes or human interest stories that will make that point come alive;
2 Find gripping facts or statistics that sum up the point;
3 Prepare a 'punch line', a rousing finish that rounds if off – it might be a quote, or an up-beat statement, but it should be memorable and short;
4 Work out the controversial aspects, and prepare your answers now, not during the interview itself.

For example, you are planning to start a dry ski-slope complex in Brick-town, and the local paper wants an interview. Your three main points are:

1 There will be new jobs created.
2 Children and adults find skiing fun, and dry skiing helps.
3 We're using a brand new type of plastic slope, that is more like real snow.

Now work on each main part. First the main facts, then the punchline:

1 *New jobs*: At least three full-timers. At our other complex in Coketown we began with three and now have six. We'll need part-timers for instructors – good skiers who would like to teach a few hours every week.

'So not only will this new complex provide lots of fun, it will also give a job to at least three people who might otherwise be claiming state benefit.'

2 *Skiing*: Dry ski slopes are amazingly good at preparing you for the real thing. For example, the current British junior slalom champion had only skied on plastic up till the age of 12.

   Skiing is one of the fastest growing participatory sports. Twenty years ago only one secondary school in 50 organised a school skiing trip; now it is one in 20. My father took up skiing at the age of 52; he can still only just make a turn but goes every year.

'Skiing is as addictive as chocolate; once tasted, most people just can't wait to experience the thrill again.'

3 *New material*: Dry ski slopes feel a bit like skiing on a plastic hair-brush. In our new slope you'll be skiing on the equivalent of 30,000 hair brushes.

   This is the first dry ski slope in the North East to be made of a new plastic that is softer and finer. Kurt Schmidt the current World Cup downhill winner says it is amazingly like the real thing.

'Our dry ski slope will technically be the best in the North East; you can ski on it just like you would ski in Zermatt or Selva, only it's a lot cheaper.'

You now have a reasonable amount of material on each point, enough to last you a 3 or 4-minute radio interview or a short article in a paper. Each point you have prepared can be brought out in answer to one question, i.e. you don't tell the interviewer everything first time, but expand on one example or fact for each question. Then when another question comes along, you bring out the next example. That way you keep control. Your punch lines are kept for a summing up of each point.

4 *Controversial aspects*: Environment (floodlights at night, appearance from distance, ugly view for locals). Knocking down a row of shops to build the centre. Skiing is for upper-class twits. Skiing is expensive. A dry ski slope is irrelevant to this area. Where will people park? The plastic material comes from Germany.

For each of these you must work out the answers. Then hope that the questions won't get asked! Sometimes you might want to confront a difficult topic head-on, in which case it should be one of your three main points.

PRACTISING

If you listen to professional speakers, especially those who are expected to ad lib, you may despair at how fluent they seem, how ready with a deflecting answer or quick jibe under attack. How do they do it?

The answer is that, generally, they practise. The Prime Minister, for example, prepares before Prime Minister's Question Time by getting his aides to think of all possible topics and angles that might come up that day. The aides then fire questions at the PM and together they all work out the optimum answers. Two hours of work might go into 30 minutes of performance. No wonder it sounds so polished!

You can practise too. One of the most effective ways is to tape yourself giving answers, whether for a broadcast or print interview. Listen to your voice: do you sound as if you care about your subject? If you don't care, why should anyone else?

Time your answers: do you ramble on for a minute, 2 minutes, 3 minutes, before you get to the point?

Count the number of times you use a technical or jargon word: can you think of a better way to explain your point?

Count how many examples and lively expressions you are using. Aim to get one good example or story into every answer.

For controversial topics, adopt the politician's approach. Get a group of colleagues to think of all the nastiest wrinkles to your topic. Then get them to fire questions at you and practise your answers. You'll be amazed at how much better you answer the third time you try.

Also work at the positive aspects of your answers: 'Yes it is true that there is still some sulphur dioxide residue in the smoke, but over the last 5 years we have spent over £2 million installing equipment that has reduced pollution by half, and we aim by 2001 to …'

CONTROLLING THE AGENDA

One way of controlling the questions is to state beforehand: 'I will not answer questions about …' This is usually totally ineffective, and merely alerts the journalist that there is a juicy story to be ferreted out; if not from you, from someone else.

But you can control any interview by the answers you give. Don't allow yourself to be side-tracked by questions that don't fit your message. It is no excuse after an interview to say: 'I wasn't asked the right questions'; you can make the questions work for you.

The politicians have their ways of doing this, which we all recognise:

'That's a very important point, but even more important is …'
'I will come back to your question in a moment, but first let me fill in the background …'
'Before I answer your question I think it is vital that people understand that our opponents are motivated by …'

Most of these blatant ways of refusing to answer the question are very annoying. There are more subtle ways and you can practise them.

THE 30-SECOND EXERCISE

This is a wonderful way to practise putting your point across quickly and effectively. It will help you keep your answers short, lively and relevant to your message. You can practise alone with a stop watch, or in a group. Once you have the idea you can practise anywhere, just for fun.

1 Decide a possible general topic ('Reading at primary level' or 'Our recent export success').
2 Decide your message – one of the main points you want to make ('There needs to be better training of student teachers in how to teach reading'; 'We are the first firm to be allowed to export yak butter into Tibet'). Write it down in one sentence.
3 Think up a question. If you are working in a group, the rest of the group think up questions on the general topic, without knowing the specific message you have in mind.
4 You then have 30 seconds to answer the question, whatever it is, in such a way as to get in your message. If the question is easy and leads into your message quickly, then use your 30 seconds to bring in an example.
5 Do it again with the same question and same message, until you are happy that you have got it right.
6 Now try all the other questions you or your group can think of, but still answer with the same message as your goal.
7 Then move on to another main point and do the same thing.

EXAMPLE

You are working as a women's group, starting a campaign about various aspects of women's inequality at work. So your general theme is 'Women at work'.

The main message you choose for the exercise is:

'There should be a change in the tax system so that working women can claim tax relief for child care.'

A possible question on the theme of 'Women at work' might be:

'Shouldn't women be at home looking after their children rather than pursuing careers?'

At first, you think there is no way that you could get from this question to your message in 30 seconds. But try this answer:

'It's true that some children may be suffering because their mothers are at work. But there are many good reasons why women work, and if children do suffer it's usually because they just aren't getting the right sort of care while their mother is away.

Many working women have to skimp on child care because they just can't afford to do it properly.

And that's because in Britain the cost of child care comes out of taxed income. But why? Wouldn't it make sense to let women claim tax relief for child care? Then children would be far more likely to be well looked after, whether their mothers are working or not.'

Here's another, even more remote, question on the general theme:

'Women claim it is prejudice that keeps them from getting promoted, but isn't it more a matter of commitment?'

Rather than getting lured into a debate on inherent intellect, environmental conditioning, the nature of prejudice, or even the positive figures showing how well women are progressing, stick to the message *you* originally identified as being what you wanted to say.

'Well, I think it's dangerous to take any generalisation and try to fit it to all situations. But I think one factor is quite important for women who have children; they feel a tug between their responsibilities for their kids and their responsibility to their work.

Good child care is very expensive, and many working women aren't perhaps as happy as they might be about their kids because they have to skimp.

We feel that child care should be allowable against tax, so that working mothers could buy better child care. Then everyone would benefit – the children, the employer, and the woman, who could concentrate on her work without worry.'

It's amazing how, with a bit of practice and imagination, you can get from any question to any message. If you can do this, then you can always control an interview, because you can side-step all irrelevant or hostile questions and bring them back to what you want to say.

It's relatively easy to keep control in a broadcast interview, because nine times out of ten you'll only get asked five or six questions at most. But it can be hard to keep concentrating on control in the half hour or more of informal chat with a reporter from the local paper. However, if you have done enough preparation, and if you keep regarding each question as a new challenge to be used for your purposes, you can do it.

KEEPING TO TIME

The time factor is vital in a broadcast interview, because if you ramble on for more than about 45 seconds, you will almost certainly be interrupted with another question. If you haven't yet got to the point, tough luck. Also, even if you are allowed to ramble, it is likely that in a pre-recorded interview your 2 minutes of answer will be edited down to 45 seconds. There is no guarantee that the reporter's view of the vital 45 seconds within that 2 minutes will coincide with yours. However, if every answer is kept to less than 45 seconds, and if every answer is made to relate to one of your two or three main points, then whichever bit of your interview is broadcast, it will still be useful to you and put across some part of your message.

Even in a press interview it is worth keeping answers shorter rather than longer. Journalists are only human, and most of us can't retain the full glorious detail of what someone is saying after the first 3 minutes. Shut up after a minute or so; let the interviewer ask another question if you haven't given enough detail. (Don't forget to check beforehand that you know how long a minute is – most people have no idea and if asked to speak for a minute will usually talk for four.)

SUMMING-UP AT THE END

Just as with a good speech, finish with a summing-up. In a broadcast interview you want to recognise the final question and use your last answer to end with something rousing.

In a press interview, finish by stating your main points to the reporter: 'So the three essential points about the issue as we see it are ...'. There's no guarantee that the reporter will see it that way, but at least you're putting across your message as strongly as you can, and there shouldn't be any confusion or misunderstandings.

It is also a good idea – for any interview – to prepare beforehand a sort of crib-sheet for the reporter. This could include vital figures, the explanation of technical terms, the full titles and names of key people, and – if you want to – a summary of your main points. Give it as he or she leaves; it will stop some of the common mistakes like misspellings, and is a further reinforcement of your message.

AVOIDING THE PITFALLS: THE JOURNALIST AS RAT

Generally speaking, most journalists are not 'out to get you', but it's as well to stay wary, especially with anyone you don't already know and trust. So here are three common pitfalls to watch for:

I KNOW I SHOULDN'T BE SAYING THIS BUT ...

People get very worried about whether to speak on the record or off the record. The simplest rule is to regard all contact with journalists as being on the record. If the phone rings, then imagine you are being recorded from the start; if a journalist walks through the door, imagine everything you say is overheard by your boss, and talk accordingly. *If you don't want it published, don't say it.*

The oldest journalistic trick in the book is to ply someone with drink so that inhibitions go; but some people start to talk merely because the journalist seemed so reasonable and friendly it seemed churlish to refuse.

If you say 'I shouldn't really be telling you this, but this new chairman hasn't a clue how to run this sort of business; at least five senior managers have already said they want to go. You won't quote me, will you?', most journalists will not quote you as the bigmouth. But that doesn't mean they won't use the story. What they will do is either use some vague rubric like 'A source inside the company ...' which leads to a witch hunt, or they will find some other way to substantiate the story (perhaps by contacting someone who has just left the organisation).

CASE STUDY Arts Council Appointment

A member of the board of one of the regional Arts Councils let slip to a journalist friend that the newly appointed director had pulled out of the job, because someone had discovered that his c.v. claim to a Princeton degree was bogus. Too late he tried to retract what he had said, and then begged his journalist friend to conceal the leak.

The journalist did so. He bolstered the story by getting confirmation from 'official' sources that the new director had indeed turned down the job, for 'personal reasons'. Then he contacted Princeton, and established that no one of the right name had attended the university. Finally he tried to contact the refusnik director, but everyone concerned – his secretary, the regional Arts Council, and the Arts Council in London – said they had no idea where he could possibly be.

All this, plus a few extra comments from supporters of the new director-elect, was put together to create a story. The original off-the-record leak did not feature, but the story would probably never have appeared at all without it.

The exceptions to the off-the-record rule are:

1 **If you want something leaked, but don't want your name put to it.** Politicians are of course masters at this; if they have a new idea to put forward but aren't sure of the public reaction, they will leak the idea to chosen journalists. The story will be published with no names mentioned and the politicians wait to see how loud the howls of outrage are.

2 **Giving background information.** Journalists will often use contacts to brief them on questions to ask someone else. If a journalist is going to do a television interview with a minister about privatisation of the NHS, then he will contact opponents for the counter-arguments. This will be done off the record, to help the journalist ask the right questions, or get a proper briefing. This can be a valuable process for both sides.

3 **Gaining journalistic understanding.** You may be in a sticky situation of some sort but you don't want the story published yet, or at least not the full story. So you explain to the interested journalists what the situation is, why discretion is necessary, and get them on your side. You promise full co-operation as soon as possible.

This tactic was used in the Gulf War with Western journalists. Reporters revealed later that the pool journalists were told the full plan of attack long before it happened; and their co-operation was requested in minimising loss of Allied life. Presumably this was done to forestall them poking about trying to discover the plan of attack and then publishing it as a scoop.

Police also use off-the-record briefings to journalists in, for example, terrorist cases, where they ask for certain details to be withheld from publication so that they can sort out hoax claims and tip-offs from genuine ones.

So certain situations like a credit crisis or an impending resignation or a cashflow problem, or even the announcement of a new product might call for an off-the-record briefing. You have to be confident of the merits of your case though: would a normal rational human being see the need for a hold-off ('If you just stay quiet for two days we should be able to put together a rescue package; otherwise two hundred people will lose their life savings').

Alternatively, have you sufficient aces up your sleeve in the way of promised future benefits to bribe them into silence? ('If you talk now, the whole deal will fall through; but if it succeeds the Russian President will be coming in person to sign the contract.') But this strategy is a high risk option. If one paper publishes, then they all will.

Generally it is best to be very careful before speaking off the record: know what you want to achieve and know whether you can trust this particular journalist.

DANGLING THE WORM

Another journalistic trick to get people talking when they shouldn't, is to go fishing. There may be a vague rumour floating about that a takeover is in prospect. A reporter will then phone up the company concerned and say, in tones of breezy confidence, 'What are the terms of the takeover?', or 'I hear that an offer of £30 million is on the table; are you going to refuse it?' Then they sit back and listen to the reaction. Anything on the lines of 'How did you know that?' or 'Well, it's not as big a figure as that, actually', and they know they are on to something.

It's easy to cope with a straight question: 'Are you under a takeover threat?', but it is much harder not to give something away if a reporter seems to have inside knowledge already. So never assume that he is really as knowledgeable as he sounds, and only give the minimum information necessary.

SILENCE IS CONSENT

One final trick to watch out for in a print interview is the 'words in the mouth' technique. This is where some statement is put to you and you are invited to agree, even if only with a nod of the head. The words are then taken and put into quotation marks as if they were your unprompted sentiments.

CASE STUDY Mrs Thatcher Hangs On

In the months before Mrs Thatcher's resignation as British Prime Minister, there was mounting speculation about when she would choose to stand down as leader of the Conservative Party.

One television interview contained a number of questions on the matter, which she parried carefully, until a final summing-up question was asked: 'So you would be prepared to go on and on as leader if you felt they wanted you to?' To which she answered, 'Yes'.

On tape, the viewers could see what had happened; but in the papers next day this exchange was reported as 'Mrs Thatcher proclaims she will go on and on', giving the impression that the Iron Lady's well-known powers of determination were now fixed at staying in power well into the next century.

It is difficult to guard against words being put in your mouth. But be very careful never to seem to agree with anything unless you really do, and put on record your disagreement, with something stronger than just a 'Well' or 'Perhaps, but …'.

If in doubt, make sure there's a recording of any interview. Take a tape recorder with you and politely tell the interviewer that you'd like a record of the proceedings. You are throwing no stones at his professionalism, but it would be useful for you to know afterwards exactly what you said so that you can report back to your superiors and/or check that you gave him the correct facts. If too much fuss is made at the sight of your recorder, then get very wary.

CASE STUDY How to Write Your Memoirs

The story goes that the British Labour Party MP Tony Benn began some years ago to take along a tape recorder to important events, in order to prepare material for his memoirs. This includes taping any interviews he does whether for print or broadcast, explaining first that it is purely for his own convenience.

The interesting twist is that he claims that ever since he started doing this, somehow he is misquoted far less often and the 'normal' misunderstandings that used to occur just don't happen any more.

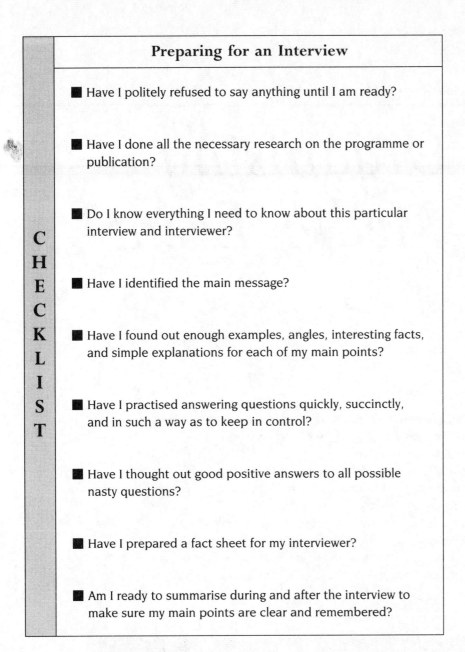

Preparing for an Interview

■ Have I politely refused to say anything until I am ready?

■ Have I done all the necessary research on the programme or publication?

■ Do I know everything I need to know about this particular interview and interviewer?

■ Have I identified the main message?

■ Have I found out enough examples, angles, interesting facts, and simple explanations for each of my main points?

■ Have I practised answering questions quickly, succinctly, and in such a way as to keep in control?

■ Have I thought out good positive answers to all possible nasty questions?

■ Have I prepared a fact sheet for my interviewer?

■ Am I ready to summarise during and after the interview to make sure my main points are clear and remembered?

CHECKLIST

12

Organising a Media Event

- Only hold a press conference or other media event whan it is appropriate.
- Send named invitations some weeks ahead, and follow up a few days before.
- Choose a time and place that will get the best response.
- Keep the event short and well structured. Shambles, however friendly, win no marks.
- Allow time for questions and informal chat afterwards, preferably over refreshments.
- Be prepared for no one to turn up, and make contingency plans.
- Treat VIPs with consideration and efficiency: thank them afterwards.

WHEN TO HOLD A MEDIA EVENT

MOST journalists recoil from the daily pile of press releases, but their bitterest bile is reserved for press conference invites. Why, they wonder, should Frou Frou Dog Baskets plc believe that any journalist is going to use three hours in order to listen to the company chairman yacking on about their increased turnover due to last year's decision to colour-match braiding to cushion? Why not just put it in a press release?

A press conference or event takes up precious time, so a journalist will only come if one of these factors applies:

- It is big news and this is the only way to get it.
- It is urgent.
- It is controversial and there is the chance of some heated argument.
- It is complex or especially interesting and the chance to ask questions or get on-the-spot quotes is important.
- There is a demonstration or a celebrity speaker or the chance of a good photo.
- An excellent lunch or expensive freebie of some kind is promised (though this is not fail-safe, and may not guarantee any more actual coverage in return for the hole in your budget).

For most organisations, therefore, a press conference will be relatively rare, a photo opportunity will happen sometimes, but most publicity should be by written release or phone. So always think through whether you should be holding an event at all and resist pressure from anyone higher up.

CASE STUDY The Shallow Learning Curve

The Industrial Society holds a number of interesting workshops and seminars every year, to which guest speakers are invited.

The aim of the Society's first press officer was to get journalists along in person to hear the speakers, and all her efforts went into creating enticing invitations to make the subjects sound as interesting as possible, and then targeting the right publications. This would be followed up by phone calls to check the invite had been received.

The usual result was that at most one journalist would arrive. Some months later the realisation dawned that this was a ludicrous misuse of time. It was far more efficient to attend the event oneself, act like a freelance by listening for all the possible angles for different publications, and then write it up for them as one or more press releases.

The press officer did this, and her coverage increased dramatically.

The moral is: *only invite the media along if you can't write it yourself.*

TYPES OF MEDIA EVENT

You can have all different sorts of media event:

- A press conference – rather than giving your news as a written release, you can tell it to an invited group.
- A news event – you organise something newsworthy as your angle, such as a protest march or a non-alcoholic drinks tasting or a celebrity cutting the ribbon.
- A photo opportunity – this will often merge with your 'event', or it may be extra, such as photographing the winning artist at home in advance of the official announcement.
- Facility trips – you invite a group to visit the village school that is about to be closed down, or the potential site of your new factory.
- A reception or lunch – for background briefing, or for journalists to meet the new chairman.

CASE STUDY The Press Event with Everything

Thames Water wanted to get maximum publicity for their £810 million investment programme in the London area. Their publicity office put together a package of ideas:

- the main announcement of how much would be spent;
- a visit down the sewers, linked with the centenary of the death of Sir Joseph Bazalgette, 'father of London's sewage system';
- the sewers chosen would be those under Fleet Street (cue for jokes about liquid lunches …);
- a rat-spotting challenge: £50 to charity for each rat seen by a journalist;
- a special lunch to present a £500 cheque to the entertainer Roy Hudd on behalf of his charity, the Ancient Order of Water Rats.

So this event included just about everything: a facility trip with a difference; good photo possibilities; a creepy slimy animal angle; a jokey challenge; and a charity event that linked with the rat theme. Plus, of course, the serious story about the need to replace crumbling Victorian water systems.

Not surprisingly, it was a resounding publicity success, with different angles being picked up by different papers. To quote just one headline: 'Why the rats have deserted Fleet Street'.

INVITATIONS

TIMING

Unless your news is urgent (a sudden crisis for example), invitations should be sent about 10–14 days ahead, so that your event will be put in the diary (from which editors and producers work when planning their day's work). If it is a very big do, you may have to invite 4 or 5 weeks ahead, which gives you a chance to test the response and go for different media targets if necessary.

NAMES

Try to send them to named people, but if you do want to send one to the news desk and one to a particular correspondent or radio programme, then say so on each copy.

For BBC radio, send at least three copies to the Future Events Unit at Broadcasting House, London W1A 1AA. This unit will circulate information to all editors and producers who might be interested, both centrally and in the regions.

GETTING INTEREST

You have to make the event or conference sound interesting, but sometimes you have to protect the story too. Check the list which gives the reasons – from a journalist's point of view – as to why he or she should come. If you can't promise any of those, then think again.

The same rules of presentation apply as for a press release. The title should sound catchy; the appearance should look professional. Maybe you know someone who is an amateur calligrapher or cartoonist (don't forget a thank you present afterwards). A personal letter is sometimes very effective; and some people swear by printed invitation cards with your logo and the journalist's name written by hand – but this can be horribly expensive.

If you can think of – and afford – what's called a 'grabber' (a gimmick or a gift relating to your event) then all well and good. It might be an astrological birth chart for the opening of a New Age shop; or an invite phrased like Army call-up papers for the trip to a military museum; or a large box which will be filled up with chocolates at the event.

But something over the top or gimmicky may backfire. Try your idea out at planning stage on a tame journalist friend or two.

GETTING A RESPONSE

It's a good idea to enclose a pre-paid reply card or envelope. This is no guarantee that they will reply, but it helps.

CASE STUDY Taxiing Them In

A reasonably well-off group had their fingers burnt a few times when even those journalists who had accepted the invitation failed to turn up on the day.

So they decided to splash out on taxis, and informed each journalist who expressed interest that a taxi would turn up at the newspaper office to take him or her to the press conference. The psychological pressure meant that they all turned up.

Make sure you give these vital bits of information:
- date;
- time of start and finish;
- place with map (showing parking and public transport);
- telephone number of venue;
- whether there will be phones, typewriters, or faxes for journalists to use;
- when broadcasters will be able to tape interviews (this is often best done before the event);
- who to contact for replies and more information;
- timetable of events if it is complicated, to help those who can attend only for a short while.

The motoring organisations will send you a free route to your location if you give them prior notice of the time, place, and where people will be coming from. They provide not just clear instructions, but also take road works into account.

FOLLOW-UP

Two or three days before the event, phone up those invited from whom you haven't heard, to check that they got the invite, and/or to gently prod them into coming. Try to have some special appropriate bait for each person you talk to ('Our representative in Prague is going to be there: he's a mine of information on how Eastern European governments are planning to organise joint ventures'; or 'There's part of the President's speech where she'll be saying some really controversial stuff about the safety record of the local playgrounds'). If they say they can't come, then find out whether they would like a press release afterwards, and whether there is any special angle or information you can give them.

It can also be wise to telephone those who have said they will come.

Journalists can get fed up with this kind of pestering, so be prepared to be very tactful and polite; but they know you're doing your job and won't grumble too much as long as you keep it short and you phone at a convenient time.

Remember that they may genuinely not know whether they'll be coming or not, since it all depends on what else crops up on the day; when in doubt the Perfect Journalist will say yes. Sensible organisers discount at least one-third of their firm acceptances.

NAMING THE DAY

WHEN

Monday is good for dailies as news is thin, but other papers will be busy. Wednesday is difficult for weeklies, and Friday and Saturday for Sundays. So a Tuesday or a Thursday is usually best to catch dailies, weeklies, and Sundays. If you are inviting monthlies, then avoid the middle of the month.

The usual time is 11.00 to 11.30, to catch most deadlines for papers and broadcasters. This also allows the event to spread into lunch, so journalists can circulate around and get their own angle on the story, and you can chat them up too.

Avoid evenings (when many journalists are still working doing the finishing touches to their pieces). Breakfast receptions are growing in popularity, American-style. They don't waste normal 'working' time, but daily journalists work late so tend to relax or sleep at 8.30 a.m.

CHECK FOR CONFLICT

If you are inviting a similar group of journalists (e.g. health correspondents, or building trade magazines, or the local weeklies), then check with one or two of them that there is nothing else clashing with your chosen day before you send invites.

Use your annual planner wall chart too, to check out clashes. Publications like the *Financial Times* will give you a guide to weekly events, and *Exhibitions Bulletin*, PR *Week*, *Foresight* and UK *Press Gazette* will show big exhibitions or other media events.

A final check, which is very cheap for a simple request, is The Information Bureau (which has taken over from the Daily Telegraph Information Bureau); they will tell you of any other events happening.

CASE STUDY Even the Professionals Get it Wrong

One of the big media stories in 1991 was the launch of two US glossy mags in British versions – *Vanity Fair* and *Esquire*.

They both decided to launch on 14 February and made expensive arrangements. *Both* then had to rearrange their events because they discovered that their key guests (media directors who are usually male) were mostly going to be having romantic events of their own with wives and girlfriends.

Esquire moved back to 13 February, and *Vanity Fair* cancelled altogether, though not before spending a reputed £35,000 on arrangements.

(Reported in *The Observer*, 17 February 1991)

PLACE

There is no golden rule whether you should hold an event in-house or outside. If there is a good reason to be in your own place (obviously a facility visit has to be at the appropriate spot) then hold it there even if space is a bit cramped or it is out of town.

If you are in a remote place, though, you may have to make arrangements for transport, such as laying on a coach from a central point.

Another consideration is atmosphere: beware of going against your overall image. A Louis Quinze room, a-glitter with chandeliers, will look very peculiar if your message is that you are desperate for more funds. This is especially important if you're hoping for photos or television coverage.

Conversely, you can add atmosphere by a bit of imagination: a tent put up beside the inner city wildlife park would be a far better place for a press conference than an anonymous hotel or office.

If none of that applies, then you need somewhere central and convenient – an hotel or hall if your own premises are distant. If you want the national press, it usually means the event has to take place in London.

Most suitable hotels will produce a conference pack. Read the small print of the contract: the penalties for cancellation, for instance. Once you have booked, put in your diary the latest cancellation date.

An organisation called Expotel publishes a free guide to conference planning, which includes around 200 hotels with details of rooms, access, parking and so on. Also, if you tell them what you need for your press conference, they'll give suggestions for suitable venues.

FACILITIES

A well-run press conference or event will have:
- parking or convenient public transport;
- plenty of telephones;
- extra rooms for interviews;
- a fax machine;
- plenty of power points for TV if invited;
- a room where the speakers can be heard and seen (avoid microphones if you can);
- an area for refreshments where people can talk informally afterwards. You don't need a slap-up lunch (though the promise of a superb meal doesn't go amiss, if your budget allows); sandwiches and peanuts will do.

ORGANISING ON THE DAY

You should have prepared:
- a table where the press will be met, given lapel badges (not that they will necessarily wear them), and sign a press book;
- a press pack with a press release in it, giving the bones of the story, quotes from the chairman's announcement, background information on your organisation, the artist's impression, etc. Give this out at the end of the speeches; otherwise the words of wisdom may get lost in a sea of rustling paper. (Though if you ask journalists, they will always say they prefer to get the press pack when they arrive so they can make notes on it …);
- a presentable room, with a table for the speakers. If you anticipate photos then think of what will appear in shot – try to get a logo right behind the speaker's head, for instance;
- some of your own folk to be on hand to fill up chairs and provide a bit of atmosphere if necessary;
- some of your senior people, with their own lapel badges, to mix with and brief journalists afterwards. Tell them to be friendly and open but proffer no more confidences than they would to someone from your closest competitors – so no 'off the record' stuff;
- your own photographer so that you can send photos and a post-event press release to the journalists who didn't come. Make arrangements for them to be printed straight away. Photos are also useful to give to those who helped at the event especially VIPs;
- an exhibition or display of the new product, if appropriate.

THE STRUCTURE OF A PRESS CONFERENCE

The first rule of any event is to *keep it short*. That means not a minute longer than one hour for the formal bit, and less is better.

A typical press conference would go like this:

10.00   Check for seating, refreshments, equipment, telephones, etc.

11.00   Staff assemble for their name tags and briefing.

11.15   Stand by to receive journalists invited for 11.30. They are welcomed, asked to sign the press book, introduced to you, and shown to a seat.

11.35   Most journalists have arrived. Seat the top table, and invite everyone to sit down. Make sure someone is still around to cope with latecomers.

11.40   Welcome them, and explain arrangements for refreshments, phones, radio and TV interviews. Say a press pack will be given out afterwards.

11.45   Hand over to main speaker, if it isn't you, for the announcement of results or the demonstration of the new gizmo.

12.00   Questions and answers. Take control again. Ask each questioner to state their name and publication before the question, and repeat it yourself if necessary. Then ask the appropriate person to give the answer.

      If there is anything controversial in the air, then you may have to decide a strategy beforehand. Before the question session, either state that certain questions are out of bounds ('Miss Gorgeous Lamonte is here to launch our dyslexia campaign, not to talk about her decision to sue a well-known paper for libel'), in which case they will probably still ask questions but you can refer back to your original announcement. Or you can state that they will get the opportunity to ask about the hostile take-over bid for 5 minutes at the end, but the first 10 minutes will only be about your sponsorship of the British moon-shot.

12.25   Final one-minute round-up, emphasising the main point of it all. Hand out press packs, and adjourn for informal chat over drinks and simple snacks.

Afterwards, get the signing-in book and check it against the invitation list to see who didn't come. If you took photos, get them printed, then send around press packs and photos to non-attendants.

If you can, use any spare time to write special angles for particular publications (a quote from your technical person for the trade press; a particular funny story, given in response to a question, for the diary page of the regional paper).

THE FULL-SCALE PRESS EVENT

A press 'event' is when you are creating some happening purely as a media exercise. It is usually done when you need to publicise a campaign, or jazz up a presentation, or get a photo in the local paper. So it exists just to create a story.

For a successful press event, you need a good angle, often a good celebrity or two, usually a good visual appeal, and a bit of luck with your timing.

CASE STUDY Going Crackers

The Industrial Society were involved in an appeal for Romanian orphanages, which was organised as a competition, including who could get most money in a week, and who could get most publicity. The IS Press Office decided to work on the publicity. Since there was only a week to do it, many ideas just weren't going to work, and a large part of the media were ruled out. So they worked on the idea of 'The Biggest Cracker in the World' as a press event in one week's time. There were a number of important considerations that made it a success:

- Official accreditation beforehand from *The Guinness Book of Records* that it was a genuine attempt. This made it easier to interest the media, and also meant the book's editor came to the event.
- The record attempt also gave shape to the affair, since one of the stipulations was that the cracker must bang.
- The search was then on for celebrities willing to take part in pulling the cracker. Neil Kinnock, the then Leader of the British Labour Party, was willing. Once he was in, other VIPs followed.
- While this was being organised, a preliminary press release was issued to the dailies, Independent Radio News (IRN), and TV to say what was going to happen. As it was a visual event and Romanian orphanages were in the news, there was a fair bit of interest.
- Credibility was helped by the promise of the Romanian ambassador to attend.
- Further press releases were sent when the cracker became an official record attempt, and the VIPs were confirmed.
- Other publicity was organised, including paid-for publicity via UNS (Universal News Service). They wrote a

news piece sent down the wire, a news feature (which wasn't taken up by any press, probably because there wasn't time for the feature editors to fit it in); and did a radio interview with the person running the competition and the leader of The Industrial Society team.

The UNS service was very successful, although expensive. For instance, over 20 radio stations ran the interview.

- As other people became involved, follow-up phone calls were made, e.g. when children from the local primary school were recruited to help pull the cracker on the day, BBC's children's news programme *Newsround* was phoned.

- It so happened that the leader of the cracker team was an excellent communicator. LBC, the London news station, came along the day before the actual event to do an interview with him and those making the cracker. This was a great success, and led to LBC doing a further set of 'progress reports' over the next 24 hours as zero-hour approached.

   This had a knock-on effect, since it gave credibility to the event and made it easier to persuade others, especially TV, to come.

- All the time, the press office was involved in check-up calls, 'Just to make sure you got our latest press release; did you get both pages?' Each phone call was used as an opportunity to deliver a 10-second spiel about the event, using the key words:

   Kinnock, children, *Guinness Book of Records*, Romania, big bang.

On the day it was a big success. The celebrities showed up, lured by the good cause and the promise that it was going to be a well-organised affair. Radio, TV, and the dailies were there, and the resulting publicity pleased everyone.

GETTING THE PHOTOS TAKEN

For a photocall, or a particular one-off event like handing in a petition, make sure you provide a specific timetable of what will be happening when. Then make everything happen 10 or 15 minutes after that: press photographers are notoriously late. Also check that the visuals are right. If it is a hard-hat area then make sure everyone around is wearing the right clothing. If you are showing off the yachting team wearing your T-shirts, bring along spares in case someone forgets theirs. And once photos are being set up, just check on what else is in shot. Do you really want the chairman posing beside his Mercedes? Do you want the scruffiest boy in the school sitting in front of the new lab equipment?

It may be worth anticipating what you'll do if lots of photographers show up for a one-off action shot. What can happen is that they all crowd round, pushing and jostling, and not only spoil it for each other but also for any other spectators. So be prepared with a roped-off area some 20 feet away into which you can corral photographers. Everyone – including them – will benefit.

Finally, have ready a briefing sheet for any press photographers. Very often they won't have a clue what it is all about, having been sent along without the original invite. Prepare a 30–50 word caption, plus an overall press pack if appropriate, and a list of the full names, titles, ages, etc., of all people likely to appear in the photograph.

See the next chapter for how to brief your own photographer.

ORGANISING OTHER MEDIA EVENTS

The overall rules stay much the same for other media events as for a press conference. You still need to meet, greet, and inform.

If it is a big do, then try to stay on top of what is happening and be ready to push journalists in the right direction. This may mean quite a lot of preliminary research.

CASE STUDY Time Manipulation

A radio reporter arrived at the first London flower show of the season. The snow was piled thick outside, and the story was obviously going to be linked to the unseasonal weather.

He went to the press room, and asked for details of how many exhibitors had pulled out because their displays weren't ready. They didn't know. Then he asked whether any exhibitors had any amazing stories about their super-human efforts to get their flowers to bloom in time. They didn't have any ideas. Well, did they know how many previous flower shows had been held in these conditions? No.

Since time was short, he had a quick walk round, did a 30-second piece on the general impression, and this was broadcast.

That afternoon, a reporter arrived from a rival radio station. The person on duty in the press room had changed, and the new one was able to answer questions, having done his homework. In particular, he sent the reporter to three people who had something interesting to say.

In the same time that the first reporter had spent wandering around, the second reporter got three short interviews. That evening the flower show got a one-minute mention on that radio station's news, with two further mentions during the week: one on the health slot about an exhibitor displaying medicinal plants, and one on the family magazine programme about ornamental vegetables.

So you can maximise coverage by putting yourself in journalists' shoes and anticipating their requests.

FACILITY TRIPS AND BRIEFING LUNCHES

A facility trip will often be a rather informal affair, but try to start with a proper briefing, then show the group around, and finish with a question and answer session.

If you have quite a large room, then split them into smaller ones of two or three and give an appropriate guide, e.g. for the new factory, give the group of local press someone from personnel; for the technical press, someone from production; for the general business press, someone involved in the design and planning.

Similarly with a briefing lunch: you need to make sure that the people around the table are useful for the journalists invited (see Chapter 7).

ANTICIPATING DISASTER

Sometimes everything goes wrong. You plan well, get your celebrities lined up, send the invites, and no one shows.

CASE STUDY Bust Out that Flopped

A group organising action for No Smoking Day made a huge model of a cigarette pack from which 50 people were going to burst out on the signal.

The two or three local papers were invited, and said they would come.

On the day, no one turned up. The 50 volunteers waited and waited, until finally the organisers sent them home very downcast and fed up. Two hours later a press photographer arrived, claiming that this was the time he'd been told, and had to be sent away. The next time they tried to organise an event involving lots of people, it was almost impossible to get people to come along and it took more than 2 years before they got over the fiasco.

The lessons are:

- Double-check with the pictures editor on the day before that the photographer knows time and place.
- If you need to have photos, then make sure you have your own back-up photographer just in case.
- Make sure your photographer is properly briefed and able to make enlarged prints straight away (see Chapter 13 for more on photos).
- Even if the press don't come, write your own release on what happened and send it along straight away to catch the deadlines, with or without a photo. As often as not, it will be used.
- If the event doesn't get covered, then still send copies of the photos or at least a thank-you letter to all who helped. This is where an in-house journal is useful: there'll be at least one place where you can get a big write-up.
- If you're not sure how many journalists will turn up to, say, a press conference, then get a few colleagues to hang around until you find out, sitting them down in the room. There's nothing more dismal than a room large enough for 50 people with two people sitting there.
- Finally, let everyone involved know beforehand that media events are chancy things. Sometimes there is no justice: a really good affair is pre-empted by some other hotter item through no fault of yours; or a pretty marginal event attracts huge coverage for no reason that you can discover. If you let them know this before the event, they are less likely to think you are just making excuses should things go wrong.

CASE STUDY Awfullest Press Event Ever

You will never have a worse event than the march held in New York in 1971 by Italian-Americans. It culminated in a rally in Columbus Circle

---

to protest that they were discriminated against because everyone thought that all Americans with Italian names were automatically members of the Mafia.

Their main speaker rose to talk, and was then shot – by a Mafia gunman.

(From *The Economist*, 6 April 1991)

GETTING ALONG THE CELEBRITIES

One of the easiest ways to lure the media along to something is to promise them a VIP.

First you have to find one. There are various ways:

- Create your own celebrity file over time from the local papers. See who lives or works locally, or has a local connection. Someone who lives near is more likely to come.
- Search your own files to see if you have had someone famous or successful working for you or as a member.
- Use an agency (see *Hollis* or *Benn's* for names) which specialises in providing famous faces or particular entertainers like clowns or Bulgarian dancers.
- Look in the reference books, such as:
  Who's Who, *Who's Who of* TV, the electoral roll, *Contact* (for actors' agents), *Athletics 19xx The International Track and Field Annual* (gives the clubs of major athletes), *Amateur Athletics Association Handbook*, *Women's Amateur Athletics Association Handbook*, *Pelham Sports Guide* (gives less usual sports such as archery, tiddlywinks, real tennis, etc.).
- MPs can be found in their constituencies, or through the House of Commons, London SW1A 0AA.
- Euro MPs have a larger constituency, but are called upon less. (The European Community Commission, 8 Storey's Gate, London SW1P 3AT.)
- Remember local worthies, such as the mayor, senior policemen, the director of social services, local government councillors, etc.

CASE STUDY Finding the Right VIP

A certain school suddenly found itself faced with a bill for £10,000. A fund-raising expert told them that their only hope to raise it quickly was to find one individual or company to donate it.

The school checked their records and found that one of the Monty Python team had once been a pupil. He was contacted, and by a stroke of luck, actually had spare cash having just received a legacy. He very nobly paid up, and the extra publicity gained by his fame enabled the school to launch a longer-term appeal as well.

Invite them by letter well in advance (months rather than weeks, if possible). Let them know very clearly exactly what you want from them and how long it is likely to take. Also outline the media coverage you are hoping for.

Make your invitation sound personal. Not 'We're asking you because you're famous', but 'I saw with interest in the paper last year that you said you began your career in painting/boxing/politics because of early encouragement from a teacher. We are trying to encourage young people by …'.

Offer to lay on transport if necessary.

If your VIP accepts, then get a brief biography and photograph from him or her in advance, and get copies in your press pack. If there isn't a biography to hand, then you'll have to write one. This is often the case with a head office bigwig. Don't just include the usual blah about when he joined the company and what august bodies he's a member of. Also put in some more interesting personal facts about hobbies, passions, strong opinions, etc. Anything that might make the press slightly interested.

Make sure you double-check all arrangements, especially the sending of maps.

It may be wise to talk to the VIP's secretary or agent, and check out on personality ('informal/huffy/likely to be late') and any special likes and dislikes ('will only drink sparkling mineral water').

On the day:
Read the papers that morning in case any hot news breaks relating to your celebrity.

Make sure that there is someone around to greet them, give them a cup of tea or their favourite malt whisky, and show them to a private place where they won't be pestered.

Be ready to organise taxis to and fro if requested.

Keep to your timings: however informal the event, it is important to keep to your side of the bargain if you promised the celebrity would be finished by three. If he or she then wants to stay on, that is a bonus but don't presume.

Afterwards, send a letter of thanks, any press coverage and photos, and any personal touches, e.g. the pictures drawn by the school kids or a reaction from the security man who got kissed.

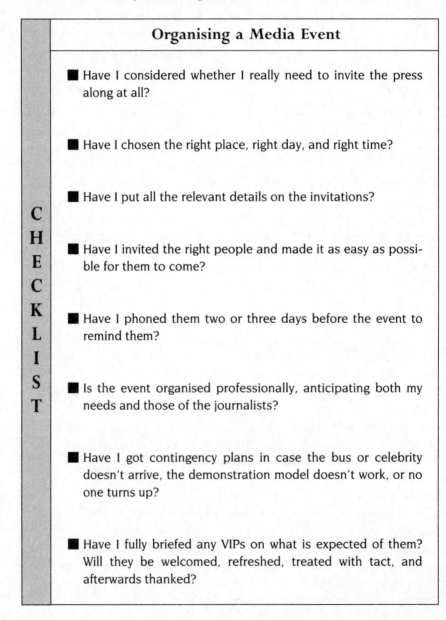

Organising a Media Event

CHECKLIST

■ Have I considered whether I really need to invite the press along at all?

■ Have I chosen the right place, right day, and right time?

■ Have I put all the relevant details on the invitations?

■ Have I invited the right people and made it as easy as possible for them to come?

■ Have I phoned them two or three days before the event to remind them?

■ Is the event organised professionally, anticipating both my needs and those of the journalists?

■ Have I got contingency plans in case the bus or celebrity doesn't arrive, the demonstration model doesn't work, or no one turns up?

■ Have I fully briefed any VIPs on what is expected of them? Will they be welcomed, refreshed, treated with tact, and afterwards thanked?

13

Getting in the Picture

- A good photo vastly increases your chances of getting coverage.
- You'll need an angle to your photo, just as you do for the story itself.
- If you are organising your own photographs, get a professional if at all possible, and brief him or her carefully.
- Don't forget to check that the logo is in shot, the background is tidy, and everyone is wearing the right clothes.
- Attach a label and a short caption to the photo but don't mark it in any way.

A PICTURE IS WORTH A THOUSAND WORDS

IF you look at most papers, especially the more upbeat ones, many stories are merely an excuse to print a good photo. The accompanying article may only be a few sentences. However, the impact on the reader is probably greater than the next-door article two columns long that doesn't have a photo.

The eye is drawn to a picture. So if you can provide a good photo yourself, or the promise of a good photo if a photographer comes along, then you have a much better chance of coverage.

These are the factors that make an arresting photo:

Drama An airplane burning; a gunman with his hostage; a fireman rescuing someone from a ninth-floor flat.

Human interest A young child hugging her mother after a long operation; a family of six evicted on to the pavement.

Humour The head dressed up as Henry VIII; a bull wearing a sombrero; the chairman pouring tea for the retiring tea lady.

Action People on an Outward Bound course clambering up a rock face; soldiers under fire running desperately across a road; horses falling at a fence.

Something different A machine photographed from very close or very far away; a city slicker in pinstripe standing on a Scottish mountain; a huge Great Dane eating from the same bowl as a Mexican Hairless.

Someone famous A film star doing something ordinary like making her lunch.

What most picture editors can do without are photos of:
- the managing director looking po-faced;
- the new branch manager looking po-faced;
- some minor VIP handing over a cheque/medal/long distance swimming certificate to an employee;
- someone presenting a huge cheque/medal/certificate to someone;
- grinning people standing in a straight line;
- two people trying to look interested at a VDU;
- a new product or machine against a white background;
- a group of people pretending to read a piece of paper;
- a pretty girl cavorting about with some consumer item.

So the two basic rules of press photography are: *a good photo will often carry a story* and *a photo needs an angle*.

GETTING THE ANGLE

Just like any piece of news, you have to find something about your photo that is going to make it stand out – its special angle. This applies whether you are in charge of your own photographer, or whether you are setting up a photocall for the press.

Don't, however, forget the message in all this. It's not particularly useful to get a photo printed unless it says the right things about you.

So always answer the question: What am I trying to say with this picture and to whom am I trying to say it? Then get on with ways to make it appeal to the papers.

Some classic ideas to work on:

Children and animals Baby drives tractor; children examine the baby deer in Richmond Park.

Contrast If the product is huge, show *how* huge by photographing it beside an elephant/local landmark/person on stilts. If it is tiny, compare to a pin/book/original model.

New and old Can you get the first X and photo it with the latest?

Picture the claim If you are launching something that is break-proof, set up a photo that shows it (a tank running over it? a strongman hitting it with a seldgehammer? a challenge to the local youth?).

Dramatise the claim If you say your city's air is not safe to breathe, purchase some gas masks in which to present your petition. If you say women should be freed from stereotyped ideas, arrange a public bra-burning (and just think how that particular image lingers on in people's minds, more than 20 years later).

If you are going to refuse to pay your TV licence because there's not enough sex and violence, then pick up your TV set and present it to the Broadcasting Standards Authority, saying you'll take it back when there are more exciting programmes broadcast.

Work the numbers If you say 30 children have been injured at a cross-roads, picture them by the roadside looking woeful.

Photo the retiring postman sitting on top of a mound of mailsacks representing one week's/one month's/one year's deliveries. Or walking down the hill with all the people on his round waving goodbye from the top.

In other words, while a picture of one thing may be ordinary, a picture of hundreds of things could be interesting.

Arty-crafty Can you think of an interesting photographic angle? From above or below? Through a hole? In close-up or far away? In an unusual place?

Role-reversal Someone in authority doing something lowly or silly or unexpected. Or someone lowly getting a chance to be in charge.

Action Rather than a cold technical photo of the new product get it in action. If necessary, get it being unloaded off the lorry, or dismantled, or being fitted: anything rather than it by itself, or being gazed at in mute admiration by someone.

The exception to this rule may be photos for the trade and technical press, where readers want to see the latest fascia of your washing machine in full unadorned close-up.

Fancy dress Whether historical, regional, or comical.

Celebrity link A nurse cuddling an AIDS patient is not news; Royalty doing it makes the headlines.

Pretty girls When all other ideas fail, bring on the dancing girls; but only as a last resort, please.

Look out for photos in papers that grab your attention, and keep a file of any that you might be able to adapt. There's no such thing as a new photographic angle any more than there's a new news angle.

CASE STUDY Too Many Cook(e)s . . .

From all over the country Cooks and Cookes were coached to Leicester – 1,200 of them – and the photographers were there to snap them.

This was a joint effort by the Coach Tourism Council and Leicester Tourism Development, to mark the 150th anniversary of Leicester-born Thomas Cook's first package holiday.

Anyone called Cook or Cooke was invited to travel by special coach to a photocall outside Leicester's De Montfort hall, and three hydraulic platforms were erected so that photographers could get the whole bunch of Cook(e)s into one shot.

Great care was taken to place the platforms and the Cooks so that pictures would include a huge banner hung in front of the hall proclaiming 'COACHING FOR PLEASURE DAY 1991 to the BIRTHPLACE OF TOURISM'.

Other angles were prepared: a stock of chef's hats; a local writer called Thomas Cook who has written a biography of his namesake and dresses up to impersonate him; and a man with a megaphone and a 'lost boy' calling out 'Will Mr and Mrs Cook please come forward!'

About 15 photographers and Central TV showed up. Nationals and the Leicester papers were interested in the mass of Cooks; papers from other regions were interested in their 'own' Cooks.

The photocall took about 15 minutes to shoot, but about four weeks to set up. On the day 20 organisers were involved, each fully briefed on their own role and having had a full run-through the day before.

SETTING UP A PHOTOCALL

Once you have decided that you can offer the chance of a 'good' photo to the press, you need to set up a photocall. Many of the basic rules are those of any press event (see Chapter 12), but there are some special requirements.

Tips for setting up a photocall

• Send a press release to the picture editor, with the usual 5 Ws (see Chapter 10). Give special details of the photo opportunities and the timing.

• Sometimes it makes sense to have a photocall the day before the press conference, e.g. if there's a product demonstration or fashion show or factory opening. Then the photographers have time to get better pictures.

• Phone on the day to check that the photographer knows the exact place and time.

• Find out whether power is required, and where the nearest power access is. If you are working outdoors this may mean laying on lengths of electrical cable. A dark room may need extra lighting too.

• If you are choosing the location, then try to choose outdoors, to minimise all the lighting problems.

• Check all uniforms, safety helmets, regulation dress, well before the event *and* just before the photographers arrive. Bring spares of everything.

• Check that everything is tidy, clean, and presents the image you want.

• If you want your product name or logo in shot, think about where you'll need to place the photographers or the celebrity.

• Allow space for the photographers to take close-ups of the chairman or the star.

• Check for inappropriate labels, name tags, etc.

• If you are demonstrating anything, then have at least one back-up in case Murphy's Law applies (if something can go wrong, it will).

• Prepare a written explanation of the event to give to the photographers, who will usually not have a clue. Give all names, titles, functions and addresses of anyone likely to appear in the photo.

• Remember that if it is vital that a photo is taken of the event, you should have your own back-up photographer, however adamant the local paper is that they will send someone.

A newspaper is usually happy to send you enlargements of any photos they publish; sometimes they will charge a small fee. They will keep the copyright on all photos, so you must get written permission if you want to reproduce or display them.

You can use these prints to send to those who took part or helped; this is all part of good internal public relations – important if you need to get people to help you again next time.

FINDING YOUR OWN PHOTOGRAPHER

If you want to take your own photos to go with a press release, you'll need to organise a photographer.

A press photo has to be a good photo. Just because Smith of Accounts takes a pretty nifty holiday snap it is not wise to let him loose on your publicity shots. If your budget really doesn't allow for a professional, then at least look for the best amateur you can, rather than leaving it till the last moment and grabbing anybody.

One half-way house is to get in touch with, for instance, the local college and see if they have students on graphics or industrial design courses (or indeed photography); they should be reasonably competent with access to proper equipment, and will be far cheaper than a professional. Or you could try the local photographers club or adult education centre.

But it is best to get a professional if you can.

Tips for finding a professional photographer

Compile a list The Yellow Pages and Thompson's will list photographers in your area. Also the National Union of Journalists (Acorn House, 314 Gray's Inn Road, London) has a directory of freelance news photographers working in each region. And publications like *Hollis*, *Benn's* and PR *Planner* have a photographic section.

Look around Not all photographers are equally good at all subjects; someone who is great for action shots will probably be no good for a technical studio shot. So look at the photographs appearing in local publications and find out who does what.

See the portfolio All photographers will have a portfolio of their work which will give a good idea of range and quality.

BRIEFING A PHOTOGRAPHER

You should have a very clear idea what you want from a photographer working for you. It's no good giving some vague instruction like 'Just get a few good action shots' because who knows what you'll get. On the other hand, don't try to teach her photography. If the professional says your idea of silhouetting 40 workmen on a ladder against a stained glass window is rubbish, then don't fight it.

CASE STUDY But Where's our Product?

A manufacturer of children's play equipment brought out a new range of swings, and set up a picture call in an attractive garden with a group of photogenic children.

The photographer was told to get pictures of the children playing. A few days later his contact prints arrived: his photos did show the children playing, but only about one quarter showed the equipment. Either the children were in close-up, or you couldn't see what sort of object they were sitting on, or they weren't even on the swings at all.

So make sure you make everything clear:

WHAT SORT OF PICTURES?

Brief thoroughly on the story angle. Do you want close-ups, long shots, pictures with the logo visible, action, smiles?

If you want a variety of different photos, suitable for various publications, make this clear: 'We want some technical product shots; a line-up of the export staff around the machine for our own in-house journal; a series of action shots with the operator; and Mrs Black the graphics designer is going to come and spray paint it for the "Ugly Bug joins in Fun Run" angle for the local paper.'

It is usually a good idea to specify a variety of shots, especially a mix of close-ups and long shots, and if a process is involved, make sure you get a sequence of shots showing the process from start to finish.

SIZE AND COLOUR

The usual press format is 6" × 8", glossy black and white, close grain. Some papers do print in colour, too. Many magazines like transparencies. Specify before the day exactly what you want. Don't assume that the photographer will arrive with the right sort of film.

If a shot is to be used as a cover, where will the heading be? And are you hoping to use any photos for a television interview as back-up stills? In which case, the picture ought to be composed to fit well on to a TV screen.

PRICE AND COPYRIGHT

Negotiate a fee beforehand: discover whether there will be any 'extras' (such as overtime if the shoot takes longer than two hours or a rush fee if you want the prints quickly). Are expenses and VAT included? What if it rains? If this will mean postponing the shoot, then negotiate a 'rain-off' fee.

You will own the copyright of the prints; the photographer will own the copyright to the negatives. If for any reason you want the copyright on the negatives, you will have to buy it from the photographer.

TIMING AND ORGANISATION

Let the photographer know as truthfully as possible how long you think it will take and what time and day.

Give full details of the location, with a map and parking place. Give a contact name and number at the location, with at least one other contact number in case of emergencies.

Let the photographer know when you want to see the results. It's no good telling him on the day that you need to send photos off at six o'clock that evening.

Where do you want prints delivered? And if you are having contact prints (i.e. negatives size) sent, make sure you have a magnifying glass to hand.

SENDING OUT THE PHOTOS

A large number of photos sent with press releases just never get used because someone has written on the back in pencil, or a photo gets detached from its release and no one has a clue which particular charity cheque story goes with this photo.

Don't mark it Don't write on the back at all; even soft pencil or felt tip can show through or mark another photo. And don't attach it to the press release with a paper clip.

Send photos in card-backed envelopes marked 'Do not bend'.

Do label it The most foolproof system is to write a very short description on a sticky label that cross-references to your main press release: 'Spot the Dog (second from left) presenting an autographed bone to Sarah Brown, 9, winner of the "Spot Spot" competition, on 12 August 1992.'

Then write a longer photo caption on half A4 and tape (not glue) it to the back of the photo. One handy trick is to tape it so that it hangs down under the photo so that picture and words can be seen at the same time. A photo caption should be fairly short, but should still answer the 5Ws (Who? What? Why? When? Where?).

It is worth writing a separate photo caption even if the photo is going with a longer release. It's much easier for the paper if all they have to do is tear off the taped story, ready for use, rather than write their own condensed version of the full release. Also you keep more control over the words and content.

Highlight people and points Make sure you identify names, titles, ages, addresses, of all key people in the photo. If there's any possible confusion, or you want to point out some special feature, make a photocopy and mark that.

Target If possible don't send the same photo to everyone, but choose the appropriate pictures for each publication. Better still, send two or three to each publication so that they can choose.

Re-use If you think there's any chance that your photo might get re-used by the publication (and many trade monthlies will ring the changes on a photo by reversing it or cropping it so that they can recycle), then put on the back: 'May be re-used with full acknowledgement'.

KEEPING YOUR OWN FILES

Keep a number of copies of all the photos you have taken, together with the original press release. Store them in cardboard-backed envelopes, with a photocopy of the print on the front and reference numbers, date, caption, and photographer's name on the back.

It's useful to have two or three prints labelled and captioned, ready to be sent immediately.

Some people keep a master file of photocopies and captions, that are cross-referenced to the original prints.

A parallel file could be made of photocopies of photos taken by different photographers, so that over the years you build up your own portfolio of people working in your area.

MUG SHOTS

You should also have mug shots of all your key people, just in case one of them suddenly rescues a busload of grannies from certain death on a level crossing, or runs off with the pension fund account. It's wise to have a smiling shot and a serious shot, to suit all possible contingencies.

The trouble with portraits is that they tend to look like police photos. People are often more natural if pictured working or doing something; if it's a good quality photo, it can always be cropped to just show the face if that's all that is wanted.

The alternative is posed studio portraits, but these do look very formal and are expensive. If you do have formal portraits, check the copyright carefully – there may be a fee for each time the picture is used. So buy the reproduction rights if necessary.

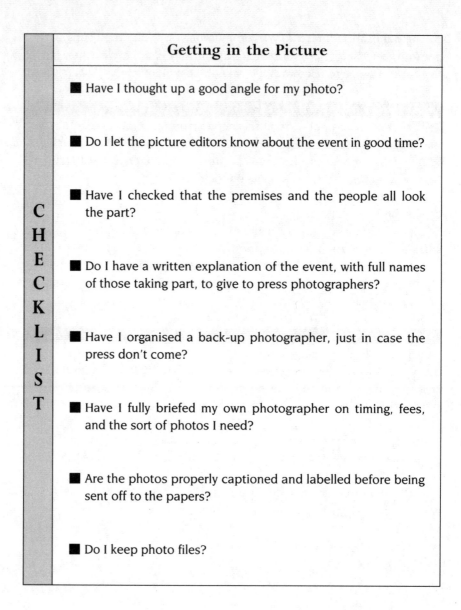

Getting in the Picture

C H E C K L I S T

■ Have I thought up a good angle for my photo?

■ Do I let the picture editors know about the event in good time?

■ Have I checked that the premises and the people all look the part?

■ Do I have a written explanation of the event, with full names of those taking part, to give to press photographers?

■ Have I organised a back-up photographer, just in case the press don't come?

■ Have I fully briefed my own photographer on timing, fees, and the sort of photos I need?

■ Are the photos properly captioned and labelled before being sent off to the papers?

■ Do I keep photo files?

PART FOUR

RADIO AND TELEVISION: THE HOT MEDIA

14

Getting on Air

- Broadcasters want lively, newsy, relevant material, suited to their particular audience.
- They especially want good pictures or sound to give atmosphere.
- Nothing is any use to them unless it is recorded, so they need interviewees able to perform quickly and effectively.
- Deadlines work to minutes and seconds; so the first person to come up with the goods is the one who will appear on air.
- Radio is relatively low-tech and casual; television is more daunting. But familiarity helps.

SO YOU WANT TO BE A STAR

THE peculiarity of broadcasting, especially television, is that it makes people 'real'. It makes the unreal seem like reality (you should see the sacks of mail addressed to the cast of any popular soap), and it gives glamour to ordinary old Mr Brown of Accounts who just happened to be around during a bank robbery and appears on the telly as a result.

Broadcasting does give a buzz; if you're looking for a morale boost for your organisation, try to get on BBC 1's *Nine O'Clock News*.

EXAMPLE The Power of the Media

The attractive middle manager of an electronics firm was asked to appear in a documentary about women's experiences at work. She knew a TV researcher from college days, and fitted the bill because she worked in a high-tech field, she was articulate and the researcher knew she'd speak her mind.

Her bit lasted only about half a minute but the morning after the broadcast, her colleagues crowded round, most impressed. Her boss asked to see her: 'You made an excellent case, Julie, about your problems; we'll see what we can do.' Within a week she had promotion.

It was as if Julie's views could only be taken seriously once she had made them on television.

WHAT ATTRACTS THE BROADCASTERS?

What a radio or television reporter wants is mostly what a press reporter wants: something that is lively, relevant, important, dramatic, interesting. They want people stories; they want local issues if a local network; national issues if a national network.

There are particular quirks, however. The types of radio and television programmes and how they are organised are described in Chapter 6, so look at that chapter if you want the reasons and background.

The added elements they look for are: atmosphere, a good talker and last-minute timing.

ATMOSPHERE

Whether it's a windblown heath for the murder hunt or a public baths for the how-to-learn-water-polo radio interview, broadcasters love actuality to give colour and atmosphere.

So if you can provide a good picture or a good sound, you are going to be attractive. As the Whale report on Broadcasting (1979) said:

'Television is pictures. It feeds on them. It must have them. There can be silence, but there must be pictures.'

Your location may naturally be visually attractive – if you make hot-air balloons, or want to promote real tennis, you're in luck. Or you may have to try to think of a visual or aural angle to add to your otherwise mundane event.

So ask yourself these questions:

- Do I have a particularly visual workplace – old, very tall, an interesting machine, a lot of interesting machines, beautiful gardens, a view, an underground vault …? If I have an event or press conference, can I bring this in somehow?
- Can I find a location that will add visual content? If I'm talking about children's education, can I use a school? If I'm promoting a new environmental campaign, which place will best prove my point visually? If I'm opening a new bicycle shop can I hire a penny-farthing and get a race organised beginning or ending at the front door?
- Can I add visual content? The classic way is to have a logo around, but there are more exciting ways. All the tricks for photos apply (see Chapter 13), but for television things ought to be moving too, or have a back-up sound element.

  Can you organise a dancing Chinese dragon competition? Or a go at *The Guinness Book of Records* spaghetti-eating record? Or a flight of doves? Or a milk-float race?
- Do I have something that sounds good? If you're organising a fête and the Baltuanian girl flautists are performing on Baltuanian flutes made from hedgehog bones, then push that with the local radio station. If your health education group is having an anti-smoking rap competition, invite the local DJ to be a judge.

  Radio likes music, interesting background noises like steam trains or fairgrounds, poetry and limericks, and strange atmospherics like coal mines and cathedrals. So be aware of the possible special sound angles when you set up an event, and tell the radio station about them.
- Can I add something that sounds good? If you want radio to be there you may need to think up a sound angle. Can you set up four of your new talking computers to sing Frère Jacques in unison? Can you organise a competition for the best company song in preparation for your new Japanese export drive, to show the Japanese that you're just as proud of your company as Mitsubishi is of theirs?

CASE STUDY You Too can Sound like Donald Duck

A reporter from the Central Office of Information came to do a radio interview with a company manufacturing diving equipment. During the preliminary chat, she discovered that the new way to stop divers getting the bends when they resurfaced was to give them a special mix of air containing helium to breathe underwater.

This worked well, but as a side-effect made their voices sound like Donald Duck. She was a freelance and grabbed the opportunity. For the COI she did a regular straight interview, but for home audiences she did a piece that demonstrated the helium effect which of course was quite amusing.

This piece went out on BBC Radio 4 and was then picked up by other presenters who arranged for their own try at hearing their helium voices. Eventually the organisation got about 30 minutes' worth of air time. Luckily for them, their story was exploited by the freelance; they could have thought it up for themselves . . .

CASE STUDY Spilling the Beans

An agriculturist working in Africa for one of the large aid agencies had devised an entertaining way of teaching villagers basic facts. He made up songs that he taught as he travelled around; they had catchy tunes and simple words like: 'Plant the yams and then the beans; put the plantains in between' to show crop rotation.

He had recordings he'd made of people singing in the fields with African harmonies of the tunes, and when he was on vacation back in London his agency suggested to the World Service that it might make a nice item.

He sang a jolly bean-planting song in the studio with guitar, which was then faded into the Africa version. And then he had a short interview about his agricultural work for the agency.

There is no way that he'd have been asked to talk about crop rotation except for the song. As it was, the song was picked up by *Pick of the Week* (the compilation of the best bits on radio and TV during the previous week), and so it got an airing on home radio too.

A GOOD TALKER

It's rare for a broadcast report not to include at least one person being interviewed. It may be an eyewitness to an accident or an environmental spokesperson or a local MP, but most editors dislike reports that are just 'voice pieces', i.e. a straight talk by the reporter giving the news,

Sometimes, talking heads are practically the only thing to be heard. Local radio survives on a diet of music, interviews and phone-ins, with the hapless guest expected to give instant advice to ignorant presenters or incomprehensible callers.

If you are a good talker, though, you will be in demand. Jargon is out. So is technical language. So are long rambling answers. What is needed is maximum clarity of thought and language, delivered with enthusiasm and pace.

Trainee journalists in BBC News used to be told that when preparing their scripts, they must choose the words and explanations that would be immediately interesting and comprehensible to 'a Sheffield bus driver's wife'. In broadcasting there is no going back; if you aren't understood on first hearing, you won't be understood at all.

LAST-MINUTE TIMING

A broadcast journalist's main worry is to get a picture or tape and to get it back to the studio. News reporters get praised by their editors for getting to a story fast and sending it back at once. A reporter who needs five takes to record his on-the-spot commentary, or spends half an hour identifying the right person to interview, will not last long in radio or television.

So the imperative is to get something on tape fast. This is often more important than the quality, though of course facts will be checked before the actual transmission, just in case. ITN has a motto: 'Success is measured in seconds'.

This means that if you have a news story breaking on your patch, the broadcasting news reporters will have a far more rushed approach than the press reporters whose deadlines are relatively relaxed. The local radio reporter, for instance, knows that if he can get the story in the next 10 minutes it can go out on the midday news bulletin: a scoop! His editor will be pleased because she likes the feeling that radio is an 'instant' medium, bringing listeners the news as it happens. So he will hassle you down the phone or in person: he will want a comment now; and if you don't provide it now, he will go ahead and file a report anyway. From his point of view, waiting till the three o'clock bulletin will make the news stale.

Similarly, if you are contacted by a radio or TV journalist because they want your comment on something else (the latest economic figures or the reports of a perpetual motion machine), then they too want it fast, which may mean in the next hour or even the next 5 minutes.

Time tends to dominate broadcasters, who have to watch every second. This can even lead to dropping an otherwise good story from a live programme, just because its timing fits. For instance, sometimes it happens at the last moment that an editor or producer has to shorten the programme, or put in a new urgent piece. Say the new piece is 1 minute 32 seconds long; then you look for another piece that length and out it goes, willy-nilly.

GETTING THEM TO COME TO YOU

The implications of all this, if you want to appear on radio or television, are:

Think visual and think aural. If you have good pictures or sound, then phone up the appropriate producers or researchers and tell them so. Don't just send out the press release and leave them to come to the right conclusions.

If you haven't got good visuals or sound, but you want broadcast coverage, try to inject some.

Promote yourself or your spokesperson as 'rent-a-pundit'. First you need to develop the skills that make for a lively interview: punchiness, pace, a clear way of explaining things, and a voice that doesn't send people to sleep.

Secondly you have to make yourself available. If you decide to go down the road of, for instance, local radio coverage, then you need to be prepared to 'waste' a lot of time. You may have to hang around in studios, or wait on the phone till they get a recording link organised, or make casual chat with reporters coming round with recorders. You may not always even get on air. Either your interview gets cut, or the reporter may contact you merely for background info. A common request is for your low-down on someone else, so that the reporter can work out some sticky questions for them.

In the end all this can be worth it. Start off, if necessary, by offering yourself for interview or comment. Listen out for anything in the news that you could have something interesting to comment on. Then phone the appropriate programme and 'sell' your contribution. If it goes well, and you do this a few times, they will start to come to you. Your name will be in the little black book of contacts, so that whenever there's a need for a quick comment from a high-street shop, or a local play group, or a company knowledgeable about Russian joint ventures, they'll think of you.

Work to their deadlines, not yours. Often their deadlines won't be too dreadful, especially if the material is features or soft news. When it is hot news, though, you have to be prepared to jump. Try to co-operate with the deadline, because if you don't you won't get on at all. Conversely, if you get a reputation for being able to provide the goods at short notice, you will get more and more coverage.

Listen to programmes and watch for opportunities. There's a wealth of chances out there, especially on local and community radio. See Chapter 6 for a round-up of different types of programme. Consider:

- What sort of guests appear in the local radio's chat pro-grammes, wedged between pop records? Is there any aspect of what I do that could fit?
- Do outsiders appear on phone-ins? Could we offer general advice on something? Is there a controversial aspect to what we do that would generate phone calls?
- Is there any legislation, plan, White Paper, announcement, new proposal, etc., coming up relevant to us? Can I prepare a response to it, so that when the official announcement is made, we can be the first to provide a coherent comment? Even better, can I contact radio or television in advance to say we'll be prepared to provide instant comment on the day?
- What specialist programmes are there which might be inter-ested in our sort of news? Check out both national and local programmes with a particular slant towards: women, health, education, the arts, business, technology, sport, children, travel, consumer ... Could I offer either hard news (new product, success, etc.) or soft (advice, research, interesting angle) relevant to that audience?

WHO TO CONTACT

Just as with newspapers and magazines, you need to contact the right peo-ple with your story or idea.

If you are generating a news story, e.g. a product launch or announce-ment of a big success, then you can send a press release in the usual way to your local radio or TV, though don't bother unless it is quite a big story. There just isn't the same amount of room in a broadcast news bulletin as there is in a local newspaper.

If you want to comment on some big story, though, then phone the news room or the appropriate correspondent. Imagine you read in your morning paper that the council has a plan to run a bypass over your car park, and you're not happy about it. Then phone the local radio news room and say you've strong feelings on the subject and would like to make a comment.

There's no point in sending a press release to them or even waiting till the afternoon. Do it straight away, get your name in there first, and strike while the news is still hot.

If you have a soft news story or an idea for a feature, then contact the producer (radio) or a researcher (television). Either send a letter or telephone, with:

- the basic information and facts;
- the particular angle that makes it good for radio or TV;
- the particular angle that makes it good for this programme;
- your contact name and number.

The other option is to get a freelance to pick up your idea, and get him or her to do the placement.

YES, WE WANT YOU

Whether the idea comes from you or from them, once things begin to happen there'll be the same procedure: you'll get a phone call and either someone will come to you to record on location, or you'll be called to a studio.

Either way it will take time and probably be nerve-wracking, so it's best to be prepared for what it will be like.

ON LOCATION WITH A TAPE RECORDER

Or: 'Have Uher, will travel'. If someone comes to tape you for radio, it is all very low-tech. Most radio journalists use a portable reel-to-reel recorder (often a Uher), with a hand-held microphone. This is because reel-to-reel tape is extremely easy and quick to edit, unlike cassette tape. You just need a razor blade, a metal editing block, and some splicing tape. An experienced person can cut out not just whole sections but also parts of words, ums and ers, and join the front half of one sentence to the back half of another.

She will look for a place to record that either has an appropriate atmosphere for the subject, or that has no background noise at all. This does not mean that you should usher her into the office that is about to be redecorated and thus is completely empty. Places without furniture or carpets sound on tape like public loos.

Try to find somewhere that isn't next door to a noisy office or the roadworks; that doesn't have interruptions (put a notice on the door and cut off the phone); and that doesn't have central air conditioning which makes a hum and can't be turned off.

You'll be asked to sit down and your interviewer will sit next to you (not on the other side of your desk like a job applicant!). She may very well sit extremely close, in order to cut out any background noise remaining. She doesn't fancy you, she's just doing her job.

The microphone will normally be held between you, at chest level, unless there's a lot of noise, when it will be held right up to your nose. Try not to be transfixed by it, nor to grab hold of it. Just speak normally and the reporter will adjust the levels.

Don't ask for it to be played back afterwards; reporters don't have time for this, and in any case, it will probably be edited down before it goes on air. You can try asking for a copy of the finished version but don't be surprised if it doesn't arrive (a reporter may be doing five or six interviews a day). It's better to try to find out when it will go out (the reporter won't necessarily know right then), and then record it off the air. Tellex Monitors will get you a copy, if you do miss it.

ON LOCATION WITH A CAMERA CREW

The invention of Electronic News Gathering (ENG) has made outside location work for television far easier than it used to be. Even so, a television crew will have a lot of equipment and it will take them a lot longer to set up and record a simple interview than the sole radio reporter with his Uher.

The minimum crew is a camera operator, sound and lights operator, and a reporter. A documentary crew will probably have a director, a researcher, a production assistant, and separate technical bods as well.

Let's imagine you're going to be recorded in your office. About half an hour to an hour before the interview, the camera crew will be setting up lights and camera. There'll be a jumble of cables and extensions, and they'll have seized anything visually interesting like a potted plant or a fancy sculpture and re-arranged it to compose a pretty picture.

The sound person will put a small lapel mic on you, perhaps just pinning it to a lapel, or possibly running the wire up the inside of your shirt or blouse (just submit to this calmly – it's his job).

You will probably be asked to sit at a particular angle; the reporter will sit with his back to the camera; and after a bit of banal chat to establish sound levels and to get some shots of the two of you talking, the interview will begin with a countdown from the camera operator.

Because of the lights it will be hot; have a glass of water handy. Even if you are told it's 'just a rehearsal', always answer for real; they may be telling the truth, they may not.

CASE STUDY I Woz Robbed

The director of a port was giving an interview about a potential industrial action. He was outside with a background of cranes and ships, and gave signs of being nervous.

The reporter reassured him, and said that they'd have a rehearsal, so that he could get used to the questions and get a feel of the proceedings. She then went into a list of questions, which he answered fairly lackadaisically. At the end she said thank you, and everyone began to pack up. 'What happened to my interview?' he asked, and she told him that they'd recorded the 'practice', and it was just fine.

He didn't feel too happy, because he hadn't really been trying but accepted the situation. He might have been right to do so; crews normally play this trick not to trip you up, but because someone nervous may perform much better under the illusion that it's not for real. But it's best always to try hard, even if it really is a rehearsal, just in case.

After the interview, you'll probably be told you can go. But the reporter and crew will remain. They'll be doing 'cut-aways' and 'reverses' and 'noddy shots' (see below and Chapter 16): all techniques to smooth the editing later.

Because there's only one camera, it will have been looking at the interviewee during the interview. So the first job will be to re-record the most important questions with the camera this time looking at the interviewer. The production assistant will have made a note of the wording, or the sound tape will be played back; then the interviewer says all the questions in a row with a little pause between each. The next job will be reaction shots: the interviewer 'listening' to your pearls of wisdom. They're called 'noddy shots' because the easiest reaction is to nod wisely.

Finally, there'll be cutaways: maybe close-ups of a pamphlet referred to in the interview or the architect's drawing.

Some advice:

- Stick around if you can during this process. Listen to the repeated questions and check that the wording and tone isn't substantially different from the original. For example, imagine this interview:

  Reporter: There are rumours that your company is about to crash; should investors be removing their money now?
  Chairman: (in rather irritated tone) It's completely untrue that we're in any financial trouble. Of course investors shouldn't be worried about their investment with us despite these ridiculous rumours, etc. ...

If a different question is recorded and inserted afterwards, it could come out like this:

Reporter: (in bland tone) What does the future look like for your company?
Chairman: (in narked tone) It's completely untrue that we're in any financial trouble ... etc.

His aggrieved response to such an innocent question makes him look a liar, or at least in bad trouble. So listen to those questions and check anything you're not happy about.

- You don't need to appear suspicious of their motives, though. Merely offer to stay in your chair to help with the 'eyeline'. This is actually very helpful to the interviewer as then he doesn't have to focus his eyes on nothing trying to remember how tall you are.
- Also keep a watch on what else is being filmed. Why exactly are they filming the dustbins at the back or the peeling poster beside the canteen?
- Hang around if anyone else is being interviewed, to make sure that they toe the company line. You can't exactly wade in with 'Cut!' should someone start dishing the dirt on the chairman's backhanders to the local Planning Committee, but your very presence will at least stop casual negative remarks. And if you hear anything more serious being said, you can demand a retake of the main interview to reply to any allegations. (You won't necessarily get it, but at least you'll be prepared for trouble when the broadcast goes out.)

IN A RADIO STUDIO

A radio station is a pretty chaotic place; the foyer may look smart but the offices are usually a jumble of papers, piles of tapes, and bins full of discarded bits of interviews.

Studios are frequently in the basement, without natural light, down endless corridors. They can be tiny, just enough room for two people to squeeze into, so you feel you are being interviewed in a broom cupboard. A typical studio will be about 3 or 4 metres square, with a table and chairs and a microphone suspended from the ceiling. The walls are brown hessian to dampen the sound, and on one wall there is a glass window looking through to the recording equipment on the other side. Here there'll be an engineer or producer in charge of the machines.

The person interviewing you may have headphones on or may communicate visually with the person on the other side. A red light will go on when things are being recorded, but it is wise to treat anything you say in the studio as 'live', just in case.

Don't bang on the table or knock your leg against it, because this will be picked up by the mic, especially if it's placed on the table. Similarly, don't have papers in front of you that rustle. If you do want to take notes with you, put them in a plastic folder so that you can pick them up or push them around without making a noise.

IN A TELEVISION STUDIO

A television studio is predominantly grey; even the rubber floor is dark grey. The set that looks so colourful and smart on screen in reality is tatty and flimsy. Everything looks chaotic and untidy, but it works very efficiently in practice.

A typical studio will have three or four cameras facing a coloured back-cloth. There'll be rows and rows of lights, obscuring the ceiling, and cables all over the floor. It may be in its own room, or more usually part of a larger studio, with other sets dotted about and the ceiling high above.

There'll be various people scurrying about, including the floor manager who is in overall charge of what goes on in the studio itself. There are the camera operators, sound engineers, autocue operators, electricians, production assistants, and general dogsbodies.

High up and far away out of sight are the Big Shots in the gallery. The producer sits up there controlling not just what goes on in the studio but also which camera shots are recorded on tape, how it is mixed, the overall timing, and so on. He or she has another technical crew up there, including video engineers, mixers, researchers, more production asistants, etc. The producer communicates with the studio crew through their headphones or over the PA system.

An interviewee may never see the producer at all. The typical scenario might be like this:

6.00 p.m.	You arrive at reception and are shown into the dressing-room.
6.40	You go to make-up.
6.55	Researcher arrives to talk through the interview, and explain that there'll be a short film to introduce the subject, and that then you'll have about 2 minutes of talk.
7.05	You are taken to the studio and sat in a dark corner. No one takes any more notice of you for the next 15 minutes and you don't see any of the people you've already met.
7.20	Someone suddenly grabs you, plonks you in a chair on the set, and fumbles about with a microphone on your lapel. You just have time to shyly smile at the famous presenter, when a man

in headphones starts to count to zero and the presenter goes all glassy-eyed. He says a few words, the monitor screen shows the film, and you're into your interview . . .

7.24   The presenter briefly thanks you, then goes all glassy-eyed again as he listens to instructions through his ear-piece. You are unplugged, the researcher arrives to take you away and thank you effusively. Off you go, with no idea how it really went.

As an interviewee, you are merely one cog in a huge machine, and it can feel very strange. But remember that they are all there working towards making the people on screen look right. So you may feel unimportant or ignored, but your interview is the end-product.

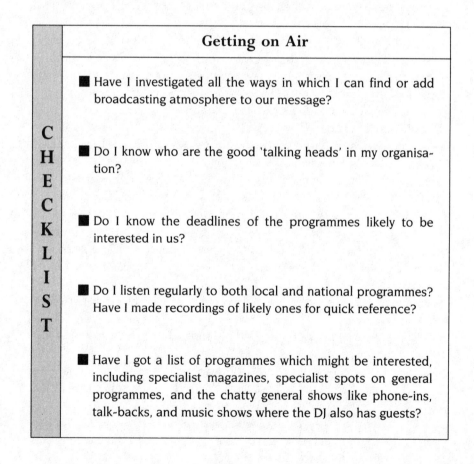

CHECKLIST

Getting on Air

■ Have I investigated all the ways in which I can find or add broadcasting atmosphere to our message?

■ Do I know who are the good 'talking heads' in my organisation?

■ Do I know the deadlines of the programmes likely to be interested in us?

■ Do I listen regularly to both local and national programmes? Have I made recordings of likely ones for quick reference?

■ Have I got a list of programmes which might be interested, including specialist magazines, specialist spots on general programmes, and the chatty general shows like phone-ins, talk-backs, and music shows where the DJ also has guests?

15

You're On! Performing in an Interview

- You don't have very long to get your message across so every word counts.
- Too many points just get lost; it's better to put across two or three well with memorable images or personal experience.
- Jargon and airy generalisations are equally tedious. Words should be simple and strong, sentences short.
- You can keep control by finding out as much as possible about the interview beforehand, and then using each question as a springboard for what *you* want to say.
- It's nearly always better to opt for a live interview rather than a pre-recorded one, because then you'll avoid all the editing pitfalls.

SO YOU THINK YOU'VE GOT SOMETHING TO SAY?

The phone goes, and at the other end is your local radio station's star reporter. He wants you to come to the studio to talk about your announced job losses. The first reaction is usually, 'Help!' The second should be to get down to work, preparing yourself.

191

Chapter 6 examines different types of radio and television programme and Chapter 11 looks at the general principles of preparing for an interview. So read those chapters before you carry on.

The main points are:

- Find out as much as you can about the programme, the context of the interview, and the theme of the questions.
- Find out roughly how long a piece he wants.
- Identify the two or three main points you want to make, in this context, to this particular audience, at this particular time.
- For each main point, work out two or three ways of making it come alive.
- Practise your answers; especially work on fielding negative questions and making them into positive answers.

Then get in your car or bus and set off, confident that you have the right attitude: 'I will put across what I want to say; I will make the most of my 30 seconds or 5 minutes of air time.'

Better still, get some media training now, before the call comes. There's only so much you can learn from reading a book and doing your own practice. Many organisations will put you under the lights or in front of a microphone, in a safe place where no one else will see the ghastly results. So if you, or someone in your organisation, are likely to be on air, look at Chapter 20 for tips on how to choose a course.

BE PREPARED

Once you know exactly what you want to say, and have practised good positive punchy answers to all the possible questions you can think of, then what do you do with all that material?

The answer is to condense. You certainly don't want to arrive clutching a wodge of papers that will only fall on the floor at the wrong time. Even worse, you'll be tempted to refer to them to find that interesting figure. One of the unfortunate conventions of broadcasting is that the interviewer is allowed notes, but the expert isn't! If you refer to a piece of paper, viewers think you don't know your business.

On the other hand, many people feel as uncomfortable without notes as without their trousers. So if you don't have enough confidence to do without notes at all, put your three key points (no more!) on a postcard or in a clear plastic folder (so that the paper doesn't rustle). If necessary, add your main examples or figures. But apply the T-shirt test – could you fit it all on a T-shirt? If not, then you've got too much. Don't be tempted to put down too much; two or three points put across well with good examples is what you're aiming for.

Come the interview, you can keep the notes in front of you for radio, but for television, you'll have to put them out of sight before the cameras roll – preferably out of reach, too.

CASE STUDY The Paper Chase

A senior executive was interviewed live on a local radio programme about his company's involvement in a financial scandal. He had prepared his case thoroughly and took along a sheaf of notes giving all the facts and figures that would prove they were innocent parties to someone else's fraud.

The first question was a general one; the second went to the heart of the matter and the executive reached for the relevant piece of paper. Alas, it went flying, along with most of the other papers, and ended up on the floor.

He was so thrown by this that he bumbled his way through the answer and the next answer as well. Though he recovered himself for the final question, the impression given was that he was on the defensive, had something to hide, and didn't know the facts. All because he had too many notes.

One other basic preparation is to remove all possible distractions. If you know that you tend to jangle the change in your pocket or click a ball point pen when you're nervous, then remove the temptation. Empty your pockets, put all pens out of reach, take off your watch …

ARRIVING ON TIME

Whatever time you are told, aim to be there at least 15 minutes earlier. It may be that you'll be offered a chauffeured car; otherwise go by taxi or be driven by a friend, so that you don't waste time parking. Make absolutely sure you know where you are going. Media people are very self-absorbed and notoriously bad at realising that other people are ignorant about television or radio. Check which studios and what the contact name will be.

HELP, I NEED A DRINK!

No, you don't need a drink. Alcohol is a depressant, and while it may get rid of your nerves it will also flatten your voice, bring out any lurking speech impediments, and dull your reflexes. The ever-flowing drinks trolley is a thing of the past in most broadcasting stations, but there may be an offer of a trip to the green room or hospitality suite for a quick drink.

Why do they offer alcohol? To loosen you up of course, to make you drop your guard. This might be a good thing from the interviewer's point of view, but it isn't likely to be great news for you. So stick to soft drinks. Even coffee and tea can be dangerous, because caffeine and tannin can affect your throat when you are nervous.

If you don't believe that even a small alcoholic drink affects performance, try this test: choose a tongue twister or a complicated poem and record yourself reading it when completely sober. Then record yourself about 10 minutes after having an alcoholic drink. See if a friend can spot which was done under the influence.

WHAT TO DO ABOUT NERVES

Nerves are not bad. Everyone has nerves, including the presenters and interviewers. There are certain famous personalities who are sick before every live broadcast, but you wouldn't know it to listen to them.

The buzz given by nerves is what makes your performance a living one. We've all heard the smoothy government spokesperson droning on in polished syntax and even more polished tones about some new initiative. It's so smooth it sounds unreal, and the impression is not competence but insincerity.

This thought is not very helpful, though, if it's your first broadcast and you're shaking like a leaf. There are various recommended procedures, all or none of which may help you:

- deep breathing just before you start;
- imagine your interviewer with no clothes on or on the loo;
- relaxing by tensing hands or feet and then releasing them;
- doing a crossword or a chess puzzle while waiting.

If none of this helps, then don't worry. Once you get started those nerves will almost certainly be forgotten, especially if you are really listening to each question and trying to grab the opportunities to push your message. The adrenalin should actually help you, because it will sharpen you up and speed your reaction time. It's there to help you win a fight with a sabre-tooth tiger; so use it to win interviews too.

One effect of nerves is a dried-up throat. It's a wise precaution to have a glass of water somewhere within reach, just in case.

Building up confidence is one of the really useful things a media training session can do for you. Just doing two or three interviews – however ghastly they were – will do wonders for your confidence when it comes to the real thing. Even a home-made session in front of a home video camera can help a bit to get over the awkwardness.

BASICS OF PERFORMANCE

What are you offering radio or television? You have only yourself – your personality and words. So what you look like or sound like are far more important than in a paper interview.

The great power of broadcasting is that people at the other end can make up their own minds about what you are telling them, without the interference of a journalist writing it down. So like it or not, what they feel about you as a person is often more important than the facts you're trying to get across.

Your aim should be to appear: competent, friendly, relevant and enthusiastic.

Ask someone what they remember of the facts of any television interview an hour or so later. You'll be lucky if they remember anything more than a vague outline of the subject: 'Something about a road safety campaign, wasn't it? Didn't he want us all to slow down or something? I think he said that at 20 mph you were less likely to kill a pedestrian ...'

Ask that same person what he felt about the interviewee, and what he was wearing: 'I thought he seemed quite a nice bloke; a bit middle-class perhaps, sort of *Guardian* reader I should think. He had dark hair and specs; wore a suit which seemed a bit silly as he was standing in the rain at the time talking to the interviewer. His eyes were a bit shifty, I should think he was nervous, but that's fair enough. Yes, he was the sort of person I wouldn't mind buying a second-hand car from. He seemed very concerned and sincere about it all ...'

It's sad, but you mustn't be too ambitious about your aims in a radio or television interview. If you can get across a general idea plus an image of you (and therefore your organisation) as competent and sincere, then you'll have done well.

VOICE

You have to sound as if you care. Enthusiasm or passion or just involvement are vital, especially in radio where there is only your voice. If you aren't interested in your subject, then why on earth should anyone else be?

The naturally extrovert won't find it hard to sound enthusiastic. The more shy may find it difficult. One main way that a voice sounds enthusiastic is in the ups and downs, so if you know you have a rather flat voice then use a tape recorder to practise putting more variety into it. It also helps to sit in an enthusiastic way, even for radio. Don't allow yourself to lean back in your chair, or slump onto the arm, because it comes out in your voice. Lean forward and stay upright.

Don't worry about an accent unless it makes you incomprehensible! In many interviews, a clear regional accent is a real help.

TIME

The average television interview is 2 minutes. How much can you say in 2 minutes?

As it happens you can say quite a lot if you put it the right way. But if you start off by giving us a run-down on the complicated financial reasons why you began the technical research on a way to use up the waste materials from your factory ... a minute and a half will have gone by and you'll have only 30 seconds left to tell us what the new wonder product is, how it means you'll be expanding, increasing profits, and taking on lots of new staff. You won't do it.

Then you'll end up frustrated because – once it's over – you realise you didn't say any of your real points.

The timing rule for broadcasting is three words a second. That means that if you are interviewed for 2 minutes, you'll be able to say approximately 300 words – the equivalent of five or six paragraphs in a quality newspaper. If you're asked to do a 'soundbite' of 10–20 seconds, you've got the equivalent of one paragraph. So it's wise to pay attention to Body Shop founder Anita Roddick's definition of a good interviewee: 'The ability to cut the crap and get straight to the point.'

Tips for interview timing

• Keep your answers short, no longer than 30–45 seconds. Any longer and either the interviewer will intervene and ask another question, or you'll have lost your audience anyway.

• Keep your answers to the point, going straight into your planned message. If you ramble you'll never get there.

• Try to have an awareness of the overall timing. In a live interview you can use this to your advantage by finishing with a good flourish. But even in a recorded interview, the interviewer will try to keep to time to limit editing afterwards, so pace your points.

LANGUAGE

Cut the jargon, cut the abstractions. Go for the word-pictures, the telling phrase. Politicians know the value of a good phrase. Think of the introduction of the 'Community Charge', with its overtones of a friendly neighbourhood united in a common purpose. The Opposition soon changed all that: they christened it the 'Poll Tax', with the negative vibes of taxation and the Peasants' Revolt.

Broadcasting language has to be simple and plain. Use the short words not the long ones. Keep the sentences short and uncomplex. Explain the meaning of any technical word you have to use. Above all, avoid using the sort of language that goes down well at internal meetings.

Certain phrases get picked up as a sort of shorthand. These phrases are often simplified versions of the truth, but broadcasting can't afford to be picky about the details. Nor should you be picky. Who are you talking to? Is it your colleagues in the office? Whatever you say they'll find fault with it, especially if you try to simplify and generalise in the way that's essential for broadcasting. But you're not going on the radio or television for them. So ignore them, concentrate on your real targets, and pitch the level of your language at the people you need to influence.

'We are building a new water storage facility with a maximum capacity of 350,492 cubic metres.'

'The new reservoir will hold four weeks' supply of clean water for our town.'

'The employment scheme guarantees a place for every school leaver in a training programme, but it doesn't mean every leaver will actually get a place, since this depends on the local skills shortage.'

'There'll be a training place for every school leaver, but if 400 teenagers all decide they want to be hairdressers then of course we'd be cruel to train them all in that, because there just wouldn't be enough jobs to go round.'

GET PERSONAL

There's a huge power in personal experience. When you can, relate your answers to something you've seen or experienced. If you can't, then at least phrase the answers as a story, rather than a list of statistics or facts.

'There are far too many children at risk every year in the Third World from gastro-enteric diseases, who could easily be saved by this simple formulation of sugar and salt to be given by health clinics in the rural districts.'

'I've just been visiting a health clinic in East Africa and saw a dreadfully sick baby suffering from diarrhoea. Her skin was grey, her lips cracked, and she trembled all the time. I thought she'd die. But after 30 hours taking the simple salt and sugar formula she looked a different child.'

The other strong word is 'you', although that can be hard to pull off in an interview. You want to present your subject as one that is important and relevant to your audience. But don't refer to 'listeners' or 'viewers' because you think that will involve them. The convention of broadcasting is – usually – that the camera or microphone just happens to be around when two people are having a talk. Break that convention by addressing the multitudes directly at your peril.

In any case, the people listening or watching don't feel like a multitude. Most of us listen to the radio in the car or while feeding the baby; television will be watched alone over a TV dinner or in the company of the family. It's a very intimate thing, and we don't know whether we are the only people in Britain watching or whether nine million others are too.

What you can do, if the programme style allows it, is to involve the interviewer by directly addressing him or her: 'I don't know if you've walked through the canal path recently, Bill, but if you have you'll know the state it's in ...' This chummy approach won't work too well with the more serious news journalist, but it's fine for a local radio or television chat show.

GETTING IN YOUR PUFF

The interviewer's dread is the MD of Junk Foods plc, there to talk about the nutritional value of crisps, who mentions Little Krispi Krunchie every other sentence. Don't go overboard mentioning your name or product; you're there to talk about something, not to get 2 minutes of free puff.

On the other hand, you don't want to go the whole time without mentioning who you are. The normal convention is that your name and organisation will be stated once in the introduction (and possibly put up on the screen in television) and once at the end. You are then 'allowed' one plug during the interview; more than that and they'll get nervous.

CASE STUDY Forgetting the Plug

A spokesperson for a marriage counselling charity was being interviewed about young people's attitudes to marriage nowadays. She was introduced by name and with the formula 'who has researched and written about marriage for over 15 years'.

She did the interview very well and mention was made of her books and articles, and of counselling services in general. But not once did she actually mention the charity for which she did most of her work.

By the end, she had made her main points and so in most respects the interview was a success. But all the glory was hers and none for her organisation, and anyone watching who might have been interested in the subject either as donor or client would have been none the wiser as to where to go.

So for many interviews, make sure that one of your three key points is a mention of your organisation and a brief explanation of what it is.

If you are told that you mustn't mention product names or if you want to plug yourself more than once, you'll have to be more subtle:

'As the Knightsbridge store with perhaps the best known name among foreigners, ...'
'It's true that beans do provide a lot of fibre, but among our 57 varieties of tinned food ...'
'Many overseas charities are very concerned about the situation, and here in Oxford ...'

This sort of cunning ploy will have to be thought out beforehand and dropped in if you get the chance.

KEEPING CONTROL

Most people's fear of broadcasting is that they'll end up looking an idiot. It's most unlikely that that will happen. After all what's in it for the interviewer? The interviewer wants: good information, lively presentation and no rambling. There'll be none of those if you are a quivering heap on the floor. The only time an interviewer might aim to really hurt you is if you are a politician (always regarded as fair game) or if you are involved in a matter of public interest such as a fraud or a disaster caused by negligence.

Most of the time interviewers will be nice and kind and helpful. But their agenda isn't necessarily yours, which is where the preparation process comes in, especially the 30-second exercise (see Chapter 11).

Tips for keeping control in an interview
• Discover the introduction to your interview. Either ask to see it if it is written down on the script, or to hear it from your interviewer. Listen for errors of fact. (Your name, title, and organisation first of all. But also figures, dates, etc.) You don't want to waste valuable air-time correcting things, so put it right before. Also listen to the tone of the introduction. Is it neutral, favourable, or antagonistic? That should give you a flavour of what is to come.

A pre-recorded interview will not necessarily have an introduction yet, but at least you can ask what they have in mind.
• Ask for the first question. You don't need to demand it; phrase it tactfully: 'Have you any idea how you'll start?' Then you'll have at least a few minutes to work out how you'll get neatly from that first question into your first main point.

- Remember the classic evasions if you don't like the question:
  - 'I can't really answer that question without looking at the reasons why we are going to ...'
  - 'Of course our opponents accuse us of doing too little, but they are obscuring the really important issue which is ...'
  - 'That's a good question, and I shall come to it in a moment, but first I have to emphasise ...'
  - 'It's true that vandalism is on the increase, but rather than dwell on debateable figures, maybe it's more important to examine why ...'
  - 'I don't have the exact details about that, but what I can tell you is ...'
  - 'What I think you mean by the question is ...'
  - 'Of course this is a very important question and you're right to bring it up, but what I think is even more interesting is ...'
- It's not just a matter of avoiding the controversial areas. Remember you want to put across your three points. So evade even the bland questions if they are leading you in a direction you don't want to go. Otherwise, time will be up, and you won't have used your chance to the full.
- If pre-recorded, ask to do again any question which you think you didn't do well. They might do it, they might not. Certainly push for it if you realise in retrospect that you said something factually wrong or misleading; it's in no one's interest for that to go out. BBC trainers always tell new radio reporters that every interviewee has the right to re-do a muffed answer. It's not so easy for television interviews, because the editing is more complicated, but give it a try.
- It's also worth giving it a try if you think a big area has been left out. Point out to the interviewer that you didn't have a chance to bring in a really good example of your product's relevance to schools; with any luck she'll think up a question that will lead you in to it. Again, this is more likely to work in a radio interview.

SYNDICATED TAPES

The ultimate way to keep control is to do it and pay for it yourself. There are commercial studios (publicised in the PR yearbooks) which will organise a radio interview for you and send it to local stations around the country. If you send out 35, there will be an average pick-up of 14 stations.

You'll need a strong angle, not just a company puff. So if you have something to say about an art exhibition touring the country or the new educational reform, then give it a strong national push.

Wherever possible give something for local interest, either during the interview or in separate bits at the end. So mention the particular artists in your exhibition from different regions and talk a little bit about each of them, so that each station can pick out their own artists and edit out the others. Use examples from all over the country if you're talking education or safety or health.

The BBC have their own syndicated radio system (Programme Services, Broadcasting House, Great Portland St, London W1A 1AA) which sends interviews down the line to BBC local radio. The BBC's syndicate system is, of course, free to you, but you have to have a strong story.

DEALING WITH INTERRUPTIONS

Why do interviewers interrupt? Some of them do it because they feel like it; it gives them a feeling of power and keeps the interviewee off-balance. If you have done your research beforehand, you might be able to spot a born interrupter and be ready.

Mostly you'll be interrupted if you go on for too long (in broadcasting terms). Just because you're trying to get your message across, it doesn't mean you should try to launch into a 3-minute speech button-holing the listeners. If you do, the interviewer will seize some chance to butt in. This isn't rudeness; it's plain boring to have one person going on for longer than about one minute, however gripping the subject. So even if you can manage to keep the interviewer out of the proceedings, you won't have done yourself any good. So if you don't want to be interrupted, keep those answers short, and let the questions break up the interview to keep it lively.

There are some tips if you are being unfairly interrupted:

- Decide whether you want to accept the interruption or not. If you've just about finished your point, then you might as well take the next question.
- If you haven't finished the point, acknowledge the interruption but politely say that you haven't finished yet: 'Perhaps I could just finish what I was saying ...' or 'Yes, that's an interesting question and I'll return to it, but if I could first continue ...'.
- Then go back and make your point. But whatever you do, don't now ramble on. Finish as quickly as you can. If you waffle on for another half a minute, you'll quickly lose your audience's sympathy and they'll be rooting for the interviewer to interrupt you again.
- If you liked the question that you were interrupted with, return to it. 'And now to answer your question about our plans for next year ...' If you didn't like it, just stop and wait. With any luck the interviewer will have forgotten what it was anyway and will ask you something else.

DEALING WITH THE NASTIES

It's best to be prepared to be put on the spot, in case you're faced with a bilious interviewer, or one whose producer has just hissed down the earpiece, 'This interview is boring – get it going!'

Once again the first rule is *be prepared*. If you know you're in a controversial business, then you'll know the nasty questions better than anyone. Don't just hope that the interviewer won't ask them. Think it through, and practise fielding questions to get from the negative to the positive.

Here are some common techniques:

Putting things in perspective OK, your chairman has just been awarded a 30% pay rise while your organisation has just refused a 5% pay rise for its workers. Put it in context:

• 'The chairman is now earning over £80,000, but let's put it in perspective. His counterparts in other similar organisations are earning over £100,000, so if we want to keep his talents – which have created 40 new jobs in the last six months alone – then he has to be paid nearer the going rate.'

• 'It will cost the company just £15,000 more to pay the chairman the going rate for his job. But every one per cent rise in wages for all employees cost £350,000 – that's money we just don't have in a recession. We'd have to cut jobs and I'm sure no one wants that.'

Confidentiality You might want to give the impression that commercial secrets will be given away to the Japanese, or lives will be lost …

• 'I'm sure you'll understand that the Stock Exchange wouldn't be too happy if I gave out information of that sort, but I can say …'

• 'We will be announcing our reaction next week, but I'm sure you can appreciate that until we really know the facts it just wouldn't be fair to the accused person to jump the gun.'

It's important in these circumstances to keep your cool, and if necessary repeat a similar formula two or even three times.

Don't know If you really don't know, then say so. There's nothing worse, though it's very natural to try to do it, than to waffle on about something when you obviously don't know the facts:

• 'I'm just here as an ordinary vet, so I really can't comment on what animal research the pharmaceutical companies are doing. But I can say that …'

• As Area Organiser for the North, I don't know very much about the incident you refer to, which happened in Devon. But when something similar happened in Manchester …'

• My responsibility is fund-raising, not overall policy, so it's not my place to comment except to say that since this month alone our donations have risen by 6% ...'

Deny knowledge or expertise, and then if you possibly can, launch off into one of your own points. If you're completely flummoxed by the question, then it's better to flatly say so and then shut up, than to attempt an answer:

• 'I've really no idea; I'm an arable farmer, not a pig breeder.'

Watch out for the follow-up question: 'But surely as a member of the board you *ought* to know about ...' or 'But you can't go and ask people for money if you don't support the new policy to ...'. If there is an aggressive follow-up like that, stay smiling and polite and deflect the question again: 'Of course the board have overall responsibility, but you really should ask the personnel director for exact details ...' or 'Naturally as a member of the Society I have my opinions, but I'm here in my official capacity as ...'.

Turn the tables The more aggressive the question, the more sympathy you will have. The interviewer wants you to rise and to say something unguarded, but you win if you keep cool and friendly. If possible, use his words against him in a polite way.

CASE STUDY Mad Gummer Disease

While John Selwyn Gummer was the British Minister for Agriculture he had to fend off questions about so-called Mad Cow Disease which had become a current health issue.

His interviewer said very aggressively: 'You've been accused of jumping up and down making noises, but doing nothing useful.'

His very cool reply was: 'If there's been any jumping up and down it's been those who have used the issue to make improper and ridiculous attacks.'

He wasted no time in defending himself, but used the expression as a springboard into his own message.

Naming the names A technique to use if you feel supremely confident of your ground, as an answer to this sort of question: 'It has been said that you are a mendacious malevolent fraud, Mr Jones. What's your reaction?'

This sort of question is impossible to answer without going on the defensive, so if you want to duck it, you say: 'Name one person who has said that.' Then sit and wait.

CASE STUDY Trials of Oz

Mrs Thatcher was being interviewed for Australian TV and the reporter obviously decided to try to make his reputation by scoring a victory over her. The interview ran something like this:

Interviewer: 'Many people say that you have an authoritarian and even dictatorial style of leadership.'

Mrs T: 'Name these people.'

Interviewer: 'You know that many people do say this.'

Mrs T: 'You can hardly expect me to reply to vague allegations. Name these people; where do they live?'

At this point the interviewer gave up and confined himself to bland questions thereafter.

STAYING COOL

The ultimate technique for keeping the interviewer off your back is to stay nice. Sympathy will quickly switch to you if an interviewer is being hostile, but if you are aggressive in response then generally no one wins. People might certainly remember the interview, but do they remember anything at all you might have said?

CASE STUDY Staying Nice

A retailers' report had been published on products made of tropical hardwood, naming certain stores that were stocking them.

The reporter went to certain of the shops and said to each the same question: 'You have been attacked in this report as helping to ravage tropical forests by selling hardwood furniture. Is this a reflection of an uncaring attitude to ecological concerns?'

A spokesperson for a famous London store, sounding very nettled, said: 'We give what the customer wants. We will not be dictated to by anyone.'

A spokesperson for a well-known furniture chain sounding pleasant and relaxed, said: 'We are very conscious of the problems of tropical forest and are looking into it to see if a more responsible attitude ...'

Which of those two remarks would you rather have associated with your organisation?

THE LAST WORD

The nicest thing an interviewee can hear is: 'Thank you very much, Mr Brown.' A wave of relief sweeps over you, and you sit back and count the score. Then you hear: 'Mr Brown of Mega plc whose company policy seems to be to put profits above people. And now over to the weather report.'

Hey! you think, I didn't say that! By the time you've gathered your wits some pretty thing is half-way through the isobars, and the chance to argue back has gone.

So never relax until you're sure that it is really over. Another favourite trick can be: 'So thank you, Mr Brown' (relief and relax), 'But just quickly, why are you spending half a million pounds refurbishing the chairman's office while telling the staff that you can't afford an indoor loo for them?' You've only 10 seconds left, and half of that will probably be filled with inarticulate fluster because you'd already switched your neurons off.

Keep listening, keep alert until the microphone is removed. If the interviewer's summing up is grossly unfair, you've got about one second to react. There won't be time to refute it properly, so all you can do is register your disapproval by a quick 'Not true' or 'That's not what I said' or 'Those are your words, not mine'. If necessary, even a 'No' or a grunt will do. If it's television, the camera may not still be on you, but for both radio and television your microphone will be on so your remark will at least be heard.

LIVE OR PRE-RECORDED

Most people's natural preference is to avoid going out live. The thought of drying up in front of millions is just too ghastly to contemplate. However, the reassurance that, 'I can always do it again if it's pre-recorded' is perhaps false. If it's a complete disaster, you can; but usually interviewers won't want to and your complacency means a less tight performance.

If you're given the option, here are the respective advantages and disadvantages to help you choose.

PRE-RECORDED ADVANTAGES

If you get really in a muddle, you can stop, take a breath and begin again.

Also, at the end you can re-record any answer you didn't like, if you can persuade the interviewer that you'll do it better next time. Generally most people feel less tense about it.

Another useful advantage that – for radio at least – your ums and ers and long-winded phrases can be edited out very easily. So you can end up sounding a lot more fluent and pithy than you really were.

PRE-RECORDED DISADVANTAGES

You can be edited, and the interviewer's idea of the significant points may not be yours. All too often the piece picked out to go on air is the one point that you didn't particularly want. Also the answer to one question can be attached to a quite different one.

So you have lost control. You can't control the timing, the introduction, the context, or the editing. You can't control who else is appearing, or check the facts in the rest of the programme.

LIVE ADVANTAGES

What you see is what you get. If there is a film before your interview you'll know it. If your deadliest opponent is going to have a chance to answer your criticisms, then you'll see him sitting there. You'll hear the introduction and will have the chance to change or anticipate it. Most importantly, the time is set. What you say is what will go out and no one can edit it, except by actually stopping the interview. So if you keep control of the answers and use well whatever time you're given, you will know that your message has gone out loud and clear.

Funnily enough, people often perform better when they know they have to get it right first time. They are sharper, clearer, and cleverer, because the pressure is on. It is very, very rare for anyone to dry completely.

LIVE DISADVANTAGES

The main one is fear: people feel more nervous when it's live, though this evaporates once things begin.

The real danger is that if you do say something wrong or stupid, then it's gone out on air, and you can't get it back. So either you let it go, with possible horrendous consequences, or you correct it straight away, in which case you may look foolish. Then British leader of the Conservative Party, Mrs Thatcher, found it hard to live down her attack on 'the people who care, the drivellers and droolers' during the 1987 election campaign. She retracted her remark immediately, but it stuck none the less.

Generally, choose live rather than pre-recorded if you can. If you have done your preparation and practice beforehand, going live should have no particular terrors, and you have a much better chance of staying in control.

If you are involved in anything controversial, it's even more important to go live, because you don't want anything to be broadcast out of context, or to be used as target practice by a clever-clogs presenter or your opponents in the studio.

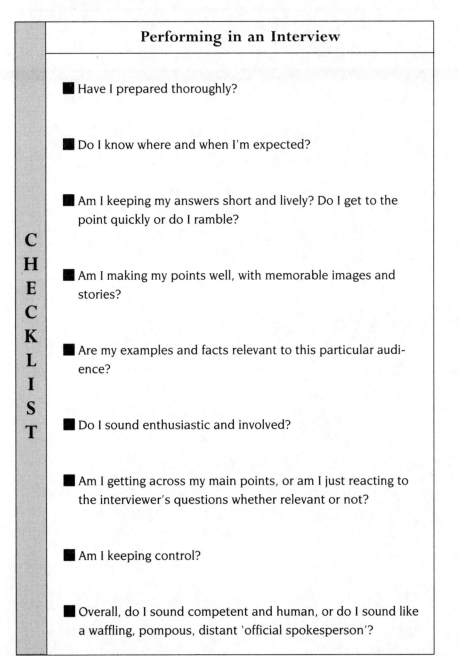

CHECKLIST

Performing in an Interview

■ Have I prepared thoroughly?

■ Do I know where and when I'm expected?

■ Am I keeping my answers short and lively? Do I get to the point quickly or do I ramble?

■ Am I making my points well, with memorable images and stories?

■ Are my examples and facts relevant to this particular audience?

■ Do I sound enthusiastic and involved?

■ Am I getting across my main points, or am I just reacting to the interviewer's questions whether relevant or not?

■ Am I keeping control?

■ Overall, do I sound competent and human, or do I sound like a waffling, pompous, distant 'official spokesperson'?

16

Appearing on the Screen

- What people see creates the most impact on television. Viewers may not remember a word of what you said, but they will remember how you looked.
- Feelings come across more powerfully than facts.
- Clothes, body position, face and gestures, all contribute to an overall impression.
- It is important to think through what image you want to project.
- Eyes reveal tension and defensiveness. So good steady eye contact with the interviewer is one of the most important techniques.

THE POWER OF THE PICTURE

A film or picture can have immense power to affect people's emotions. The claim that the Vietnam war was lost on American television may or may not be true, but certainly television stories can change attitudes and affect events.

Television cameras relayed horrific pictures of what Allied bombing had done to Iraqi convoys at the Mutla gap during the 1991 Gulf War, and it was US President Bush's anxiety that television would witness even worse should the war continue that led him to ignore military advice to continue attacking the Iraqi army. The consequence was the continuation of President Saddam Hussein as leader of Iraq in charge of still formidable forces which he could turn on to his own people.

More positively, immediately after this war the sight of the Kurds fleeing into the mountains with all the misery that followed led to public revulsion against them being left to a miserable fate. Not merely humanitarian aid followed, but also a Government policy was quickly cobbled together to create safe enclaves for them. Without the television images it's unlikely that anything would have been done so fast.

You are unlikely to be involved in anything so dramatic; but even an ordinary television interview does have that extra dimension of the image and the subliminal messages that you send out to the viewers.

SPECIAL POINTS FOR TELEVISION

Everything in the previous chapter about language and control is relevant to television. But you've got one extra dimension when you appear on screen, and that's what you look like.

Image is all, and that includes clothes, face, shifting eyes, and how you sit. People are very quick at picking up the subliminal messages from your appearance, and make possibly unfair judgements. You can do your best to avoid the worst mistakes.

CASE STUDY Has this Man no Friends?

A member of the International Petroleum Exchange was interviewed for television about oil prices. He stood in a room of VDUs, surrounded by colleagues, sprouting his expert stuff. Unfortunately his collar was sticking up around one ear the whole time.

A quick check afterwards with other people who'd seen the news bulletin revealed that everybody had noticed the collar; and that no one could remember anything he'd said because they were all speculating on the lurid reasons why not one of his colleagues had told him he looked ridiculous.

WHAT TO WEAR

You've two considerations here: the programme style, and how you want to come over. Watch the programme or think about the audience; if it's to young people then wearing a suit may look unbearably stuffy. Also consider the studio background. If the décor is yellow, you'd best avoid wearing yellow. Then consider what sort of image you want to put across. Do you want to look like Mum? Do you want to appear an authority figure? Should you be dressed in your professional clothes (white coat, pin-stripe suit, uniform) or in your off-duty clothes? Are you representing yourself or your organisation?

Most people on television want to appear competent but human, which means appearing smart but not glitzy, with nothing either too powerful or too outrageous.

Tips for dressing for television
• Don't wear a new outfit. Choose something that you know you'll feel good in.
• Choose natural fabrics that won't show sweat.
• Very dark colours look sombre. A dark suit has the image of 'City financier', especially with a pin-stripe. Straight black and white makes life very difficult for the cameraman because of the extreme contrast.
• Bright white isn't a great idea either, except in small quantities. Pastel or coloured shirts are best.
• If you have a dark skin, it is especially important to avoid light colours, because your face may get blotted out by the contrast. So wear medium to dark tones.
• Avoid stripes or checks, especially narrow ones which can create an op art effect on video. If you really like something with a stripe, then by all means try it out, but take a replacement garment along just in case.
• Avoid anything really flashy, like a loud tie or a diamanté brooch, or anything that might distract such as an initial tie-pin or dangly earrings. You want people to be listening to you, not working out which school you went to or whether you're a Rotarian.
• For women, an informal suit is often a good idea rather than a dress. Go for clean lines, with clear patterns or plain colours. A very frilly blouse can give a negative impression. Some media advisers swear by bright red because it's such a vibrant colour; others say avoid it at all cost. Mrs Thatcher decided that clear blues suited her and the medium. At least a touch of bright colour somewhere is a good idea; you don't want to look like burnt porridge.
• Check on the length of your skirt – too much thigh is unlikely to help your message.
• If you have glasses, don't remove them unless they are light-reactive (in which case you'll look like a hit-man). If you think you'll be appearing on television a lot, it may be a good idea to spend some extra money on non-reflective lenses which help a bit.

Before you go on:

• Make a few faces in the mirror to check whether you've got any spinach on your teeth. You'll feel pretty silly if you have.

• Once you're sitting, use the studio monitor to check on whether you've got a collar sticking up or dandruff on your shoulders. Check too that there's no expanse of hairy leg to be seen. There will often be an establishing shot at the beginning to show you sitting down in the studio. If you wear short socks or popsock stockings, your credibility could be blown.

• If you're on location, get a friend to give you the once over for basic neatness.

CASE STUDY Checking the Props

As well as clothes, don't forget the accessories. Chris Moncrieff, the Press Association's Westminster man, relates that just after the 1987 election he was at Downing Street.

Denis Thatcher came downstairs clutching a copy of the *Financial Times* then Mrs Thatcher arrived, holding *Harpers & Queen*. She was told camera crews were lurking outside, so she snatched Denis's FT, wrapped it round her glossy magazine and sauntered out to face the press.

SITTING DOWN

You'd have thought that sitting down is the easy bit, but don't you believe it. Your body posture gives you away as much as your actual answers. You want to appear keen and open; not defensive or hostile. Sit down, get your behind in the back of the chair (or perched on the edge of it if it's an over-stuffed monster), sit up, and then lean forward just a few inches. Those few inches make the crucial difference; if you sit back you run the risk of looking defensive or oh-too-casual. But sit forward, and you look involved, concerned, interested.

This shouldn't come as a surprise. Imagine watching a couple in a restaurant. He's sitting forward, leaning with his arms on the table and intensely looking at her. How would you decide what his chances were? You'd look at her posture. If she's also leaning towards him, animatedly gesturing, you'll decide that they're getting on fine. But if she's leaning back in her chair, her body slightly turned away, her hands floppy or her arms crossed ...

If you feel natural with your legs crossed, it does create an interesting body line. But don't get your body twisted, with your legs one way and your arms another; keep to a discreet leg cross, with your body straight not leaning to one side. It may be safest to keep your feet firmly on the floor, with your hands initially crossed on your lap until you relax enough to start using them naturally. Don't worry about gestures; you don't want to look like a wild dervish, but if you don't gesture at all you look very wooden. So just do what comes naturally. If you do have large arm movements, the camera will pull back a bit to fit them in.

By the way, it's best not to grip your hands or entwine your fingers. Under tension the knuckles are a dead giveaway. Folded arms give a bad impression too.

Whatever you do, don't sit back with your legs akimbo in the Mighty Crotch position. This is not a pretty sight.

STANDING UP

If you are doing an interview standing up, then watch the angles of the shot. You don't usually want to be filmed from down below (for instance, you at the top of a flight of steps with the camera at the bottom). Not only will all the hairs in your nose be revealed, but also you might give the impression of a looming, authoritarian figure.

It's not a good idea to be filmed too much from above, either. The bald patch shows, your nose sticks out, and you look small and diminished. So if the cameraman starts setting up either of those two extremes, find out why and check that you're happy with the reason.

Another problem can be a big mismatch between the height of you and your interviewer. If the interviewer is much smaller than you, you look as if you're talking down your nose at people in a superior sort of way. Much taller and you look like a hopeful schoolchild. So if that's the case try to find a setting where one of you can naturally stand on a step to even things out.

THE EYES HAVE IT

We read a lot from people's eyes, and a shifty look at the wrong moment will be interpreted as evasion or fear or the sign of a downright lie. It may be nothing of the sort. A television studio is a complicated place, and things and people will be moving about the whole time. There may be a television monitor in your line of vision where you can catch glimpses of yourself; another guest is being manoeuvred into place; the floor manager is making weird signals at the presenter. It can be very difficult not to let your eyes flicker.

So keep looking at the interviewer, however unnatural it may feel. Until you're confident it's best not to look away for thought either, because if you do it too much you look as if you're not actually involved in the conversation. In particular, never look at the camera itself. In Britain, at least, you have to pretend the camera isn't there.

CASE STUDY Animal Magic

Archbishop Makarios was interviewed for BBC Television in the 1950s, some time before he became leader of Cyprus. At the time he was suspected by the British authorities of being heavily involved in terrorism, and his interviewer asked him a question about whether he supported terror as a means of gaining independence. His eyes shifted heavily to the right as he paused and weighed the question; then he gave a bland reassuring answer denying involvement. The result was that he looked as if he were lying.

The sting in the tail is that the journalist who tells this story relates that, many years after seeing this interview, he interviewed Makarios in similar circumstances, sitting in a Cypriot village square. He put an awkward question to the Archbishop, by then leader of independent Cyprus, about the treatment of Cypriot Turks. Again there was the heavy eye flicker, followed by the bland answer.

However, this time at least, there was a perfectly innocent explanation for the shifty look. Off camera, a dog had just ambled up and had a pee on the Archbishop's black robe!

MAKE UP

Lights flatten out your face, and drain colour from it, so that's one reason why television performers wear make-up. The other reason is that lights pick up shine from your skin. This is interpreted (whether viewers know they're doing it or not) as nervous sweat. So if you really are sweating, whether from the heat or from genuine terror, you'll really look in trouble!

In a studio, you'll probably be taken to be made up by an expert. Men will usually just have a bit of powder applied, though if your face is very pale you might be asked if you want some colour. You can always refuse, though they know their business better than you do. Make sure you have an extra good shave before you go to record, and if you have a heavy growth, then even take your shaving things with you. The other option is to have make-up on your upper lip, as British Prime Minister John Major does.

You don't need any more make-up than that, though actor Michael Caine says he always wears mascara on television or film, because he has blonde eye lashes and he doesn't like the piggy eye effect under bright lights.

Women can choose the amount of make-up they'd like. If you want glamour make-up for the first time in your life, then the make-up artist will oblige, though the full works will take time. If you have a favourite eye shadow or lip-stick, then take it along. If you don't normally wear much make-up and prefer a natural look, tell the make-up person and she'll go gently. But it's worth remembering that what may look a lot of gunge on your face in the mirror, will look far less on camera, and a bit of emphasis on the eyes and mouth will add sparkle to your face. So don't panic.

On location there won't be anyone from the make-up department to do it for you. It's worthwhile doing it for yourself. Men should swallow their macho pride and bring in a powder puff to the office; women should put on a bit more colour and eye make-up than they would normally. If you've got a loo with bright neon lights then go and look at yourself in there and see whether your face looks washed out or shiny.

CASE STUDY Tricky Dick

One of the most famous television confrontations was that between John F. Kennedy and Richard Nixon in the 1960 US presidential elections.

The idea of a debate between the two candidates was a new one, but JFK's advisers were wise to the medium and he had proper make-up. Nixon scorned the notion and appeared without.

Once the debate between the two candidates was over the pollsters did their stuff and asked voters who had 'won'. What was interesting was that radio listeners were either undecided or put Nixon ahead. But television viewers were overwhelmingly in favour of Kennedy; Nixon's sweaty upper lip and heavy five o'clock shadow made him appear sinister and nervous, whereas Kennedy looked cool, calm and in control.

After that, Nixon always wore make-up. But it was too late; from then on cartoonists always drew him with a heavy shadow and he never threw off the image.

THE END

There's a huge temptation to give a big smile, or even leap out of your chair at the end. You hear the thank you, and your feelings of relief are made all too apparent.

Stay looking at the interviewer at the end; keep in the same body position; and whatever you do, don't smirk.

PROVIDING VISUALS

If you're involved in a straight interview it can be a good idea to take along any pictures or pamphlets or models relevant to the subject. So if you have some good historical photographs or an artist's impression of the new factory then take them with you.

Don't conjure them out of your briefcase during the interview itself because it's practically impossible to get a good shot of something being held – the angle will be wrong, or there'll be a shake. Give it to the researcher and they will set it up on a stand, ready to cut to it when it's mentioned. This is a good trick to keep control, too. If the visual is any good at all there's a huge temptation to use it, so the interview is bound to be steered in that direction.

If you want to give out an address on air it's not a bad idea to bring that along too, well printed with your logo if you have one. Make sure that it's the right shape for television: a rectangle in roughly the same proportions as a TV screen. If it's the wrong shape it can't be used.

AFTER THE INTERVIEW

Editing an interview is difficult for television, especially when videotape is used, which is why an interviewer will try to record something which can be used as it stands, without cutting bits out from the middle. However, the crew will make provision for editing by taking a number of shots which can be slotted in afterwards if necessary.

'**Cutaways**' These are shots of something else relevant to the interview such as a close-up of the machinery mentioned by the interviewee, or the artist's impression of the new bridge. They may also be a close-up of the interviewee's hands on the steering-wheel as he drives along. These shots will be dropped into the interview, to disguise an edit or illustrate a point.

A '**two-shot**' This is a wide shot of the interviewer and interviewee talking together, often shot from behind the interviewer's head. Try to find out when the crew are taking this shot; it may be while you are chatting beforehand with the interviewer, or it may be after it's all over. You ought to know, because whatever expression you think you'll be wearing for the real interview should be the same for the two-shot, especially if it's a serious subject. Either before or after the interview proper, you're likely to be smiling a lot more at the interviewer. So if this is filmed, and then slotted into the middle of the interview during which you are looking very sombre and concerned, it will undercut your message.

'**Reverse questions**' These are when the interviewer's questions are filmed again, but this time the camera is pointing at him or her and not at you. This helps with editing, and also lets the interviewer tidy up the questions (and so appear smarter and slicker than they really are ...). You should try to hang around during this process, offering to stay sitting so as to help the inter-viewer get the right eye-line. Then you can hear the questions and make sure those being re-recorded really are the ones you were asked.

DOWN THE LINE

One further aspect of interviews is that you may be asked to record 'down the line'. For radio, this is easy because we are all familiar with telephone conversations, where you don't see who you are talking to. In television you have to talk to a lens and most of us get very peculiar even when asked to pose for the family photo album, never mind a television camera.

Television down-the-line is very unfamiliar. It's the situation where the presenter says 'And now to Jiminy Cricket by satellite from Disneyland' and she turns to a television beside her on which Jiminy Cricket's face appears.

To the viewer at home it looks as if the interviewer and interviewee are talking 'through' the monitor screen; in fact, Jiminy Cricket can't see her at all and can only hear through an ear-piece uncomfortably lodged in the ear out of shot.

What has happened is that Jiminy will have arrived at a studio, been wired for sound, and given the ear-piece. He is told which camera to look at and then has to wait for anything up to half an hour. Perhaps he will be able to see the rest of the programme on a studio monitor, perhaps not. He may even be told to address a pot of flowers or a bored looking techni-cian sitting to the side of the camera; it depends on whether the producer wants him to appear to look directly out of the screen or to look to one side, as if at the presenter. It may even be that he has been directed to a self-operate studio where he has to read a list of instructions and do it all himself, with no one else in sight.

Once the interview starts, Jiminy has to give his all to a piece of glass or a spot on the wall. The ear-piece may not work very well, and he certainly won't get any of the normal encouragement we take for granted in normal conversation, like an occasional nod or 'Uh huh' or 'Yes'. The interviewer will keep quiet except when asking a question and he can't see any reac-tion. All this makes a down-the-line interview very hard.

Tips for giving interviews 'down-the-line'
• If you feel more comfortable addressing a spot on the wall than looking directly at camera, or vice versa, then say so. It may be that they can't accommodate you for technical reasons, but at least give it a try.
• Stay alert all the time, especially at the beginning of the programme when a run-down on the contents is often given, and during the introduc-tion to your own interview. At those times, make sure you're looking at

your appointed eye-line with a steady gaze, and not checking your notes, eyeing up the attractive sound engineer, or picking your teeth. That's because the producer may decide to quickly jump to you for just a second or two, before going back to the presenter.

• Keep your face neutral while waiting, especially when your name is said at the end of the introduction which is the usual time to switch the picture to you. It's common to smile nervously, but it looks very silly if the presenter says, 'And in our Manchester studios is Mrs Boothney' (cut to shot of Mrs Boothney grinning inanely) 'who is owner of one of the restaurants accused in the survey of ripping off the public'. (Mrs Boothney's smile freezes.) 'Why are you adding a service charge of 20% to your customers' bills, Mrs Boothney?' (Mrs Boothney's smile now looks like rigor mortis.)

CASE STUDY Selective Deafness

If you are in a tight spot in a down-the-line interview, one way out is to suddenly have difficulties with your ear-piece.

A trades union spokesman was being grilled on a hard-hitting news programme. At the third aggressive question he suddenly put his hand up to his ear and said: 'I'm afraid I can't hear you.' The interviewer repeated the question; the TU person repeated that he couldn't hear. The interviewer was obviously fed up by this time, so asked a different, more friendly, question. Miraculously the ear-piece now worked and the TU person was able to answer.

This is not a technique to over-use.

THE SOUND-BITE

You may be asked for a short soundbite for radio or television, especially if the broadcast is for a news programme. What the reporter wants is 10–20 seconds from you about the subject which can be slotted in to the programme without any introduction. So her question won't be broadcast, just your answer. They want you to get it right, so you may find yourself doing it two, three, or even more times, which the non-professional finds extra difficult.

Of course, if it's a door-stepping kind of soundbite (as you walk down the steps of your office from the strike meeting to the waiting car), you'll only get one go, but at least in that situation you can usually ignore the question and have some sort of statement prepared.

Tips for giving sound-bites
• Still look at the interviewer rather than the camera.
• Don't start with any reference to the question. So you don't begin: 'That's a very interesting point ...', or 'The answer to that is ...', or 'Well ...' or 'No, it's not true that ...'. They want a statement that will stand on its own like: 'Our reaction to the Government's plan is ...', or 'We are very enthusiastic about the management buy-out because ...'.
• Keep it short, no more than 20 seconds, which is around 60 words or three normal sentences. If you ramble on, you'll be asked to sharpen it up.
• If you are asked to do it again, try to inject the same enthusiasm as well as the same content into each try. Treat it as an acting performance, and start again fresh. You may very well feel silly repeating the same formula again and again, but they will only use one take. So you have to make sure that each take has the right message and words in it.
   If you start to get flustered or start fumbling your words, ask for a pause and take a few minutes' break. That will often do the trick.
• If they do film it again and again, don't feel it's necessarily your fault. It may be a bus passing by drowns the sound, or a faulty cable connection, or a small boy pulling faces.

CASE STUDY A Bit of Hype is Necessary

Five weeks after becoming British Prime Minister, John Major was waylaid by the BBC political correspondent as he stepped out of church near Chequers. At the time British troops were getting into position for the Gulf War.

The reporter shouted: 'What's your Christmas message for the troops in the Gulf?' The answer was: 'Christmas is the message to the troops and to everybody. Thank you very much. Have a nice day.' This answer was so innocuous that it failed to make the news bulletin at all.

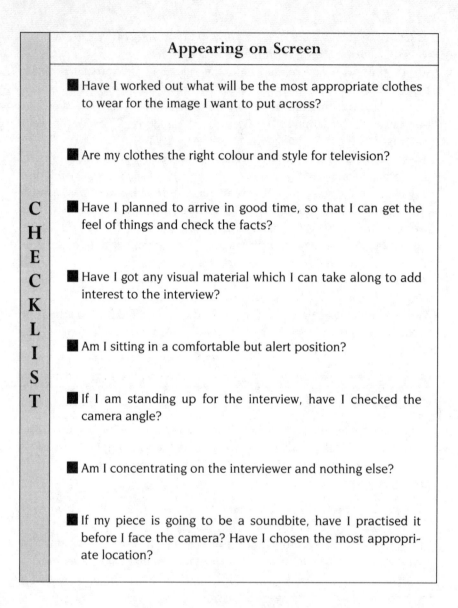

Appearing on Screen

■ Have I worked out what will be the most appropriate clothes to wear for the image I want to put across?

■ Are my clothes the right colour and style for television?

■ Have I planned to arrive in good time, so that I can get the feel of things and check the facts?

■ Have I got any visual material which I can take along to add interest to the interview?

■ Am I sitting in a comfortable but alert position?

■ If I am standing up for the interview, have I checked the camera angle?

■ Am I concentrating on the interviewer and nothing else?

■ If my piece is going to be a soundbite, have I practised it before I face the camera? Have I chosen the most appropriate location?

C H E C K L I S T

PART FIVE

TROUBLE
AND CRISIS

17
Complaining

- It is easy to over-react to what you read or hear about yourself.
- The best remedy if unhappy is to contact the journalist directly and ask for another, more positive, airing.
- Writing a letter for publication is also effective.
- If necessary you can work your way up the complaints ladder, with a libel action as a final resort.
- At all stages, stay calm, polite, and reasonable in your demands. Keep all the evidence and correspondence.

WHEN TO COMPLAIN

WHAT are the things that tend to irritate people? It's often something minor, like a misspelt name or a wrong title. It may be one or two negative points about your organisation in the middle of an otherwise favourable article (and it's only human to dwell on the negatives). Or the complaint may be something really serious: a total misquote or even fabrication, or a grossly wrong estimate of your potential losses which – if true – would imply you were about to fold any minute.

Most of the time you are better off not complaining. Swallow hard, accept the occasional mistake or negative comment, and carry on being co-operative with journalists. No one, but no one, gets favourable coverage all the time; and very often making a big fuss over something relatively trivial just means that more people are aware of the original unfavourable comment.

Certainly don't get too hot and bothered about names and titles. You'll get into trouble when you're described as 'The Chairman of Higgle Piggle Ltd', when in fact you're the chairman of the social committee; but no one else in the outside world cares one bit.

Even wrong facts or misquotations aren't necessarily worth making a fuss about, unless they are crucial to your operation and leaving them uncorrected will really harm you.

It's a bit harder to know if you should gripe about true but negative comment. That's where an article about your environmental record spends most of its time examining your one chemical spillage two years ago, and only mentions in passing all your awards, safety schemes, and overall excellent attitude to the environment. You can't deny that the spillage happened, but the balance seems unfair.

In that sort of case, before you decide whether to make a fuss, check if whether what sounds awful to you seems quite so bad to someone else outside your organisation.

CASE STUDY My Stitch-up's Better than Your Stitch-up

A large hotel organisation, with an excellent reputation for training, was approached by a fairly new business magazine for a feature on their training policy and methods.

The organisation asked to see a copy of the magazine, since they weren't familiar with it, and were sent an issue with a long article about a popular chain store's developmental methods. This looked fine to them, so they agreed to the feature and let the journalist loose to talk to employees.

But when the article was published, they were really unhappy. They felt that they'd been stitched up, with comments like this one from a senior manager: 'I sometimes wonder if the top management really take training seriously, since it happens a lot that outsiders get jobs rather than the insiders who have been attending the training to do that job.' They couldn't claim that anyone had been misquoted, but felt that they'd been misled by the store's article to believe that the treatment would be a lot softer than in fact it was.

The interesting part is, that to an outsider, the overwhelming balance of the article was favourable. Any more and it would have sounded like a company puff and lost credibility.

Even more interesting is that the store's people had had a negative reaction to their article! They hadn't liked it, thought it had too many niggling comments, etc., etc. But the hotel organisation had thought it fine …

Which all goes to show that your heated reaction to some bad coverage may be way over the top. We are all very quick to spot personal criticism, whether of ourselves, our children, or our organisation. But most outsiders won't have even noticed it.

However, it is worth doing something about a complaint if you feel you're going to be badly damaged in some way if you don't put things right. There's an escalation of methods:

- personal contact with the journalist concerned;
- contact the editor or programme producer;
- write a letter to be published;
- make a formal complaint;
- contact the Press Complaints Commission, or the equivalent broadcasting bodies;
- sue for libel.

Just make sure before you start that you know what you want to achieve, and what you might stand to lose. If your motivation is merely to show your boss that you are Doing Something About It, whatever It may be, then try to resist the pressure. Getting too involved in a nasty complaint loses friends, takes a lot of time, and could even cost a lot of money.

YOUR RIGHTS

The situation in print journalism has been in some confusion, because the report of the Calcutt Committee on Privacy and Related Matters, chaired by David Calcutt, QC (June 1990), recommended the abolition of the Press Council in favour of a new streamlined Press Complaints Commission. The report said that if this didn't work in curbing the worst excesses of the press, then statutory control of some sort would be introduced.

The recommended Calcutt Code of Practice lays down professional and ethical standards which papers should stick to, but most of its provisions haven't been properly tested yet in practice. But if you can prove that your rights have been trampled on, then you've got a powerful case with the paper's editor, or with the Press Complaints Commission.

Recommended Calcutt Code of Practice

• Newspapers and periodicals should not publish inaccurate, misleading, or distorted material. If a 'significant' error is made, it should be corrected promptly and with due prominence. An apology should be published whenever appropriate.

• You should have a right of reply to criticism or alleged inaccuracies (but nothing is specified about the format of this, so you can't necessarily demand a front-page column all to yourself).

• You have a right to normal privacy. Making enquiries about your personal life, or publishing information about your personal life, is allowed only if it is in the public interest or is with your express consent.

• Journalists aren't allowed to obtain information or photos through trickery or by pretending to be someone else. (But note that although they can't lie if challenged, there's nothing about having to volunteer that they are journalists, except in the case of making enquiries at hospitals.)

• Journalists mustn't trespass on private property (a revealing photo of the chairman shredding company documents is perfectly allowable so long as it's taken from the road, but not if the photographer climbed over the wall – but the 'public interest' defence still applies, so if the chairman is destroying vital evidence of a fraud the photographer can climb where he likes).

• Journalists mustn't harass or intimidate, or persist in phoning or questioning after being asked to stop. (A tricky one this, and it will be interesting to see if it has any force.)

• The press should not print photos which are likely to cause or increase distress (already tested, in the aftermath of the British Hillsborough football stadium deaths in 1986 when some papers printed pictures of the victims).

• Children under 16 are not to be photographed or interviewed without the presence or consent of a parent or other adult responsible for the child.

The Press Complaints Commission has a written code, listing all these and more. Also, most responsible newspapers have their own house rules, such as telling reporters that they must identify themselves as such before asking any questions.

On the other hand, some papers still have the equivalent of the 'picture snatcher' employed by Express Newspapers under Lord Beaverbrook's regime – a large and highly trained journalist whose job was to steal photos off the mantelpiece should the family refuse to sell.

You do not have the right to control the final version or exercise editorial veto (unless you can somehow negotiate it beforehand, which is well-nigh impossible).

You also do not have the right to retract something after you've said it because you've realised it's damaging. If that happens to you, you can do your best to get it squashed by employing charm, threats, hints that you won't pass on any more stories, etc., but you can't force them not to publish.

COMPLAINING TO THE JOURNALIST

In general, this is your best first step. Phone up the person who's done the dirty deed, and calmly put your problem to him or her. Use normal tact – journalists don't like being put in the wrong any more than anyone else. Start off with a bit of buttering up and then go into your little problem.

The response very often will be either: 'Yes, I know, wasn't it dreadful? It wasn't me, it was the sub'; or 'Oh dear, well I do see your point; are you sure you said "four thousand" and not "forty thousand"?'

If it is either of those, then don't immediately spring like a wounded tiger and demand huge retractions next issue. You won't get them; and if you try to screw a retraction out of the journalist you may make an enemy. You're much better off asking him to come and do another, more favourable, story as soon as possible, as a way of showing repentence. With any luck, the new story will put the original error right. You get more coverage; the error is corrected in a subtle way; and the reporter isn't made to feel a fool.

COMPLAINING TO THE HIGHER-UPS

If you don't get anywhere by talking to the journalist concerned, you can approach the boss. Once again, present your case calmly and rationally. The editor of a paper is unlikely to be very sympathetic to your complaint that a name was spelt wrong, but may be very concerned to hear that you have been misrepresented, or that a confidential document was quoted, or that unscrupulous methods were used to get a story. Contrary to public belief, most editors don't particularly want their journalists to be rats (or at least to be exposed as such), and they issue guidelines on behaviour. Also they'll be very interested if a journalist has been sloppy in his facts; the last thing they want is lots of libel writs winging their way towards them.

You can ask for a retraction, but there are two problems: where it appears, and the emphasis given to it. Retractions often get published on page 29 in tiny print between the small ads. This isn't a lot of good to you because no one's going to see it.

So if you have a seriously good case, emphasise that any retraction has to appear soon, on the same page number as the one the offending article appeared on, and given adequate prominence. If you feel really macho, demand to see the copy before it is published and hint that you'll remove your advertising from the paper and/or sue if not satisfied.

You can ask for a 'reply' article written by you, but you're unlikely to get one except under legal pressure.

Most complaints are not going to be serious enough to make an editor do any of this, so you'll probably be better off asking for another article soon (as above), or for a 'news' coverage of your reaction ('Factory manager denies job loss rumour') or that a letter should be published next issue.

CASE STUDY Great Corrections of our Time

FROM THE GATESHEAD POST:

In a report on page 5 of last week's *Gateshead Post* on a proposed new traffic office for Saltwell Road, Coun Norman Lakey was quoted as saying: 'I'll deal with the inspector, don't you worry about that.' Coun Lakey asks us to point out that he said: 'I understand that each planning application should be dealt with on its own merits.'

(Reported in *The Guardian* Diary, 28 September 1990)

This may be a case where leaving well alone might have been a better idea ...

WRITING A LETTER

This is a much neglected way of making a complaint, but it's one of the most effective. Just write a good letter to the letters page, putting your case. There are lots of advantages:

- the wording is under your control;
- it will appear very soon after the original piece you didn't like;
- it will be read by the same people who read the original;
- you have the chance to make positive points as well as just refuting the original mistake.

It's wise to let the publication know that a letter is on its way, either by informing the overall editor (see above) or the features editor. They won't necessarily make any promises, in case your effort is unbearably awful, but they probably will publish it.

When you write your letter, don't start off with: 'In all my years as a judge of champion leeks I have never read such a load of unmitigated rubbish and false accusations as you printed yesterday ...'. You want to begin by putting the readers in the picture:

'Yesterday's farming column made a number of allegations about the way that champion leeks are judged at the County Agricultural Show.'

If possible, throw in a compliment before getting down to business:

'I always turn immediately to this column for its interesting and informative approach, ...'

Put your complaint in a calm rational way:

'... but yesterday I was disturbed to read allegations that judges take bribes in the form of free compost from certain competitors. I've been a vegetable judge for 20 years and the only bribe I've ever been offered is a pint of beer before the competition.

In any case, all measurements are open to inspection, so that any competitor who feels cheated has only to pick up a tape measure and do his own calculations.'

Now see if you can throw in a bit of free public relations while you're at it:

'Leek growing is a fine old northern tradition, with more and more youngsters taking it up. It is healthy, environmentally friendly, and very sociable.'

And then some summing up:

'I'd be sorry if the atmosphere of leek competitions should be soured by misplaced suspicion about corruption in high places. Maybe your reporter would care to attend our next competition to see for himself how impossible trickery would be.'

Such a letter is reasonably short, reasonably interesting, and gets across quite a few points.

Other things to watch when writing a letter:
- Don't begin with a list of moans, whinges, or an attack on the morals or professional competence of the journalist.
- Be aware of deadlines. Letters tend to be prepared quite early in the cycle of a paper, so get it to them soon, e.g. by Monday for a weekly paper, by mid-morning of the day before an evening paper.
- Keep your overall length down. A short interesting letter is far more likely to be printed than a long rambling one which

they will have to take the bother to edit. Also, the shorter it is the more likely that it won't be edited. So choose one or two main bones of contention, rather than addressing every single one.

- If you have a positive action you want done, then say so.
- One way to add impact and increase your chances of publication is to have a collection of signatures; make sure each person also prints his or her name clearly so there's no problem in establishing who they are.

GETTING HEAVY

If you're not happy with the response you're getting, then you can start turning up the heat.

Write a formal letter to the editor, or even better, get a solicitor to write one, laying out your complaint in legal terms and implying that you mean business. Copy it to his managing director, or group editor, or whoever you think might have influence. State very clearly the minimum recompense you want, and why you're not satisfied with the reaction so far.

Many national papers now have an ombudsman; if so, contact him or her.

THE PRESS COMPLAINTS COMMISSION

Your next step is to contact the Press Complaints Commission (PCC), which has replaced the Press Council. They do not have power to enforce their code of practice, but papers at the moment are very conscious that if they aren't seen to be getting their act together, statutory regulation is on the cards. And none of them wants that.

The PCC, which started on 1 January 1991, is run by a body of 16 members, of whom nine are editors. It's geared for quick decisions, rather than the long drawn-out hearings of the Press Council.

- They have a privacy 'hot-line' to forestall publication of damaging material; so in theory you should be able to stop something really bad before it is even printed.
- It can consider complaints of unfair treatment and unwarranted intrusions of privacy.
- It can recommend and possibly word suitable apologies to a complainant by the offending publication.
- It will investigate a complaint, and initiate an ajudication if necessary.

If you want to complain to the PCC, send the original article and any further correspondence to them.

LIBEL AND SLANDER

The golden rule is 'Don't'. Entering into a libel case is costly, time-consuming and frequently counter-productive. For every huge sum paid to a celebrity there are many more plaintiffs who come to grief. Most papers are very careful about what they print, and national newspapers have lawyers on their staff whose only job is to check material for possible libel.

On the other hand, you do have the right to defend yourself from malicious and unfair attack. Libel is when the offending remarks are in writing or broadcast; slander is when they were spoken. You have to prove that what was said was defamatory and that it was actually circulated to a third person (so you need the original article or broadcast). But you also have to be ready against the defence of justification, fair comment or privilege.

If you think you really do have a good case, then consult a solicitor before going to a libel counsel. A really stiff letter showing you mean business may do the trick, and will be a lot cheaper than starting libel proceedings.

COMPLAINTS ABOUT BROADCASTING

The situation for broadcasting is slightly different, because broadcasters have to be authorised to go on air and so are under control; whereas anyone can legally publish anything, so long as it doesn't fall foul of libel or obscenity laws.

You have certain rights about a broadcast, as laid out originally in the Independent Broadcasting Association's (IBA) Guidelines and the BBC's own code of practice, and continued by the new bodies:

- You should be told the general theme of the interview, the introduction, and the first question.
- You should know in advance whether it will be one-to-one or in a group, live or pre-recorded, and when it will be transmitted.
- You should be told when you are on or off-air, and anything uttered before or after the interview proper should not be broadcast (but note that this didn't save President Reagan when he quipped during his voice test that 'Bombing of the USSR will start after five minutes'. His voice may not have been used, but the juicy information was leaked all the same).
- A telephone conversation cannot be recorded without your consent first, and it must be made clear that anything said might be used in a programme.
- You have the right to go back and correct something, even if the programme has been recorded.

- You can refuse to talk to anyone who gets through to you without warning and demands comment.

You don't have a right of veto over questions or answers, unless you can claim that such questions are unfair or are probing into your personal life. In general, there's no point at all in even trying to veto a particular line of questioning. If you say: 'I'm here to answer questions about our new factory; I will refuse to say anything about the news that one of our products has been accused of being carcinogenic', what do you think any respectable journalist will do? Better not to bring up the subject at all, but be prepared for that line of questioning just in case.

You also can't demand a list of specific questions, where you will appear in the running order of the programme, or that you should see a recording or a transcript of the programme before it's transmitted. Above all, you have no right of veto over whether your piece will be used. Once you agree to it, you are effectively handing over control.

For most people the main fear is that your words will get mucked about after the recording during the editing process. Either something will be taken completely out of context, or your words will be mauled about in some way.

It's very unusual for this to be done deliberately, but it can happen that a small piece of a longer interview will be picked out that isn't representative of the whole, or that two different sentences will be stitched together in such a way as to distort your original meaning. It's especially easy to do this in radio.

It's quite common for the second half of a statement to be cut, and if that second half was a modification of the first statement, then the wrong impression might be given. ('It is true that the Venusian Spaceball Club has had a policy for the last 50 years not to admit Martians, bug-eyed monsters or bi-peds, but it's extremely likely that next solar cycle we'll be changing that policy.' If this sentence is cut after 'bi-peds', it would sound far worse.) There are, however, editing guidelines too:

- A shortened version of an interview should not misrepresent the interviewee's contribution.
- Due weight should be given to any qualifying remarks that may perhaps weaken the force of an answer, but to which the interviewee is likely to attach importance.
- The context in which extracts from a recorded interview are used is also important (e.g. if someone comes along to talk to you about the profitability of running a battery chicken farm, and then puts your happy face talking about last year's profits just before a gruesome shot of chickens pecking each other to death ...).

FIRST CALL FOR BROADCASTING COMPLAINTS

First let's look at trying to stop something being broadcast. Ring the producer or reporter, explain your concern, and put your case. If it's just a matter of not liking the questions you were asked, or feeling that you didn't give very good answers, you probably won't get anywhere. But if you can show you were misled, or that you said something factually wrong or potentially damaging, then you should get some sort of a hearing.

If you're not happy, go to the overall editor or senior producer; and then to the head of department, and if necessary the controller. At each stage be polite but firm, and say what action you want taken immediately, because time is of the essence.

You can't do much more at this stage. Formerly you could go to the Independent Broadcasting Authority, which had the power to stop transmission or order a re-editing. The new authority, the Independent Television Commission, doesn't have this power.

For the BBC you could try the Director-General's office or the General Advisory Council, but it would have to be a pretty important matter for you to do this.

The more usual complaints come after the programme is broadcast. First of all, think whether you really want to travel down the formal road. What will you gain? If it's hard to get a paper to retract something, it's well-nigh impossible to get any apologies on television or radio. So try a little gentle prodding of the programme first: state your case calmly and suggest that they should redress the balance by coming and doing another piece about you soon which will put things right. If you're not happy, lodge a complaint by phone. Keep a note of the time of your call, what was said, and the name of the person you spoke to. Better still, record the conversation.

Make sure you have a copy of the programme. If you don't have your own, then get one from Tellex Monitors, either in transcript or broadcast form (if your complaint is to do with context or pictures, then make sure you get the pictures).

Write a formal letter of complaint to the programme, and copy to the programme controller. If necessary, write to the programme controller and send a copy of all correspondence to the MD.

SERIOUS BROADCASTING COMPLAINTS

Your final levels of complaint are to the various broadcasting organisations:

The Independent Television Commission which is the regulator and licenser of all non-BBC television services. It cannot preview programmes, so can only decide after the event if a programme has transgressed licence conditions.

The Radio Authority has the same function for non-BBC radio stations.

BBC General Advisory Council covers complaints for both TV and radio.

Broadcasting Complaints Commission will look at matters of factual accuracy, unfair context, etc. Their rulings take time and effort, with an initial process of written evidence, and if taken further, a series of formal and informal sessions when each party makes separate submissions. Its only power is to force an offender to publish a summary of the complaint and the Commission's findings, and often a publication of the adjudication in the *Radio Times* and TV *Times*. It cannot force an apology, a right of reply or a remedy.

Broadcasting Standards Council can tackle complaints about violence, sex, and matters of taste and decency – such as bad language or the treatment of disasters.

As with the press, go into the murky waters of libel action with great caution. It's far better to get an injunction before the programme than take action afterwards.

CASE STUDY Death of a Princess

This particular *cause célèbre* at the start of the 1980s illustrates the perils of making too much fuss. The programme claimed to show the story of a Saudi princess executed for her adultery, and on the way talked a lot about sexual hyprocrisy, the ill effects of fundamentalist Islam on Saudi society, and the power of the royal family to bend the rules.

Not surprisingly the Saudi authorities didn't like it. First they tried to get the programme banned, and when that didn't work, they made their distaste known through diplomatic channels.

As a result, an interesting but flawed programme became hot news. The original fairly small audience grew to tens of millions and the programme was shown world-wide. Even in Saudi Arabia itself, where the programme was of course banned, there were numerous pirate copies circulating.

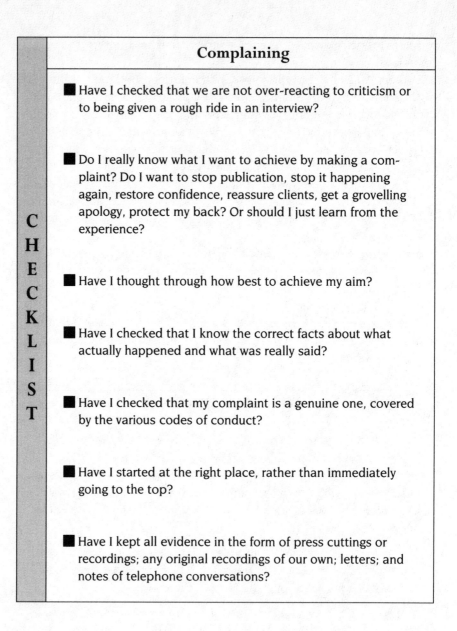

Complaining

C H E C K L I S T

■ Have I checked that we are not over-reacting to criticism or to being given a rough ride in an interview?

■ Do I really know what I want to achieve by making a complaint? Do I want to stop publication, stop it happening again, restore confidence, reassure clients, get a grovelling apology, protect my back? Or should I just learn from the experience?

■ Have I thought through how best to achieve my aim?

■ Have I checked that I know the correct facts about what actually happened and what was really said?

■ Have I checked that my complaint is a genuine one, covered by the various codes of conduct?

■ Have I started at the right place, rather than immediately going to the top?

■ Have I kept all evidence in the form of press cuttings or recordings; any original recordings of our own; letters; and notes of telephone conversations?

18

Preparing for Trouble

- It is always best to prepare for disaster before it happens.
- You should have a crisis team organised who meet regularly to work through all aspects of trouble and disaster.
- Sample documents can be prepared in advance, together with files containing all the information and plans you might need.
- If you know trouble is looming, then prepare ahead for it so that you are managing the timing and information flow right from the beginning.

THE one time that senior management will really love the idea of media relations is when disaster strikes. As the factory burns to the ground emitting poisonous fumes across half the county, they'll shriek for you, in the fond belief that a smoothy spokesperson can somehow save the day.

When you are overwhelmed by events, left in the dark about what's happening so you have to make wild guesses, and accused by journalists of incompetence, prevarication, cover-up, and lack of compassion; then they come back at you and say it's all your fault the press were so nasty.

It doesn't have to be so: by looking ahead and taking sensible precautions, a crisis ought to be containable. It certainly shouldn't be made worse by bumbling and fumbling. It's a matter of sensible management practice. You have to: *anticipate, prepare* and *perform*. Get a good system in place before crisis strikes, and you'll be far more likely to perform well on the day.

ANTICIPATING TROUBLE

Very few disasters are completely out of the blue. You can't anticipate that your oil terminal will explode on any particular day, and you obviously take all sensible precautions to make sure it never does, but it shouldn't come as a complete surprise if it blows up.

Even less surprising is any trouble that comes your way because you are laying off employees, or closing down a particular work site, or are announcing dreadful half-yearly figures. In such a case, you should be able to think through – before it all happens – how you will announce the news and manage, as best you can, any criticism that is bound to come your way.

Yet very few organisations have really sat down to think what they would do if trouble strikes them. Either they think it never will, or they decide that they'll face that problem once it happens because they can't afford the time to worry about it now.

Alas, if something really bad comes your way, you won't have the luxury of being able to calmly sit down and prepare a plan. You'll be involved not just in managing the crisis itself, but also in fending off reporters and phone calls and worried employees, and any mistakes made at the beginning will be hung around your neck like a rotten albatross for the rest of the troubles.

So what sort of crises should you think about? There are three sorts:

1 Definite trouble (strikes, redundancies, closures, etc.).
2 Possible trouble (product tampering, employee injury, attacks by opponents, etc.).
3 Horrible disasters (fraud, deaths, crashes, fire, etc.).

The first two can be fairly well anticipated and prepared for, so that what might be unpleasant at least won't turn into a total crisis through mismanagement. Even the horrible disasters can be thought about and some sort of preparations put in place. After all, the more horrible it is the more likely the media will come running and the less time you'll have to do anything.

WHAT COULD HAPPEN TO YOU?

The first thing to do is to work out a list of all the troubles that could hit you, from the most ordinary through to the most ghastly. For instance, let's say you're in charge of the Tower of London; what are the contingencies you might have to prepare for? First, the fairly possible ones in a sort of escalating list:

- falling number of visitors;
- cut in grant;
- increase in entrance charges;
- road works outside that block the entrance creating a 4-hour queue;
- burst water main that blocks entrance creating a 5-hour queue;
- strike by cleaning staff;
- ticket sellers accused of pocketing money;
- majority of Beefeaters ill so Tower has to be closed;
- visitor has heart attack and dies in the Quad;
- child falls off wall and is seriously injured;
- food on sale outside is contaminated with salmonella;
- lovers try to jump off battlements in suicide pact;
- madman attacks Beefeater with knife;
- berserk Beefeater attacks visitor with an axe;
- bomb threat leads to evacuation.

Then what about the improbable ones:

- strike by the Beefeaters;
- destruction of King Henry VIII's armour by pacifist;
- theft of the Crown Jewels;
- sickness of all the ravens;
- poisoning of all the ravens;
- Beefeaters accused of sex/drug orgies;
- terrorists seize the building;
- terrorists blow up the building;
- overcrowding in the Crown Jewels queue creates panic and injury;
- fire creates panic and deaths;
- a corner of the Tower collapses and kills tourists;
- a helicopter crashes on the Green and explodes in a fireball.

For each of those crises, there ought to be some sort of plan worked out – not too rigid, but at least a blueprint to be turned to immediately the crisis looms.

Create your own list of troubles, from the probable to the seemingly impossible, and have a think about them. Some day all of them will happen to someone.

CASE STUDY Murder

The Industrial Society was unhappily involved in a murder case, the so-called 'Cross bow murder'.

A young woman, Diana Maw, was found dead with a cross-bow bolt in her head. The bizarre murder method, together with speculations about 'love triangles' and such like, created huge media interest.

She happened to be a management adviser working for The Industrial Society, and though her death had nothing to do with her work, journalists phoned and came snooping around to see if they could pick up any juicy clues. For some days the press officer's time was totally occupied with protecting other staff from intrusion, and answering press queries.

A murder is not exactly high on most contingency planning lists, but it just goes to show that you never quite know what could be around the corner.

So here are some more quickies to think about: computer crash, kidnapping, unwanted takeover bid, pollution, rumour about bankruptcy, major supplier goes bust, financial scandal, sex scandal …

Also don't forget outside problems that might have a bearing on you. This might include legislation proposals, EC rules, environmental disasters elsewhere, or a scandal in a similar field.

CASE STUDY Who Else Can We Go For?

A London children's hospital had a case of rape, when someone infiltrated a ward. The papers reported the original incident; many of them used the story as a peg to look at hospital security generally. So the day the story broke, reporters were roaming various hospitals trying to get inside to see how good security measures were.

In the event, most hospitals came out of it badly and names were named.

> In such a situation, it's wise to be on your guard for this sort of behaviour and put everyone on extra alert immediately whether it's a security, safety, or consumer issue.

Lastly, don't bring disaster on yourself. One classic example is the downfall of Gerald Ratner of British jewellery chain-store fame. He proclaimed at a serious business dinner where he was the invited speaker that one of his products was 'crap'. This merry quip aimed at his peers was of course picked up with glee by the papers, and thus his customers. It's difficult to tell how much they were affected by the news that Ratner's jewellery is crap, but certainly the next half-year figures showed that sales had dropped compared to competitors'.

In the following case study, the company concerned didn't check their product.

CASE STUDY A Natural Mistake

A clothes company sent a sample T-shirt to various fashion editors, with a release claiming that they use only 'natural fibres' in their up-market products. Unfortunately for them the label inside clearly stated: '50 per cent synthetic polyester', a point picked up with interest by the journalists.

The spokeswomen tried to retrieve the situation by apologising and saying that they had ordered 100% cotton, but by then the damage was done. Their products weren't attacked, but the story was printed in diary columns and the like as a bit of a giggle.

In both those cases there need never have been any crisis at all, had the people concerned been a bit more careful.

THE CRISIS TEAM

You can't cope with a crisis alone. There are too many things to do all at once, and many different skills will be needed. So it's important to have a crisis team organised beforehand, who have occasional meetings to talk through their plans, and who all know their tasks should trouble happen. Such a team won't be just for disasters; they should also be thinking about the management of any bad news, from the sudden illness of the chairman to a full-scale industrial dispute.

A basic committee might consist of the chief executive officer, the works manager, the personnel manager, the health and safety manager, and the media person. There might also be a services person, to look at the communications side. If there are several locations, then each should also have at least one person on the team so that they can make an input and also know the policies.

The crisis committee should meet regularly to update the crisis list, examine any possible troubles coming up, and plan procedures. They should all know each other's home phone numbers, and at least one person should always know who is on holiday, who is the deputy, and any information that could help track someone down at weekends or evenings. They must know the roles of each person – who will be the spokesperson, for instance; who will brief the staff; who will be in charge of any written statement? Policy should be clear, too; what will be the order of priority, what can and cannot be said to the press?

Certain things can be planned ahead, just in case:

- Basic press releases on the most likely problems, e.g. if you are a food production company you could prepare releases about food poisoning, product tampering, contamination of a product, etc. Then it is very easy to fill in the particular details on the day.
- An emergency press pack, giving details of safety records, security precautions, evacuation plans, etc., as well as normal background material and photos.
- Copies (kept up to date) of installations, work sites, lists of key people at each location, safety equipment, etc.
- Message pads suitable to log incoming and outgoing calls, especially to the press, so that each conversation is recorded and timed, with full notes on what was said to whom, and follow-up calls, etc.
- Work out whether the switchboard could cope with a flood of calls. How would calls be routed? Where would extra help come from?
- Prepare a list of who must be told about a crisis, and organise who will tell them. It's vital that people know quickly what's going on and what they have to do.
- Prepare a list of outside organisations which might help. Obviously that starts with the police and the other emergency services. But also other local employers, or other employers in your industry, or sympathetic MPs, or local community health doctors. You might need third-party support.

> ## CASE STUDY Sweet Talk
>
> A very well-known sweet nearly choked a child to death, and the media began an attack on its size and shape which could have dropped sales.
>
> The confectionary firm concerned decided to call in a consultant paediatrician to brief the press on how children behave. In particular, he made the point that most children suffer accidents because their carers' are distracted for a time. Attention then shifted to parental behaviour and the need to watch children like a hawk so that they don't swallow pins, climb furniture, turn on the gas, etc.
>
> Using an outside neutral expert was far more effective than using a company spokesman.

- Where would you put an emergency press room? It needs lots of phones, fax, etc.; refreshments for those on long duty (even a mattress sometimes if things are really bad); and a place nearby where journalists can be talked to singly or in a group. If you don't have a room that has all those things, then think how you would organise it at short notice. Where would you get the phones from, for instance? And the extra people to man them?
- Train ahead, e.g. the media spokesman needs to go on a media interview course.
- Test occasionally. Certain industries take testing very seriously; for example the UK Department of Energy organises an exercise every year in a different North Sea oil location. This is played 'for real' with computer simulations, over a number of days, and the results are circulated throughout the whole industry.

    You may not be able to go to such extremes, but try an exercise once in a while, even if it's just to see how many of the crisis team you can actually locate on a Saturday night.

Get all this in writing in one place, which everyone on the team knows about. Don't rely on the hope that 'Old Fred will know what to do'; he might or he might not. In any case, you all need to know what Fred will do.

SAMPLE PRESS RELEASE

Here's an example of a possible contingency press release which can sit in the files until it's needed. Obviously it's quickest to have sample documents on a word processor disk.

The Bannerman Corporation confirms that an incident (state what it was) happened at its (place) building at approx. (state time) today.

At this stage specific information about exactly what happened is not available, but a detailed press statement wil be issued as soon as this is feasible. This will probably be by (state time).

We will be holding a press conference this afternoon at (state time and place) when the Director-General will answer questions.

Further press information will also be available by telephoning the following numbers (give telephone numbers) and asking for the Press Room. An information pack on the Bannerman Corporation can be faxed on request.

PREVENTING A DRAMA FROM BECOMING A CRISIS

There's a whole world of news management out there, where the bearer of bad news makes sure that first it's presented in the best possible light ('the numbers of unemployed are still going up, but the rate of increase is going down'), and secondly that the news breaks at the best possible time for their purposes. It's the opposite of normal press work – you want to achieve the littlest coverage possible. Governments do it all the time, but even the royals have a try.

CASE STUDY Losing a Story

In October 1990 there was an announcement that the British Royal Family had increased its spending by 20%.

The announcement was timed for 7.30 in the evening, probably in the hope that the press would miss it. Indeed, radio and television didn't pick it up because there wasn't time to get any actuality coverage; and the quality press had more or less gone to bed by then, so they didn't cover it except as a brief mention.

The only big coverage was from the tabloids, which have a short lead-in time and are geared up to sudden last-minute stories with up to 24 remakes of their pages every night. And since they were pretty pro-Royal, the story was fairly gently handled.

If you have something unfavourable coming up there are various possible strategies.

CHOOSE YOUR TIMING

Choose to issue a press release with bad news the day before a big event such as the Budget. If that's not possible, then release it late at night, or on a Saturday so that the Sundays don't have much time to do a lot of coverage, and the news is stale by Monday.

More positively, think ahead to the reaction and time it to suit you, as in the case study following.

CASE STUDY Time Management

When Ernest Saunders announced the takeover bid by Guinness for Arthur Bell, he announced it late on Friday, briefing financial journalists and stockbroking analysts at a press conference.

The news thus got a lot of publicity in the Sunday nationals. But by then Saunders was in Edinburgh, so that when the Scottish papers picked up the story on Sunday, he was available at a hotel to talk to the Scottish press about the implications for Bell's, a local firm.

By the time Bell's woke up to the situation, Saunders had already put his case and set the agenda. They had to work twice as hard to put their side of the story.

LEAK THE NEWS

A little judicious advance warning can work wonders with bad news about profits or jobs. Everyone tends to react unfavourably if a big blow just arrives, so it's better to prepare the ground. You can issue a press release with the news that the dividend 'may' be cut or jobs 'could' be shed. Or – the more usual way – you gently hint to the right journalist that something is in the offing. That paper will probably print the speculation; and others will follow.

Be prepared to be quizzed about exact figures, so decide beforehand how you'll deal with that. You also have to decide whether the damage caused by such speculation will be less than the damage caused by a sudden announcement.

However, a gently leaked piece of bad news can defuse a crisis before it begins: your share prices won't suddenly dip, your employees won't feel quite so astounded. (Note that listed companies have to give the Stock Exchange – and only the Stock Exchange – any information that might affect the market. So a real leak to the papers in advance of the Stock

Exchange is illegal, while a gentle hint may not be.)

One final ploy used sometimes is to leak an exaggerated figure. It's a dangerous plan which can backfire, but in essence, what is done is to let it be known that the yearly figures will be horrendous, or that hundreds of jobs are going to be lost. Then when the real situation is revealed, things look quite good by comparison.

PREPARE YOUR STRATEGY

If you know something bad is coming up, then prepare for it:

- Get press releases ready, emphasising your side of the story, or putting the best gloss on it.
- Prepare for any trouble arising, such as threats of industrial action, so that you know before they happen what your response will be.
- Have your crisis team all ready and briefed and in place for when the news is announced.
- Prepare a brief for all spokespersons, with a list of the likely questions they'll be asked and the model response they should make. Make sure they have mastered that brief, and have had plenty of time to clarify any doubts beforehand. So hold meetings to discuss all possible contingencies.
- Try to anticipate what any opposition will do, and prepare a response. So if you think they'll hold a press conference to put their point of view, make sure you get a friendly journalist or a mole to find out what time it will be, so that you can be ready to hold your press conference half an hour later, or issue a refuting press release in time to catch the same edition of the papers. You want to be the ones who always have the last word.
- Prepare a list of contacts, friends, enemies, and all the people you might want to influence about your news. Assign one of your people to each person or group you want to talk to immediately after the news breaks. Give a target time for a phone call.
- Prepare in advance follow-up letters to customers, members, employees, suppliers, donors, etc., to be sent immediately the news is public, explaining what it all means for them.

If you do all this, you'll find that what might have become a crisis should flow relatively smoothly. You may still get tough questions or adverse publicity, especially if the bad news is going to affect a lot of people, but at least nothing you do will be making it worse. With any luck you'll have thought through the best way to show the people who matter that you've been doing your best – that you don't want to lay people off, but otherwise even more jobs are at risk; you don't want to close down a certain production unit, but it's dangerous because the buildings are unsafe; your exam results are bad, but set in the context of the area as a whole they aren't quite so awful, and by next year the new head will have really improved things with her wonderful dynamism.

CASE STUDY Winning the Bottle

A big dairy firm had plans to close down one of their bottling plants in East Anglia. This would mean 140 jobs lost, and though the company was going to set up a job shop to help those made redundant, it obviously couldn't guarantee that everyone would find another job.

Management anticipated that the closure would be newsworthy, and decided to plan ahead. Their policy was: 'We must pre-empt basic questions by issuing as much useful information as possible to interested groups. We must also be prepared to answer their reasonable questions in a positive and helpful manner.'

They prepared a 30-page plan, 2 months ahead of the planned announcement. It had in it:

- a list of all those likely to be interested in the announcement (trade unions, local press, agricultural press, local MPs, etc.);
- the press statement announcing the closure;
- the full details of the closure;
- full details of personnel, production, etc. of the closing dairy;
- information on previous closures around the country;
- a map showing all their major dairy sites;
- 20 sample questions and model answers;
- an action list showing exactly who would contact which interested group or person either before the announcement or on the day of the announcement – this showed not just the names, but also how they would do it (meeting, phone, or letter), and when (9.00 a.m., 12 noon, etc.); also any follow-up plans;
- names and addresses of local MPs;
- home telephone numbers of the senior dairy managers involved.

Such a plan was drawn up well in advance, because the company had plenty of time to work it all out. But there's no reason why a lot of such information shouldn't be on file in preparation, so that if a crisis looks like erupting (such as industrial trouble or an industry-wide scandal) and you have a few days grace to think ahead, quite a lot of the work is already done.

It seems that someone in British Gas really pressed for the positive approach in the following newspaper story. By anticipating possible trouble arising from the inquest, British Gas have turned what could have been very negative reporting into almost a success story ...

CASE STUDY British Gas Learn

TRAGEDY PROMPTS SAFETY REVIEW

British Gas has stepped up safety checks on gas central heating systems in homes throughout the Midlands after an inquest heard how a man died of carbon monoxide poisoning in his own home.

And it has ordered all its fitters to go on a refresher course to make sure they know every aspect of the job. Inquiries by British Gas and the Health and Safety Executive linked the man's death with wind conditions which had appeared to make the flue inefficient. The jury returned a verdict of accidental death.

(*Evening Mail*, 11 February 1991)

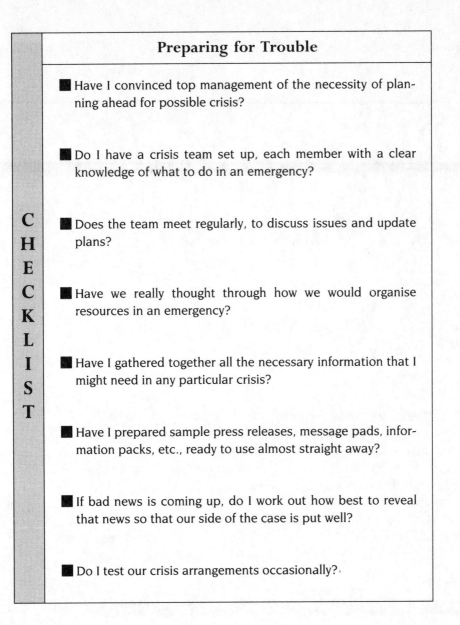

Preparing for Trouble

**C
H
E
C
K
L
I
S
T**

■ Have I convinced top management of the necessity of planning ahead for possible crisis?

■ Do I have a crisis team set up, each member with a clear knowledge of what to do in an emergency?

■ Does the team meet regularly, to discuss issues and update plans?

■ Have we really thought through how we would organise resources in an emergency?

■ Have I gathered together all the necessary information that I might need in any particular crisis?

■ Have I prepared sample press releases, message pads, information packs, etc., ready to use almost straight away?

■ If bad news is coming up, do I work out how best to reveal that news so that our side of the case is put well?

■ Do I test our crisis arrangements occasionally?

19

Plagues and Pestilences

- Like the Spanish Inquisition, you never know when bad news will strike.
- The more you have prepared beforehand, the less disastrous it will be.
- Act fast, act first, act adequately.
- It's usually better to assume the worst, and take huge steps to put things right, than to seem to be slow and grudging.
- Put people before products.
- Tell the truth and nothing but the truth. You don't necessarily have to volunteer the whole truth.

THE NIGHTMARE COMES TRUE

IT'S 6.00 on a Monday morning; the phone goes; it's the school caretaker with the news that the school is on fire and he thinks he saw three youngsters running away whom he recognised as pupils ... Or it's Monday morning; you open your newspaper to find that your company has been voted the worst employer in the region, and that you are described as 'unfriendly, unsafe, unclean, and usually mean'.

The nightmare has happened. Now it's time to activate all your crisis plans and look out your emergency files. The media may come running any moment, and you don't have a minute to lose.

'The first twenty four hours are critical. If you aren't geared up and ready to inform the public you will be judged guilty until proven innocent.'
(Donald R. Stephenson, Director of Public Issues for Dow Chemical Canada Inc. Quoted in Michael Regester, *Crisis Management*, Hutchinson, London, 1989.)

CASE STUDY Lucozade

In November 1991, the head of communications at SmithKline Beecham was contacted by Scotland Yard for an urgent meeting. The Anti Terrorist Branch had information that the Animal Liberation Front had plans to poison Lucozade bottles.

The chief executive was told of the threat and his strategy was: 'To understand it; to minimise the risk; and to ensure that the crisis team was prepared.' The chairman of the consumer brand division immediately set up an 'incident room' with 20 staff. At 6.30 the next morning the police announced that they'd arrested a number of people, with a news embargo till 7.00 a.m.

Calls started after three minutes. By 7.15 a Lucozade spokesman was talking live to local radio, and another was on Radio 4's *Today* warning listeners. 1,500 calls were received in the 'incident room'. And the head of communications spent the next two days coping with a stream of reporters' questions.

Luckily for Lucozade, no poisonings were reported. But all loose bottles and those in open cases were poured away, costing around £5 million pounds. The company then announced that Lucozade was safe to drink, and sales resumed.

Within a week shares had recovered to 3p above their original level.

THE BASICS

The lessons to be learnt from Lucozade are:
- Every minute counts.
- You need lots and lots of people because so many things are going on at once.
- You need to find out the real situation quickly.
- The message put across must be clear and positive.
- You must be caring and careful.

- You must be seen to be caring and careful.
- Action taken at the beginning of the crisis is worth twice as much as any action taken days later.

GET THE CRISIS TEAM INVOLVED

The first step is to inform the crisis team, or a group who will be your team if you haven't done the preparations you should. Get them together, if that can be done quickly. They should be released from their normal jobs; you can't manage a crisis and also be going to all the usual meetings, however important.

Activate the crisis room. Where are you going to put the phones, the files, the photocopier, etc.? You may need lots of phones if it is a big incident; at least one line should be for outward calls only, in case the lines get blocked by in-coming calls.

You may need lots of people; inform them and start to organise them. If things look bad, start thinking about a 24-hour duty roster; and how to organise breaks for the crisis team people so that they don't get exhausted after two or three days.

ESTABLISH THE FACTS

You need to know what has happened, and what is continuing to happen. Someone should be immediately assigned to find out the facts, and record carefully all information. Initially find the details of the incident, who raised the alarm, who saw anything and how it was found out.

If the situation is a long-running one, you need to constantly review the facts, and try to anticipate events as well.

If you don't know the facts, then don't make them up or speculate on what you think they might be. Above all, don't make any public statements that might return to haunt you, unless you are sure you are on safe ground.

CASE STUDY 'Poisoned through Bungles'

On 6 July 1988 a lorry driver discharged 20 tons of aluminium sulphate into the wrong tank at the water treatment works near Camelford in Devon, England. As a result, the drinking water of 20,000 people was contaminated. Three years later the incident was still a matter of burning interest to the local community, believing that the water had caused long-term serious damage to their health.

In particular they felt bitter at the water authority's bland reassurances that the water was safe to drink before they knew any of the facts.

Within hours of the original mistake, people were phoning in to complain of 'black, foul-tasting water'. The stand-by officer was not available for three hours because he was at a dog-training class, and when he was contacted, he told the switchboard operator 'Don't say anything too much'.

Next morning the authority's water operations controller went on local radio to say the water was completely safe. In fact, the authority had no idea what had gone wrong. No samples of domestic water had been analysed and it was another two days before the aluminium sulphate mistake was discovered. Even then, public health doctors were not consulted and the community were not told the truth.

The authority said they had had an internal investigation, had decided there was no health risk, and did not make the full nature of the incident public because it would cause undue concern. But ever after, their explanations were suspect, and the community's trust lost.

BRIEF THE STAFF

In a really serious crisis, the media may know about the incident almost as quickly as you do, so you may not have much time before they are phoning up for confirmation, or even arriving at the door. So let the staff know what has happened and what is being done. Tell them that they shouldn't talk to anyone, however plausible, and explain why it is important that all news comes from one source only. In particular, brief the front-line people: the switchboard, reception, and gatekeepers.

Switchboard should know what is happening almost before anyone else. It's important that they know who might be calling and what to do. They must be told to be very discreet, and refuse all blandishments to reveal any information. All press calls should be put through to the press room, as should any calls from the general public. Calls from employees or relatives should go to the employee relations person. Ordinary calls to people involved in the crisis team should be routed to their offices.

If there is a terrorist threat, or a blackmailer, then obviously the police should be informed. But until they come to give advice, people on the switchboard should be aware of standard questions to ask, in case the caller refuses to speak to anyone else.

Such questions for a bomb might be: When will the bomb explode? Where is it? What does it look like? Where are you calling from? Can you give proof that you are from the group you claim?

For a blackmailer: How many products are contaminated? How are they contaminated? What signs are there? When did you contaminate them? How did you contaminate them? Where are you phoning from? What action do you want us to take?

It's unlikely that all or even any of those questions will be answered, but clues may be dropped all the same. So the telephonist should note the exact timing, exact wording and information, and any impressions of age, sex, accent, and background noises.

SEIZE THE INITIATIVE

Decide on a good time for a press conference or when you can issue a statement. Make it earlier rather than later; even if you don't yet know the full story it's better to get your partial view of events out rather than let speculation or attack get out of hand.

You want to establish early on that you are an authoritative source of news and that you are being as open and helpful as possible. If you feel you really can't yet talk about your side of the incident, then see if you can find another angle to go for: if your chemicals are polluting a river, then bring in an industry spokesperson to talk about general principles, or a doctor to talk about public health.

As soon as you can, follow up your first release with a full statement, but stick only to the known facts. The press will be speculating quite enough without you adding to it.

Express concern, state what is being done, and give information on any other bodies you're co-operating with, to add credibility.

You also want to try to seize initiative by making the story one that suits you, so that the more positive angles get used rather than the negative ones. 'Company reacts quickly to critical safety report' reads better than 'Warehouse a safety nightmare, says factory report'.

CASE STUDY Eau Dear!

Source Perrier had a nasty jolt in 1990 when benzene was discovered in their water. Mineral waters sell on their image of health and purity, and a decision was made to recall immediately all bottles of Perrier water world-wide.

At once this decision became the story, which was no bad thing for Perrier, since the last thing they wanted was too much speculation on where the benzene came from. Their original explanation was that a worker had used the wrong sort of cleaning fluid for the bottling equipment.

In fact, they later discovered that the benzene was coming from the gas pumped to the water above ground (itself taken from another underground source) to make it fizzy. This gas contains benzene, which is filtered out before bottling. For over six months the filters had been faulty.

The problem for Perrier therefore was to keep away from public airing any close look at what mineral water contains (not all minerals are good for you), and how so-called 'natural carbonation' works.

But the recall of 160 million bottles took the news, as Perrier water disappeared entirely from the shelves for 8 weeks. When it was re-launched, it quickly re-established its brand leadership, and within a year was back to over 90% of its original sales.

One other interesting point is that Perrier's competitors kept quiet through all this. No one wanted to muddy the reputation of any 'pure spring water' because an attack on Perrier's purity could easily rebound on all mineral water manufacturers.

BUY TIME

Once you have decided when you're going to say something, on your terms, then refuse to say anything substantial till then. You can buy time by telling all callers when the press conference/press release/statement will happen. *Then shut up*. It is one of the hardest things to do. You have mayhem around you; you want to co-operate; and you are being asked specific questions. But having decided that you aren't going to say anything until you know a bit more and have time to work out your best response, you must stick by it.

Watch in particular for specific questions 'just verifying facts'. If a journalist says with great confidence: 'I hear six people are dead', the temptation is to respond hastily, 'No, it's not as bad as that, thank God; only one person died and the rest are in hospital'. He then has the information he needs and not at all in the way you might want to reveal it.

So every question must be fielded politely but firmly with the statement that 'We'll be making an announcement at five o'clock; please come along then or phone in'.

WORK OUT THE APPROPRIATE RESPONSE

You don't want to escalate a crisis; if this is a local problem then don't start alerting the national media unless you really want them in on the act.

Similarly, if your prelimary investigation of the facts seems to show that you don't actually have anything to worry about, then you want to dampen news rather than encourage it. So going overboard with a huge press conference, large numbers of experts, dozens of press releases day and night, will only fuel speculation that you are really worried despite your assurances that you aren't.

CASE STUDY Sexy Slurs

A famous British girls' boarding school had a nasty shock early one morning when a copy of the tabloid newspaper *The Sun* was shown to them. A two-page spread, with picture, claimed that a certain young man had been in the habit of climbing into the school for 'nights of love' with his girlfriend. There were allegations of smuggled drugs and drink as well, and the overall impression was that the girls spent most nights in lurid orgies.

The fear of the school was that the quality press might pick up the story and thus give it credibility, so their concern was to quash it if possible.

The senior teachers checked the claimed route of entry (which seemed impossible even for an athletic youth), and read the article at assembly to the girls. They discovered that the young man named in the article had indeed visited the school under normal visiting procedures. The girl named had later left the school under a cloud.

By this time they were fairly confident that the story was untrue. Reporters from other papers who phoned up were told to wait until 11.00 a.m. From then on the school read over the phone a very bland statement saying that, while they took the allegations seriously, there was no evidence of any truth in it (and they briefly explained why).

This did the trick: no other nationals even ran the story, and the local paper only ran it under a headline 'School slams sexy slurs'.

A letter was sent to parents some days later.

KEEP THE RECORDS

From the very beginning, log all contacts using your pre-prepared crisis message pad. You want to have down in detail:

- who;
- what was asked and said;
- when;
- any action taken;
- any follow-up.

You also want to keep carefully filed all statements made to the press, all press releases, and any broadcasts. This is important at the time, so that you don't contradict yourselves; it's also important later when everything is over and you need to evaluate what happened.

APPOINT ONE SPOKESPERSON

It's very confusing and dangerous to have more than one message coming out of an organisation in a crisis. So it's important that only one person is giving the news and fielding the questions.

The more serious the crisis, the more important that your spokesperson is someone high up with a lot of credibility. Journalists are very suspicious of the 'PR man' in these circumstances, and want to speak to someone in authority.

But it's not just journalists: if it's an issue of public health, injury, or death, then the public, too, want to be reassured by someone they can trust. So bring out your top person, and tell everyone else to keep quiet.

SHOW A HUMAN FACE

It's very easy in a crisis to get so involved with defending yourself that you forget to show you care.

Someone is injured, say, in an accident. It is vital that you show that your major concern is not with the legal liabilities, but with the injured person and the family. So the first thing you show is that you are concerned about the person's welfare; one of the first things you do is work out what you're going to do for that person, and then tell the press.

CASE STUDY A Bunch of Flowers

An Asian factory employee was knifed at work in an incident with racial overtones. He was quite badly injured and hospitalised.

The manager was very concerned about him, and one of his first actions was to put him in a private room, at the company's cost, and to reassure his family that he'd be on full pay until he recovered.

However, the manager also wanted to dampen down the racial aspect of the incident. So he organised time off work for some of the man's (Asian and non-Asian) workmates to go and visit him in hospital. Pictures duly appeared in the local press, and the emphasis of the story was more 'Well wishers go to see Ahmed' than 'Asian man set upon by factory racists'.

CASE STUDY The Dog that Didn't Bark

A manufacturing company had a faulty product that had a one in three hundred chance of exploding a few minutes after being turned on.

They were hastily recalled, but meantime six did actually explode and one killed a dog. In their relief that no people had been hurt, the company ignored the dog; they didn't contact the family concerned nor state any public regret.

As a result, the original story about the exploding products – which was bad enough – became the story about the heartless distant company and ran for twice as long.

DO MORE THAN IS NECESSARY TO PUT THINGS RIGHT

It's best to adopt a 'worst possible scenario' approach to any bad incident. That means that you expect the worst and plan for it. If necessary you do far more than is strictly needed, because it's better to be seen to be over-reacting on the side of safety and concern than to seem niggardly and grudging. (This is not the same as over-reacting to the media, which is usually to be avoided.)

So if your product is suspect, right from the beginning do – and be seen to be doing – far more than ought to be necessary to protect the public. If you are accused of pollution, then immediately spend money and resources to put it right, and more than put it right.

If in the end the size of the problem turns out to be less than feared, then at least you can't be criticised for being over-cautious. But if it turns out that you have done too little at the beginning, and it looks as if you only got your act together under the pressure of events or public opinion, you will be damned for being uncaring, money grubbing, and stupid.

CASE STUDY Cyanide, Dear?

One of the most famous crises is that of Tylenol, the American anal-gesic manufactured by Johnson & Johnson. On 29 and 30 September 1982 cyanide-laced Tylenol tablets caused three deaths in the Chica-go area. Johnson & Johnson immediately recalled all their Tylenol bottles nationwide, and spent half a million dollars warning doctors, distributors, and hospitals.

Eventually it turned out, after four more deaths, that the poisonings were only in the Chicago area, so that the company need not have reacted so strongly.

But they gained great credibility from their actions. As the Wall St Journal said: 'The company chose to take a large loss rather than expose anyone to further risk'. As a result, when they later launched a 'tamper-proof' bottle and claimed that Tylenol was now absolutely safe they were believed by the public, and within five months Tylenol had won back 70% of its orginal market share.

NEVER 'NO COMMENT'

It is nearly always a mistake to say 'No comment' to a reporter's questions about some crisis. Whatever may be the situation in a court of law, in most people's minds a 'no comment' sounds defensive at best and guilty as hell at worst.

It's much better to have prepared a 15-second formula for both press and broadcasting journalists which will sidestep any aggressive or probing questions:

'My immediate concern is to get the injured people looked after; once we've done that, we'll fully investigate how it all happened.'

'Yes, we've heard the allegations about the fraud. Our first priority is to protect our shareholders and until we've done that we'd be foolish to speculate on anything else.'

There's nothing in these statements that can return to harm you; and you can't be accused of 'no commenting' either. The trick is to utter the words, and then move on. Refuse all invitations to answer any more questions with a nice smile and a shake of the head. Then move to the car – fast!

The other problem with a 'No comment' response is that a reporter chasing a story can't afford to leave it at that. Editors don't take kindly to stories filled full of 'no comments'. So if it's a good juicy story the reporter will go elsewhere to get it, even if it is to the window cleaner's cousin twice-removed.

Much better to get your version in, putting the positive point of view and telling everyone what you're going to do about it all.

KEEP SMILING

It's very hard to keep smiling when all around you is tumbling down, but it is essential to do it if the cameras are rolling. Tight lips, a harassed answer, and the viewers immediately come to the conclusion that you are in big trouble.

It's better to adopt the attitude 'Yes it's a drama, but not a crisis', than to go all grim and worried. Even if you are involved in casualties or deaths, you should still try to be positive – for the sake of the families as well as your own public image – while if it is anything to do with business confidence or financial troubles, it is vital to keep a slight smile of confidence on your face (however worried you're really feeling).

A camera crew will be a nuisance during a crisis, but you mustn't show that you are annoyed or fed up. Treat even stupid questions with courtesy, and be ready with a cheery formula to get you out of the room or down the steps once you've had enough. *Showing stress can be interpreted as being unable to cope.* It isn't fair that stress is read as incompetence – but who said life is fair?

CASE STUDY The Mirror Crack'd

On 5 November 1991, Robert Maxwell the media tycoon was found dead in the sea off the Canaries.

On the day of his death, the full extent of his empire's financial troubles was not yet known, so the media's immediate reaction was to go for the 'Who dunnit?' angle – was it accident, heart attack, suicide, or even murder?

The television news bulletins ran extended programmes that evening, examining Maxwell the man, asking for reactions from those who knew him, and looking at his business interests to see if suicide might be a possibility.

ITN's *News at Ten* did a live interview with Richard Stott, editor of the *Daily Mirror*. Mr Stott was seen outside his office as his name was announced by the newscaster Trevor Macdonald, turned away from the camera presumably talking to someone else.

Trevor Macdonald: Can you hear me, Mr Stott?

Richard Stott: (*as he turns round, his mouth set in a very thin line*) Yes.

TM: Your office must be a sad place tonight. Now, the circumstances of Mr Maxwell's death are still a mystery. Can you tell me this – had the pressure on him become simply too much?

RS: No. (*His eyes flick to the right.*)

TM: But it's well known that the company was in a great deal of debt and it wasn't exactly a bed of roses. (*Mr Stott is looking down at his toes through all this.*) These were circumstances in which a man of even comparable stature might have cracked.

RS: (*Raises his head slightly, but his body is still turned away from the camera.*) There are no debts within Mirror Newspapers. You're talking about a company that makes between 80 and 100 million pounds a year – rather a lot of money. (*Said in very dismissive tone.*)

TM: So you know of nothing that would have made him crack under this pressure?

RS: (*His eyes flick again.*) Absolutely nothing.

TM: And did anything happen in the last two days which might have in any way changed his mood?

RS: Not that I know of. I spoke to him last night and he was in very buoyant mood because I told him that once again we were going to pass *The Sun's* circulation.

TM: Everyone said he was very much in command of operations. Can the empire survive without him?

RS: The *Daily Mirror* is a national institution. Of course it can survive. (*Said very scornfully, but his eyes flick left and right.*)

TM: Mr Stott, thank you very much.

RS: Goodnight. (*Said very quickly, eyes down, as he moves off into the night.*)

Just about everything that Richard Stott said was undermined by the manner in which he said it: abrupt answers, twisted body position, nervous eyes that either flickered or looked at his boots. His mouth was set tight throughout, and the general impression was that he'd rather be anywhere than in front of that camera.

It may have been that he genuinely believed everything he was saying, and that the reason he came across so badly was that he just wanted to be getting on with his job of coping with the crisis.

However, he was so ungracious that it looked as if he had something to hide. So as the next few days passed, and it became apparent that Robert Maxwell's business dealings had been even shadier and shakier than first supposed, any normal viewer would have felt justified in their initial impression that the Mirror Group was in bad trouble too.

HOLDING A PRESS CONFERENCE

A press conference, either right at the beginning or as part of the continuing crisis, is a good way to put your view across. A press conference puts a human face to your concerns better than a written statement ever will. You can use it to create interest, especially for radio and television who want some actuality footage. And the question sessions – while daunting – at least mean that you can clear up possible misunderstandings.

Once you've made your initial response to the events, then hold a press conference every day at the same time and place, so the media know what to expect and can plan for it.

Once things die down a bit, you can lessen the frequency.

Basic tips for a crisis conference
• Prepare thoroughly beforehand; don't wing it.
• Keep them short; not longer than 40 minutes unless absolutely necessary.
• Introduce your people, and then carefully explain the situation, what is being done, and who else is involved. Don't speculate if you don't yet know precise facts, or bring up your past mistakes; let others do that.
• If there is any injury or loss, express regret and concern right at the beginning. Show that you care.
• Answer questions one at a time. If you can't answer, say so and give a sensible reason. Then move on to the positive, with: 'But I can tell you that …'. Try to anticipate questions and prepare the answers.
• Leave at the end in a businesslike fashion. Don't be lured into any more answers on the move. But don't look as if you are escaping, either. Keep a calm smile on your face and politely decline with 'I'm sorry, time's up, and I have to get on with the job fire-fighting/contacting relatives/seeing the Minister/putting things right, but you'll have another chance tomorrow.'

PUTTING WRONG STATEMENTS RIGHT

One sort of a crisis is when you discover you are implicated in something that in fact is none of your business. But you may suffer all the same unless facts are put straight.

If this happens, then get moving straight away to get the story changed.

Pull in bigger guns if necessary: trade associations, employers' organisations, 'experts' of any kind.

Contact the media and find where they got their wrong information from. Tell them the true story and ask that they don't perpetuate the mistake in future editions. Then keep going back to source and put it right there.

If the mistake persists, then so must you. Keep at it. If you don't correct it as early as possible, you'll find it around forever, because other journalists doing their research later will find the wrong information in the press cuttings and will repeat the original mistake.

CASE STUDY Child-minding

Newspapers one morning broke the story that a 'child-minder' had murdered a child in her care.

A member of the Childminders Association phoned up to report this to the Association, and they phoned the police. They were told that the accused was not a registered child-minder, but the baby-sitter. So the Association phoned the media to tell them so, and also found out that it was a news agency which had reported it in the first place. So they phoned the agency too.

The first two editions of the papers went out with the 'child-minder' tag; further editions had changed it to 'baby-sitter'.

The Childminder's Association didn't do it, but it might have been a good idea to then contact radio and breakfast television for the next morning, to use the dreadful incident as a way of reminding people of the importance of checking references, using registered child-minders, etc.

The very fact that newspapers used 'child-minder' and 'baby-sitter' as interchangeable terms would prove the point that few of us are as careful as we should be when employing someone to look after children.

WHEN IT ALL GOES WRONG

If you don't have preparations made ahead, and if you botch up your campaign, then don't be surprised if there are tears all round. Even worse, one disastrous crisis will return to haunt you ever after. Pity Gulf Oil Corporation, when an oil tanker blew up in 1979, killing about 50 employees. This was ghastly enough, but all statements and action by the company was tainted by two previous incidents in 1974 and 1975, when oil had spilled into Bantry Bay. Both times the general manager had speculated on the amount of oil spilled before knowing the facts. Both times his guess was far too low.

As a result, Gulf Oil's credibility with the press was lousy. During the 1979 incident they not only had to cope with an horrendous crisis, they had to cope with a media pack who automatically distrusted every word they said.

So to finish this chapter, let's look in more detail at two case studies: the BSE beef scare in 1990; and a postal dispute in Northern England in 1989.

BSE Burgers

In early 1990 a health scare about beef alarmed the Ministry of Agriculture, Food and Fisheries (MAFF). Cattle were dying from a mysterious brain disease called bovine spongiform encephalopathy, or BSE for short. This was promptly dubbed 'mad cow disease' by the media. The scare was whether the disease could be passed on to humans in meat from infected animals. Sales of beef plummeted, farmers were in panic, and the MAFF stepped in to stem the crisis.

They made numerous basic errors.

RE-ASSURANCE THAT TURNED OUT TO BE FALSE

They said that BSE couldn't be transmitted between animal species. This was soon shown to be false when infected sheep offal was nailed as the probable source for cows, and researchers managed to give pigs and other animals the disease by feeding them infected sheep.

Well, said MAFF, that doesn't really matter, because humans can't get it from infected animals. After all, we've been eating infected sheep for centuries and centuries and hardly any people develop the human version of BSE (which is called Creuzfeldt-Jacob's disease). Unfortunately this was quickly shown to be false, too, when further research showed that up to 9,000 people a year (250 times the previous estimate) die of Creuzfeldt-Jacob's disease.

Ah, they said, but public health doctors agree with us that beef is safe. Upon which, many eminent doctors stood up and said they weren't so sure.

By this time, the MAFF's credibility was full of holes with the public who had no idea who to believe. In an attempt to stave off panic, it had made too many confident statements that just weren't justified by knowledge at the time.

HOPING FOR THE BEST

Rather than assuming the 'worst case scenario', it was hoped that somehow the problem would all go away. Merely reacting from day to day, they didn't insist on better geneological records or ban breeding from offspring of BSE cases. Pigs and chickens could still be fed sheep and beef offal.

It all looked as if they didn't really take the problem seriously, and certainly weren't too concerned that, should BSE surface as an issue again in 5 or 10 years, their lack of action then would be held against them in the future.

SLOW RELUCTANT ACTION

The MAFF gave the impression of only taking positive action under pressure. It was slow to make BSE notifiable, or destruction of 'mad cows' compulsory. At first, farmers did not get full compensation for destroying infected cows, so stories began to break about farmers turning a blind eye to staggering animals and sending them to market anyway. Only then did the MAFF raise compensation rates to full market value.

Meanwhile, France, Germany and Italy banned all British beef until more research had been done on its safety or otherwise. This may have suited their nationalistic instincts, but it also sent a message to their consumers that public safety was more important than farmers' pockets. The reverse message was coming out of the MAFF.

MAKING ENEMIES

In a situation like this, where evidence is scanty anyway, you don't gain by attacking the other side. The then agriculture Minister, John Gummer, hit out at all those – scientific experts, vegetarians, foreign ministries – who took the view that beef was dodgy. Instead of calmly acknowledging their arguments as legitimate but probably misguided, he made personal attacks on their motives, even swiping at vegetarians as 'wholly unnatural' and going against the Bible.

GOING FOR GIMMICKS

One of the most immediately recognised media images of 1990 was John Gummer feeding his daughter a beefburger, to show how safe they were. You can see why someone thought this was good idea: to counter attacks on the line of 'But do *you* eat beef, Minister?', and to involve his little girl to create instant appeal. In fact it created instant yuck, and beefburgers were instantly christened BSE-burgers.

What the public wanted was an adult approach, not a cheap gimmick.

NO AUTHORITATIVE SOURCE

There was no one source of information at the MAFF nor any crisis team or crisis plan. Journalists had no structure to work to, or person to call on, and responses to enquiries were slow and cumbersome. This was partly lack of foresight; partly a bureaucratic attitude to information. A sort of 'Nanny knows best' philosophy ruled.

As a result, journalists filled the gap with other opinions and even wild rumours. Not just scientists and doctors were asked for their comments, but also magazine and newspaper cooks, vegetarian societies, school and hospital caterers, and anyone with an axe to grind, however crackpot.

OUTCOME

Three months later, 25% of British people said they weren't eating beef, and a Commons select committee's pronouncement that beef was 'safe' was treated with scorn by the media.

In early 1992, it was shown that the sorry tale had even reached Russia, when a gift of British beef was refused by customs officials on the grounds that they weren't sure whether it had BSE, despite having an EC health certificate.

Two years after the initial scare, sales of beef were still 15% less than they were before the BSE crisis broke, intensifying an already apparent trend away from red meat.

POSTMAN PAT'S STRIKING DAY

An original minor industrial dispute in one of the Royal Mail's regions escalated from a local trouble to a region-wide strike. This was partly due to mis-handled public relations.

A postman was frightened by a vicious dog and therefore failed to deliver some letters. But instead of following the proper procedure of informing his supervisor, he re-posted the letters in a letter box. When this came to light, he was reprimanded. For various reasons, his Union didn't like what happened, and over the next four days both sides began to fix their positions. Eventually postmen throughout the region were on strike for 15 days.

Management's point of view was that there was a proper procedure for what to do if the post is undelivered for any reason, and this postman hadn't followed it. He had been fairly and routinely dealt with. However, their case got completely lost in a media blitz of Brave Postmen Battling Ravaging Beasts while unsympathetic managers sat tight in their safe offices. Once the strike began to bite and people were losing out on their mail, sympathy stayed with the Union rather than the Royal Mail managers.

How did this happen?

CAUGHT ON THE HOP

The management were completely unprepared for the Union's decision after 4 days to involve the media. They hadn't adopted a 'worst case scenario', so had no plans on what to do. From then on, they were always reacting to the other side and never regained the initiative.

LACK OF SPOKESPERSON

Only two managers were around, because two others were on holiday. As a result, no one was appointed to manage the crisis full-time. Journalists would phone and be told that someone would ring back. When no one did, this was interpreted as 'declined to comment'. When going home time came, communication ceased. No one gave home numbers to the press, or thought to use mobile phones to keep in touch.

Also, because managers were having to do their normal jobs as well as cope with the press, news conferences were always at a different time each day, which created yet more work in telling the press when to come and led to all sorts of confusion.

NOT GETTING THE MESSAGE ACROSS

The PR people were used to 'good news' stories about sponsorship and long-service awards. They had never dealt with a crisis. The management were used to crisis, but had never dealt with the press.

Only management attended the vital meetings so they wrote the press releases. But their lack of experience meant that they failed to grasp the important communication points and wrote ineffective press releases. And the PR people weren't sufficiently sure of their ground to intervene.

NOT HAVING THE RIGHT INFORMATION READY

As the dispute got worse, many smaller localities were involved each with their own local media. But these small papers were unfamiliar to the PR people who were used to only the bigger papers. So each time another locality became involved, it took management a number of days to catch up on papers' names, deadlines, phone numbers, etc., and meantime their story wasn't being told.

ENGAGING IN A WAR OF WORDS

Rather than addressing the issues only at a balanced and authoritative level, the management reacted angrily to what they saw as irresponsible Union behaviour. When the Union brought up what seemed to management silly issues, or even worse, leaked details of confidential industrial tribunal hearings, the response was bitter and acrimonious. They'd have been better off keeping an Olympian calm.

No cool person was entrusted with checking every press prelease before it went out, to censor all emotive words.

OUTCOME

After the strike was over, the Royal Mail's management sat down and examined what had gone wrong. To their credit they used the whole experience as a learning exercise, and later undertook crisis training and began a crisis policy.

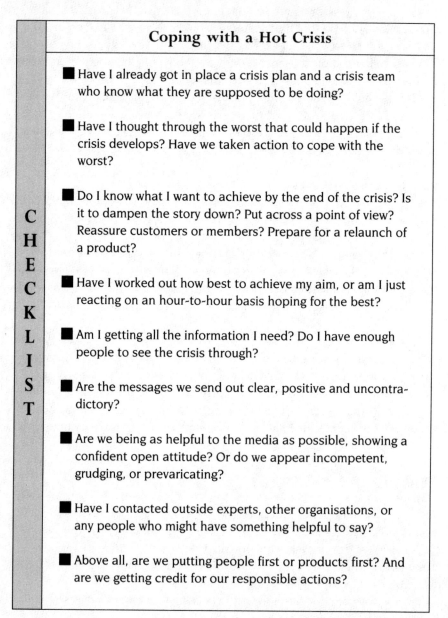

Coping with a Hot Crisis

CHECKLIST

■ Have I already got in place a crisis plan and a crisis team who know what they are supposed to be doing?

■ Have I thought through the worst that could happen if the crisis develops? Have we taken action to cope with the worst?

■ Do I know what I want to achieve by the end of the crisis? Is it to dampen the story down? Put across a point of view? Reassure customers or members? Prepare for a relaunch of a product?

■ Have I worked out how best to achieve my aim, or am I just reacting on an hour-to-hour basis hoping for the best?

■ Am I getting all the information I need? Do I have enough people to see the crisis through?

■ Are the messages we send out clear, positive and uncontradictory?

■ Are we being as helpful to the media as possible, showing a confident open attitude? Or do we appear incompetent, grudging, or prevaricating?

■ Have I contacted outside experts, other organisations, or any people who might have something helpful to say?

■ Above all, are we putting people first or products first? And are we getting credit for our responsible actions?

PART SIX
SPECIAL CASES

20

Using Professionals

- The most usual outside help comes from public relations agencies, media trainers, and press cutting agencies.
- Any outside professional will only be as good as you allow them to be.
- Unrealistic expectations will cause grief, so it's important to know exactly what you think an agency or trainer will do for you.
- If you have a thorough brief before you make contact, you're more likely to get a good service.

DO WE/DON'T WE?

PROFESSIONALS and experts don't come cheap in any field. They charge you by the hour; they charge you by the job; and they charge you by the expenses.

So the question is whether they are worth the money. Can you do the job yourself cheaper? Can you do it at all? And what will a professional bring to the task that you can't?

Whether it's using a PR consultancy or a cuttings agency or a media trainer, it's important to know your objectives and how it all fits into your overall plan. So sit down and make yourself a list of what services you think a professional could provide, and what you'll do with them. If this makes sense within your budget, then go to a number of professionals who provide those services, and check out that they really can provide the services you want.

In PR, for instance, outsiders sometimes think that by paying a lot of money you are buying an expert who will be 'your' press and public relations officer, and do the same job as a full-time insider. This just isn't so; you still need someone to find the stories and do the liaison and build up the internal communications and brief the PR person. A consultancy can't and won't do that for you. If you have unreal expectations of what a professional can do, then you'll have a very unhappy and expensive time.

THE PUBLIC RELATIONS BUSINESS

The public relations industry is a thriving part of the economy. In 1986 *The Economist* reported that it was then the fastest growing sector at 48% growth, and up till 1990 it was expanding at about 25% a year. Business drops in the PR industry during times of recession, but once the economy picks up the PR business resumes its growth.

There are a lot of PR firms out there, some attached to advertising agencies, some large specialist firms, some very small with just two or three people. They are all anxious to persuade you to use their services.

The usual reasons for using an agency are:

- Because it is thought to be cheaper than running a full in-house PR department.
- For specialist expertise, such as organising a house journal, raising sponsorship, or promoting financial stories.
- In times of extra workload, such as publicising a big exhibition.
- As part of a crisis team.

Certainly one of the problems with press work is that it tends to erupt like a volcano occasionally, so that you suddenly find the work load is doubled for a few days or weeks, and then it tails off again. If you can't co-opt from within, you have to look outside to one of the 1,200 or so agencies.

But if you are considering a long-term relationship with an agency, you need to know the advantages and disadvantages first, before laying out a substantial retainer and their subsequent high hourly rate.

Advantages of a PR Agency

- They have knowledge of all forms of media, and have contacts already made. They should find it easier to keep watch as to which papers and magazines are being produced, and who are the right journalists to talk to.

- Press material and events should be professionally presented and be targeted at the right people.
- They can give independent, unbiased advice, unaffected by office politics.
- Because they are not immersed in the technical details of your product or industry, they are often better at expressing things in layman's language and seeing the newsworthy angle.
- They are usually centrally located, either in London or in the main city of a region, which can be useful in day-to-day media work or when organising media events.
- Because of all this, an agency may be in the end more cost-effective than some internal bumbler messing it up.

Disadvantages of a PR Agency

- They are remote from the source of the stories, and can only be as good as the information fed them. Certainly an agency will find it difficult to pick up the human interest snippets that an insider will discover by casually chatting to people at lunch or walking the job. Also it is just too expensive for an agency to attend routine meetings or visit the regions.
- Some journalists are intrinsically suspicious of anything with a 'PR agency' feel to it.
- An agency may try to justify its fat fee by saturating all media with news releases, just to show how hard they are trying on your behalf.
- Of necessity, they can provide only a partial service. You will be only one of a number of clients and, unless you pay for it, their services will not extend to evenings or weekends.
- An agency may not have the same specialised knowledge of your industry as you do, especially when it comes to technical matters.
- You pay for every minute they spend on your business, every phone call, every meeting with your own people or with a journalist on your behalf.

Overall you get expertise and good presentation from an agency; you get insider knowledge from an in-house person. An internal person can cut corners because he or she already knows people and information, and can dovetail press relations work with other work.

For example, a visit to an area branch to research a trade exhibition stand could also include finding a sales success story for the in-house newsletter; discovering that one of the local employees has just been awarded a medal for bravery; and meeting the new branch manager so that her biographical details and photo are now on file (and she is now briefed to be a potential source of information in the future). So one visit could generate in-house material, an article in a local paper, a personnel profile in the trade press, and useful contacts.

On the other hand, the internal person may well have other jobs to do as well as press and public relations. He or she may not be a very good writer, or may not have the time to go off for drinks with journalists to get chummy. Or the stories that you want to promote are just the occasional biggies, like a product launch or the AGM, and it makes more sense to get a really good professional effect two or three times a year than let Joe the Marketing Man mess it up.

HOW TO CHOOSE AND USE A PR AGENCY

If you do decide that you could use a PR agency, you will find names and addresses (and often a list of their main clients) in *Advertisers Annual*, *Hollis Press and Public Relations Annual* and other such publications.

Tips for choosing a PR agency
• Draw up a shortlist of three or four agencies, based on word of mouth and who their clients are. You want to find agencies with experience in your line of business.
• Get your own act together. You must know exactly what you want from the agency, how much you have to spend, and who will be the people on your side working with them.
• Contact your shortlist and visit them for initial discussions. Present your brief and see what impression you get.
• Check out the finances. Ask them what their mark-up rate is for services like hiring a photographer or using a courier. The norm is 17.5–20%; it may go as high as 50%. Ask to see the figures for an account with services similar to the ones you're asking for; this will help you get an idea of the real eventual costs, which will inevitably be higher than the ones quoted.
• Check out who will actually be running your brief. Often the initial chat-up will be with the top executives, but the actual work will be done by someone else. So make sure the negotiations are between the people on both sides who will be doing the work, so that the chemistry is right.
• Check the expertise. Anyone can set themselves up as a PR agency, so it is worth investigating qualifications such as a CAM (Communication, Advertising and Marketing) diploma or membership of the IPR (Institute of Public Relations). Not all good people do have formal qualifications, though, so have a good hard look at their experience, especially in your

field. Ask to talk to some of their clients.

• Check the number of staff. A very small firm may not have the resources for a long-term campaign, or may even have to resort to an answering machine when under pressure. But a small firm may be cheaper and might try harder for more limited projects. A large firm will have the resources, with the overheads to match.

Once you've taken the steps outlined for choosing a PR agency, ask two agencies to present a detailed proposition, fully budgeted, setting out the workloads, the man-hours, and the various costs. A good firm will normally ask for an expansion on your initial brief, unless you've been unusually thorough. Then make your final choice.

WORKING EFFICIENTLY WITH YOUR AGENCY

A PR agency can be only as good as you allow it to be. Sometimes the attitude is: 'Don't tell the PR consultants; they don't really belong and they'll only blab it to the press'. If that's going to be the situation, then you might as well stick to internal PR. All the good practice of letting the media person have full trust and access applies to an agency, too (unless their job is only supposed to be limited, e.g. organising a particular press conference).

- Have a person in your organisation who is first-stage contact with the agency. Make sure that person is available all the time, or that there's a back-up. This is obviously especially important if your agency has a crisis brief. If they see an unfavourable press article which requires instant response, they'll need to consult fast.
- There should be regular monthly progress meetings, with reports circulated afterwards to those concerned.
- Allow the consultancy to meet people and visit locations.
- Decide who in your organisation has authority over press releases, and keep the chain of approval short. Once again, have a back-up in case of emergency.
- Send the agency information on products, staff changes, research projects, internal newsletters, copies of speeches, relevant committee minutes, sales literature, annual report and accounts, list of agents or stockists, etc. Keep on sending them.
- Keep the agency informed on potential or actual problems, such as general ones for the whole trade or industry, or particular ones of your own, such as industrial disputes, anticipated bad figures, relocations, redundancies, etc. This aspect is usually one of the hardest to get top management to agree to, especially when it comes to sensitive or confi-

dential information. But how can an agency do its job if it doesn't know the whole picture? Especially, how can you draw on its expertise in managing bad news effectively if you don't give advance warning?

A PR contract will usually run for a year, and 8 months into the contract you'll be deciding on your next year's plan. Have circumstances changed? Do you want more from your agency or less? Are there any special projects coming up?

One agency sends out this questionnaire to its clients each year, which is certainly one way of concentrating the mind:

1 In which areas are you most satisfied?
2 In which areas are you least satisfied?
3 Are there any of the consultancy's activities which you would like done differently?
4 Would you like the consultancy to do anything else?
5 Would you prefer it not to do something which it is now doing?
6 Do you think the consultancy is clear about your level of satisfaction?
7 Do the consultancy make clear what it wants or expects from you?
8 Does the consultancy make clear about your expectations of their involvement in your organisation?

Unless you are very satisfied, it's worth changing your agency every so often because there's a tendency for them to get stale. On the other hand, over time they will have got to know you and it can be wearing to have to start all over again.

At the very least, you should get a properly laid out plan every year from your agency, and get one or two other agencies to set out their ideas every two years. Even if you stick with your original team, it will keep them on their toes and may provide some fresh angles.

MEDIA TRAINING

If you think you are going to appear a fair amount on radio or television, or a certain spokesperson will, then it's a very good idea for that person to have some professional training. It's also worth thinking about preparing for a crisis. Even if you don't normally expect to be interviewed, radio and television may come running when you're in trouble, and in that case it'll be too late to start thinking about training.

Many organisations do media training. A good interview course should cover the basic principles of appearing on radio or television:

- how to identify your message;
- how to prepare for an interview;
- how to appear lively and interesting;

- how to keep control;
- how to look and sound.

During a one-day course, you should get plenty of experience in actually doing interviews of different types; with playback and analysis. Listening to the theory of how to do it, or even seeing other people have a go, will never substitute for doing it yourself.

It's important that each person on the course has a chance to have a number of goes at being interviewed, because one of the main advantages of such training is in building up familiarity with the technical equipment, as well as gaining confidence in handling the material. It can be a false economy to try to cram too many people on to a media course; you're better off getting a few people properly trained.

HOW A MEDIA COURSE WORKS

Most training organisations who do media interview work will concentrate on the television aspect, though if you think that radio is more likely to be your thing, then you should be able to organise a radio course more cheaply.

Television courses are expensive, because they usually involve either using or setting up a television-style studio with lights, camera operator, lapel microphones, etc. This is quite important to give the feel of the real thing. Lights make you hot; a lapel mic gives a different sound quality from a distant microphone; lots of technical people about makes for distraction and tension; and the quality of the playback means that you can really see what you and your clothes would look like on television.

They are also expensive because there is usually a limit to the number of participants. The ideal number is four to six people, which means that each person should be able to do at least four interviews. More than six and you start to cut down on each person's experience.

Like most training courses, media courses can be 'public' ones, where you'll go to the training organisation's building and take pot-luck with the other participants, or you can arrange an in-house course just for your own people. Whether public or in-house, you'll either go to a professional studio, where everything is laid on; or a camera crew will set up 'mini-studio' in an ordinary room, in the just the same way that they would if you were doing a location interview for real broadcast.

Of course, if your budget just doesn't stretch to several thousand pounds per day for a course with knobs on, then you can usually arrange a course using ordinary closed circuit television (CCTV) with only the trainer there. It won't be quite so effective, but is far better than nothing. If you do arrange such a course, it's very useful to provide an extra person to operate the CCTV during the recording sessions. Otherwise other course members have to do it when they ought to be either watching each other's efforts or preparing for their own next interview.

TYPICAL CONTENT

During a day's session you'd expect some or all of the following:
- a piece to camera (without questions, so it's like an ordinary presentation);
- one or two straightforward interviews on a one-to-one basis;
- one or two difficult interviews;
- an interview down-the-line (with the interviewer in a different room, communicating through an ear-piece);
- taking part in a panel confrontation.

The trainer should be able to point out general principles about preparing and practising for an interview, as well as helping with individual faults.

STYLES OF MEDIA COURSES

One point to think about when doing your research for which course to go for, is the overall style. There are two main approaches by media trainers:
- Let's sock it to them and show them how lousy they'll be without putting in the preparation.
- Let's build up their confidence gradually so that by the end of the day they can handle the pressure.

The first style tends to be adopted by trainers who regard themselves as big names, so if you pay a lot of money to get someone who is a practising broadcaster you may get the confrontative approach. The second style tends to be used by media trainers who are hired by training specialists.

With the confrontative approach, at the beginning of the day each interviewee is thrust into the lights without preliminaries, and an interview is begun. The interviewer aims to see blood on the floor, and will usually succeed. A shaken and terrified participant slinks away to sit down and enjoy watching the next victim.

The aim is not so much to make the interviewer feel clever, but to bring home to people that if they don't work hard at their preparations, and if they don't use the right controlling techniques, this is what could happen to them. So after showing everyone how idiotic they might appear if they get it wrong, the interviewer then picks everyone up, works them through more interviews to show them what to do, and by the end of the day, they should have regained confidence.

The trouble is that some people never regain their confidence. That awful first experience stays with them, and succeeding interviews instead of building them up just depress them further. So by the end of the day, their firm resolve is never to appear on television, ever. It may be that this is a sensible decision, or that a lot of money has been wasted.

So the confrontative approach works well with people who have had some experience already and think they're pretty good at it; or with someone who is a bit cocky and needs to be taken down a peg or two before they'll pay any attention. It doesn't work well with timid souls or (usually) with those who've had no media experience at all.

The confidence-building method will start gently with a piece to camera or a gentle interview about some very non-controversial topic. This will be used to explore general principles about language, image, voice, and so on.

Then the trainer will move on through progressively more difficult situations and topics, at each stage consolidating what's been learned. The idea is that as confidence and experience build, the participant will be learning how to cope with more and more pressure, until by the final horrible interview he or she will discover that it is possible to cope, however tricky the topic or aggressive the questions. This approach works well with most people, but particularly those who don't have experience or who don't have much confidence about public speaking or presentations. It should also help those who want to learn about coping with difficult interviews, but may not feel 'pressurised' enough, and for those who think they know it all already and won't listen until they've been proved wrong.

So it's wise to investigate potential courses to determine which approach they take and decide which will fit your participant or participants best.

HELPING THE TRAINER TO HELP YOU

A good trainer will ask for a very thorough briefing before the course about your organisation, your message, your potential problems, etc. Don't look on this as a waste of your time, but co-operate in sending the material asked for.

If you don't send full information, or only send it at the last minute, then the trainer won't do such a good job. Some people seem to think that a 'real' broadcaster can just pluck questions out of the air on the spot. Of course some interviews can be done like that – interviews on the lines of 'What does your organisation do? How is it funded?', or 'What happened at the scene of the accident? How many people were injured?' But if you want to get prepared for in-depth interviews, and especially if you want to be put under pressure and prepare for controversial topics, then you must give the interviewer sufficient information for him or her to put together sensible realistic questions.

If the interview were for real, the reporter would have access to press releases, press cuttings, police reports, etc., which would be used in the preparation of the questions. So for a training session to work, you may have to provide sample press releases, past press cuttings (favourable and unfavourable), internal reports, and a spoken briefing to make sure the trainer can really put the tough questions.

Therefore, if you are asked to send 'information on the organisation', don't just send the Annual Report, or state 'I'd like to be interviewed about redundancies due to relocation'. How on earth can an interviewer ask realistic questions if that's all the information she has?

PRESS CUTTING AGENCIES

A press cutting agency will look out in the media for any reference to your organisation, or to any key words you might want to specify. This obviously saves you a lot of time and effort in searching through papers and magazines, but the system is never perfect.

The Industrial Society press office did a check on two different press cuttings agencies over the same period, and discovered that there was only a 70% overlap, i.e. each agency was missing at least 30% of the coverage. Agencies tend to have their own favourite publications, and – contrary to the fond belief of press officers – do not look at every single publication in the United Kingdom.

So you may still have to keep your own lookout, even if you use an agency, especially in the obscurer trade and technical press.

Tips for choosing and using a press cuttings service

• **Keeping costs down** The first thing to do is to work out what you think your likely amount of coverage will be. Do you expect ten items a week? Ten a month? Ten a year?

Some agencies, especially the big ones, charge both a retainer fee and a fee per cutting. So if you are expecting a lot of cuttings then this could work out very expensive. Others charge on an all-in six monthly basis, or a flat fee for a certain number of cuttings. You should work out the various charges, using your estimate of how many items you think you'll get, then choose which system will be cheapest for you.

• **Depth of coverage** Overall, most agencies provide a pretty similar service. They will monitor the national papers and big magazines well; they will all be patchy about local papers and small circulation trade publications. However, it is probably true the more you pay, the better quality you get.

If you are really only concerned with local papers, then use a local agency – they'll be cheaper, and they'll be thorough with your regional press.

If you're concerned with technical press, then ask around in your business and see which agency other similar organisations use.

If it's essential to you that you see everything that is published about your organisation, then you'll need to use at least two agencies. Choose two that have a different sort of profile; make sure that you get enough information from each agency about which publications they regularly monitor, so that you can choose two with as wide a spread as possible.

• **Briefing** Once you've chosen an agency, then give them a thorough briefing on the publications you think your news might appear in. This is no guarantee that they'll check them all, but it helps.

In particular, send them any press releases you are issuing, or let them know which journalists attended a press conference or seem likely to publish something about you. If you can, get a named person in the agency as your regular point of contact, whom you can brief when necessary.

Once again, telling the agency in advance what to look out for is no guarantee that they will do it, but it gives them and you a better chance.

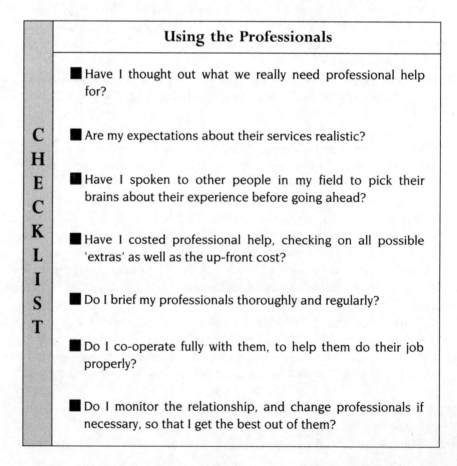

Using the Professionals

C H E C K L I S T

■ Have I thought out what we really need professional help for?

■ Are my expectations about their services realistic?

■ Have I spoken to other people in my field to pick their brains about their experience before going ahead?

■ Have I costed professional help, checking on all possible 'extras' as well as the up-front cost?

■ Do I brief my professionals thoroughly and regularly?

■ Do I co-operate fully with them, to help them do their job properly?

■ Do I monitor the relationship, and change professionals if necessary, so that I get the best out of them?

21

Special Thoughts for Special Cases

- The general principles laid out in earlier chapters apply to special sectors, but there are special factors, which are looked at here.
- A lot of it comes down to knowing your market.
- The more specialist your field, the more likely that you can make good contacts with the specialist journalists.
- Many press persons don't bother – but all specialist journalists say they welcome meeting anyone in their field.

INDUSTRY AND PRODUCTION

THE OVERALL PICTURE

Most industries still regard the press with great suspicion. They believe that journalists will misquote, misrepresent, and misunderstand, and in any case are only interested in strikes and disasters. At best, the chief executive officer will delegate all press work to a press person and then think that the job is done.

In fact there are lots of good news stories that the industrial and general press want to pick up. This is especially important when you think of the overall image that people still have of industry, which is reinforced by television. What's the usual stereotype of a businessman in a drama? Greedy, uncaring, or criminal.

TIPS AND GUIDELINES

One reason for the bad press given to British industry is its facelessness. Many companies refuse to be quoted, or will keep media work at the level of a 'company spokesperson'. Those companies where there is an identifiable top person tend to do better.

As Bill Deedes, Editor of *The Daily Telegraph* said at an Industrial Society Conference in 1986: 'There is no substitute for good relations between high executives and people they know and trust in the media. The more the chief executive is available, including via his home telephone, the better the company will fare in the media.'

The MD of BP Chemicals International holds monthly off-the-record meetings with four industrial journalists at a time, and anyone who wants to discuss something for publication can have an on-the-record interview with him personally.

Other companies have open days when journalists are briefed by senior people, can ask questions, and can then more or less wander at will around the premises (though usually 'minded' through the process, just in case). This works wonders in educating them about what the company does, how it works, and its achievements and problems.

Such openness may lead to immediate coverage, but more importantly it means that journalists know what's going on. This should eliminate gross errors, and also is invaluable should trouble strike. If journalists know that you are usually open and friendly, with nothing much to conceal, then they are far more likely to credit your statements and actions in a crisis.

Let it be known that you are always available for comment. Jim Prince, operations director of Vickers Defence Systems in Leeds, said: 'We prefer to be interviewed by the media before any topic covering our business is broadcast or published. If we refuse to be interviewed, reporters may go ahead and write an article on limited or erroneous information.' Vickers have a system whereby any approach from the media is first handled by public relations staff, but if an interview is granted, then a nominated manager does it at the site.

Any major announcements should be told to staff first. This is partly courtesy, but also good sense. If you establish a system of team briefing or videos which tells the workforce good news and bad, then when the press come to cover a story there should be a consistent message coming through. This is especially important for bad news, like redundancies or losses, when it's vital for management to explain what's happening and why, before the press start sharpening their pencils and come looking for trouble.

Don't forget journalists' needs. *The Guardian*'s Labour and Industrial Editor, Keith Harper, says: 'I have always considered that industry is its own worst enemy because it reacts far too slowly to the needs of the press. You are left hanging on the end of the line or put through to someone who doesn't know how to handle press enquiries' (Industrial Society conference, 1986).

So make sure, if you don't have a full-time press officer, that the switchboard knows who to put calls through to, and that all people who might be called on to give information to the press know that what is required of them – prompt, clear comment or facts. If someone promises to phone back before a deadline, then it must be done.

Lastly, don't expect miracles if you decide to add press coverage to an event at the last minute. Media lead-in times can be measured in weeks or months, especially for the technical press. So make sure that press and publicity ideas are built in to any planning right at the beginning, so that everything can get organised in good time.

PARTICULAR MEDIA

One group of journalists vitally important is the Labour and Industrial Correspondents Group. Make sure they are on your mailing list and that you contact them directly to find out who's a member in your area.

Most papers have a business section which will print stories of interest to business folk. Foster contacts with the business editor as well as individual reporters. It's worth being aware of who reads what. Only 8% of business people read *The Guardian*, for instance, so if you're trying to influence on a business-to-business level you'll be better off talking to other national dailies.

Local papers may have a daily business section, or a supplement. They will often run extra supplements on local industries and employers, so check with the planning manager or features editor to find out when these are coming up and see if you can get included in some of the articles.

Of vital importance is the trade and technical press, because there you'll find your suppliers, customers, potential employees, and your investors. Know who reads what, and make sure that you have a reputation as a willing informant, so that you become a regular source of informed comment or analysis.

Radio and television have business programmes and special items after the main news. Contact the editors directly. Watch for the particular audiences: BBC 2's *Money Programme* is much more down-market than Channel 4's *The City Programme* which is aimed at senior executives and financiers.

Also, don't forget general interest programmes like Radio 4's *Women's Hour*, which will be interested in anything to do with women or families; BBC 1's *Tomorrow's World* which wants to hear about innovations; or *New Ideas*, the BBC World Service's technology programme.

If you have anything you want promoted overseas, you have the Central Office of Information as well as BBC World Service. The COI is interested in new products and technology, interesting research, export successes, membership of trade delegations, overseas visitors, and anything else that might be of interest to people abroad. Contact them in London or in one of their regional offices, and they will write a press release for you and/or arrange a radio or television interview.

STORIES AND ANGLES
The press will want to know about:
- new products or research;
- market research or surveys;
- top people coming or going;
- local or national success;
- annual figures;
- job creation or loss;
- new or improved premises;
- initiatives with young people, women, old people, etc.;
- school/industry links;
- interesting training schemes;
- employees doing interesting things out of work;
- charity events;
- competitions and awards.

They'll also want to know about strikes, disputes, pollution, explosions, lawsuits ... Make sure that they know something about you during good times first!

TRADES UNIONS

THE OVERALL PICTURE
In some ways, the picture is not so different from that of industrialists. Bill Sirs of the Iron and Steel Trades Confederation, said at an Industrial Society conference in 1986 that until he became General Secretary the policy on press relations had been to tell any caller that there was nobody in. If the caller persisted he would be told that the person involved had just gone out, and any further calls would be met by the statement that the official had nothing to say anyway. He, however, believes that accessibility is vital, in good times as well as bad, and makes himself available to the

press for any comment. He also makes sure that the Union puts its case all the time, not just during strikes, so that journalists and the public know where the Union stands on issues affecting the steel industry.

One problem for unions is making a distinction between publicising themselves as employees and publicising themselves as union members. This is probably a false distinction. If you're a fireman doing something heroic or involved in a charity effort, then it's worth publicising. The general public will think better of firemen, so that if you then are involved in a dispute the goodwill lingers on. Don't worry that one activity is 'work' and the other is 'union'.

There's a suspicion that all journalists are merely press baron lackeys. This is not necessarily so, even if the journalist is from an anti-union paper. Industrial correspondents try very hard to put both sides of the picture, which they can't do if the unions refuse to talk to them.

It's worth remembering that reporters, even senior ones, have bosses too. During the early 1980s' miners' strike the management of the National Coal Board (NCB) were going directly to the national editors to reveal their strategy or reactions. The specialist correspondents found themselves on the side-lines, and unable to present balanced coverage.

Many of them became extremely angry; for instance, Donald MacIntyre, the labour editor of the *Sunday Times*, demanded that his byline be removed from stories about the strike. This, however, cut no ice with the miners. They refused to speak to industrial correspondents of papers which printed hostile leaders or feature articles. While this was very understandable as an emotional reaction, it meant that no one at all was putting the miners' case, except Mr Scargill, the miners' leader, himself via 12-second television soundbites.

TIPS AND GUIDELINES

Don't forget to publicise your 'positive' activities. All too often the only time people see or read a union spokesperson is in the context of a dispute. Not unnaturally, unions get associated with trouble. So tell the press about your other tasks in health and safety or training or equal opportunities. When you are co-operating with management, then publicise that too.

The general secretary or the local branch person should be available and accessible. Keep an open-door policy, and give your home phone number to journalists.

Trust is built up over time. Volunteer yourself to press and broadcasting to talk on general issues. If there's a food scare about, for instance, and you have catering workers among your members, then see if you can choose someone to go and talk on local radio about what your union is doing to ensure proper standards. Don't leave it all to the management.

Always remember who you are wanting to influence. Is it members or management or the general public or the government? Sometimes you may have to resist a dig at management in favour of a soft word aimed at reassuring the general public.

During a dispute or negotiations, make sure that you give time to reporters, even though you've just had several hours of talks. This may well take over an hour, especially if you are giving separate broadcast interviews (which is a good idea and increases your chances of longer coverage). Even if you don't, management probably will …

Be predictable in your flow of information during a dispute. Make sure the press know who is the spokesperson, and when he or she will talk each day. Where possible, arrange a set time and place for a press conference each day.

It may be worth taking a tip from Sir Michael Edwardes' use of the media when he was Chief Executive of BL during the 1970s. The BL management would always announce any controversial move – especially during a dispute – in the morning, via the local evening newspapers and radio and TV. Their news would then appear on lunch-time bulletins and in mid-afternoon papers. Any early announcement could be reinforced later for the national papers. The great advantage was that the news broke, and BL had set the agenda, before the unions had a chance to react.

Here's a contrary example: during the miners' strike the NUM (National Union of Miners) issued a report on the economics of the pits. It was a complex, important document challenging the NCB's whole economic case. They issued it late afternoon, with a broadcast embargo until after that evening's edition of Newsnight which was going to run an exclusive report.

The prospect of the exclusive scuppered all other publicity, because newspaper labour correspondents had a bare half an hour or so to digest the contents of the report before their deadlines, and the rest of the broadcast media didn't want to examine it very much the next day when it had become 'stale' news. The popular papers largely ignored it, and the qualities skimped it.

So bear in mind the timing of statements, and especially that radio and television are the quickest to react.

Don't forget to keep monitoring the media during any troubles. Someone should have the job of making sure that all news bulletins and interview programmes are listened to, so that you can be quick to respond if necessary. Record them too, as well as your own interviews.

However, don't go too mad with the media. There can be a danger that both sides in a dispute are so concerned with getting media coverage that they negotiate via the media, rather than with each other. This is usually a recipe for raising temperatures and prolonging things.

So tell the media what's going on, but don't start making new offers or producing new evidence through interviews. Also, it's best to resist temptation to reveal secret sessions or what happened at confidential tribunals. This may work well temporarily to influence the public, but will only encourage management into tit for tat.

STORIES AND ANGLES
Stories and angles to use are:
- successes of members at job;
- health and safety;
- environment;
- women and ethnic issues;
- training and young people;
- reaction to issues in your industry;
- reaction to government policies;
- reaction to European initiatives.

… And, of course, disputes, negotiations, and industrial action.

CHARITIES AND THE VOLUNTARY SECTOR

THE OVERALL PICTURE
There are a quarter of a million registered charities in Britain, with 4,000 new ones each year. Their turnover is huge – around £17 billion. With so many, it's hardly surprising that there's confusion about who and what they all are. Reaching potential helpers, donors and clients is part of the job; the other part may be to change public attitudes. Either way, press and broadcasting can help.

Charities need the media, yet they also have a contempt (often well founded) for the media's trivialising and frivolous ways. Those involved in the voluntary sector are emotionally engaged in their work, and it is hard to see the need to 'sell' a serious message through a silly stunt.

Yet somehow they have to reach the public and win hearts and minds. So press relations are embarked upon, but with a grudging attitude. This makes it difficult for the press person.

Obviously some charities are more glamorous than others; those dealing with the mentally ill or the disabled have a particularly difficult time, because of society's (and journalists') prejudices. A study by the Spastics Society showed that the medical 'problems' of disabled people completely overshadow political and social issues relating to disability. It's easier to concentrate on individuals than to examine a whole society.

Another difficulty is that of complexity. Many charities do not have one simple message to concentrate on, because the problems of cancer

research or animal vivisection or child abuse can't be reduced to one simple formula. Yet that is what is needed to make an effective press campaign.

Newspapers will concentrate on fund-raising, charity issues and personal interest, neglecting complicated research or social implications.

There's also a 'brand image' problem. There are so many ecological
groups, educational groups, medical research groups, animal welfare
groups ... Their work overlaps, their messages overlap, and the media,
never mind the general public, just don't know who's who.

International charities have a particular problem because they need
both to raise lots of money and to change attitudes, and the two don't
always merge happily. Charities like Oxfam are torn between emphasising
the 'poor starving baby' image (which raises lots of money) and the 'self-
sufficient proud farmer' (which doesn't raise any money but shows that aid
is not a hopeless cause).

Lastly, the voluntary sector is volatile and dependent on fashion. One
year Third World aid is in; another year it's women's refuges and rape crisis schemes. So from being flavour-of-the-month, a certain charity or
group of charities will become stale and has-been for a number of years.

TIPS AND GUIDELINES

You'll first need to convince those in your own organisation that media
work is important. Without that, you'll never get real co-operation.

Try compiling a dossier of coverage of an organisation similar to yours –
either similar in its field, or in its size or locality. See how the media treats
it; find out if you can the effect that coverage has had. Have membership/
donations gone up? Have there been any notable successes for
campaigns?

Work through your own press cuttings – have there been any notable
successes as a result of media publicity? Are there any gross misunderstandings about your subject which ought to be put right? It's always very
difficult to find solid evidence that press coverage actually achieves anything, so in the end you have to rely a lot on anecdotal evidence and gut
feeling.

One important thing to get straight is what you want to achieve by better media relations. Do you want to change attitudes or behaviour? There's
a difference: think of drink-driving, for instance. You could change people's behaviour by campaigning for lots and lots of random breathalyser
tests, so that a motorist knows he'd have a fair chance of being caught if
he drinks and drives. But changing people's attitudes is harder; the ideal is
that it becomes just as socially inept or immoral to drink before driving as
it is to pick your nose in public or hit your spouse.

It may help to know which of these any media campaign is likely to do. Given that complex issues are difficult to get across, keep your aims realistic. Also be aware that the quality press tend to be more interested in issues than the popular press are, which is good for raising money, but not so good for changing mass attitudes.

It is vitally important that you stay honest about your 'product' when you talk about it. If you gloss over the corrupt politics of the developing country receiving famine relief, or exaggerate the polluting effects of a pesticide, then your opponents will be on to it in a flash, and the debate will concentrate on opposing arguments rather than the issue itself.

Know exactly what it is that makes you different from your 'competitor' charities. Is it in the scope of your work? A particular set of clients? A famous founder or tradition? A connection with a particular place or person? Does the public at large know this? Do journalists know? Any misunderstandings need to be cleared up. Any particular strengths need to be emphasised.

Organise journalist lunches to explain issues, and who or what you are. If you do have any famous names attached to you, then try to capitalise on that. Famous names don't necessarily want to be trotted out for all public occasions, but often they're happier to be meeting journalists on an informal basis to talk serious issues, than to be opening bazaars and fending off autograph-hunters. One of the unfortunate aspects of the glamorisation of certain charities through innovative events like Band Aid and Comic Relief, is that many people now expect a celebrity to be around: 'It can't be much good if you can't get a celebrity involved' can be the attitude. So you may have to try extra hard.

If you are flavour-of-the-month for a while, then go with the flow. But once you become last month's news, you may have to change tack for a while. Bring out your lesser campaigns, your local issues, your sidelines. You'll get nowhere by trying to flog issues that the media see as 'stale', so you'll get frustrated and the press will get fed up with you. You might as well give in gracefully, plug other stories, and wait a bit before pushing your main line again.

Don't forget the value of being 'rent-a-pundit'. Offer yourself or a spokesperson as instant comment on anything which relates at all to your field. Phone up the local radio station on the morning after an old person is found frozen to death, and offer to talk about what ought to be done or should have been done. Don't wait for them to phone you.

Phone the papers with an instant quote, or a local example of something that is creating national media interest. Even if they don't take you up on your ideas, they'll start to think of you when they are doing stories on your subject, and then they'll come to you.

You can point out this aspect of your work to wavering colleagues: very often if a paper comes to you for something, it won't be for a quote or for anything that will be attributed to your organisation. The journalist may just be picking your brains or asking for other good people to contact. That doesn't matter – each time a journalist is on the phone to you, you are educating him or her, and in effect campaigning for your message. So log these calls, and tell people about good examples.

Don't forget the power of newspaper letters pages. If you can't get a journalist to take up your ideas or comments directly, then draft a good letter. Or you can get supporters to write letters covering different aspects.

Lastly, don't try always to go it alone, especially for any issues which are wider than just one charity. Try to keep contacts with other press persons or high-ups in related organisations, so that if something crops up which affects you all, you can put on a joint campaign which will often be far more effective than just one group working alone.

EDUCATION

THE OVERALL PICTURE

Papers and the media love kids; schools and education are also 'important' issues which affect many people in the community. So if you are concerned with children you are already one jump ahead. Education as a whole is a hot issue nationally too, so if you have a local angle to the national story, you'll have a good chance of getting your views known.

The main problem is one of time. Teachers are over-stretched enough as it is with classroom work, preparation and marking, admin, testing, etc. They may feel the last thing they need is yet another job. Yet somehow it ought to get done, because changes in the education system mean that every school has to market itself now in a way inconceivable 10 years ago.

What with the publishing of exam and truancy results, and the introduction of more and more parental choice, each school has to look to its image, either to promote its successes or explain its 'failures'. A school with a bad reputation will rapidly find itself no longer a school at all. One way of promoting a positive image is to use the media.

On a lower, but important, level is the matter of publicising school events such as fund-raising sales. Obviously most of those attending will be hearing about it by school grapevine, but if it's a big do you may want a wider catchment area and local paper publicity can help.

There are also wider educational implications: it may be a matter of affecting public opinion about a general educational issue, for example, a proposal to change the balance between coursework and exams in GCSEs. Or to explain exactly what are the options for teaching reading in primary schools, to clear up the hopelessly polarised picture presented by most newspapers. Such issues are not just the concern of one school, but many, which may mean the case goes by default since no one school will bother to enter the argument.

The usual person who gets burdened with the press job is the deputy head, though he or she usually already has the longest working hours. It may be better to delegate it, or even set up a press committee (including the PTA) so that no one person has to do everything.

TIPS AND GUIDELINES

Don't assume that when journalists get it wrong they are doing it out of malice or from a cynical disregard for a good story. Sometimes that may be so, but it's more likely to be that they don't understand the issues.

So it may be in your interest to educate them. Don't just cultivate journalists when you have a 'story'. If possible, try to get them into the school for a briefing. Either organise a simple lunch for a group of local paper correspondents, so that they can look round the school, talk through the topical issues, etc., or choose the most likely candidate (e.g. education correspondent of your regional daily) to invite. One head meets the education reporter of the local newspaper for coffee every Tuesday morning.

Explore the idea of publishing children's work in the paper. This may be on an *ad hoc* basis, should someone write a particularly funny poem or interesting article, or some papers occasionally run a school page, where pupils take over the editorial control.

Keep an eye on general issues. If there's a flavour-of-the-month topic in the national news, such as class sizes or ethnic mix, then see if you have something to say on the matter. This may be to put right misconceptions, or to use your local experience to back up the national picture. You can phone the local paper and tell them you have something interesting to add. If the paper isn't interested in quoting you directly, then write a good letter (but not too long!) to the letters page.

Don't forget the usefulness of the 'local angle to national story' for promoting your school activities and work. This may be a big sporting event (link to your school's relevant sport), a shock-horror report on child accidents (link to your accident prevention teaching); or a grumble about how badly British people speak foreign languages (link to your language activities or school visits or pen pals).

Of course lots of other schools are doing similar things – all the more reason to get on the phone fast and get your idea in first. Who said that you have to be original?

Papers like competitions, so if you are entering national competitions (like Young Engineers or a writing competition) then make sure you publicise it, even if your people don't win anything. Better still, get something in before results are announced, on the lines of 'James and Suzi are really hoping to do well in the "Recycled outfits competition" with their brilliant entry made out of 1,200 can rings ...'.

Play the numbers game: the 100th pupil to get an A grade in Maths 'A' level, or the 1,000th to enter the Duke of Edinburgh Awards scheme.

The LEA Press Office is there to help you out, especially if you're in trouble. Make contact with them and talk through local issues while everything is calm. In a real crisis call them in fast, and if possible before anything actually appears in print or on air. They will have more clout than you if it's a matter of putting pressure on a paper to withdraw or modify a story.

PARTICULAR MEDIA

As well as education correspondents and women's pages in most papers, there are also specialist papers for young people, like the *Early Times* and the *Young Telegraph*. So keep an eye out for stories of interest to them or for any participation on offer.

If you are doing anything visually interesting don't forget the children's programmes on TV like *Newsround* and *Blue Peter*. They have the usual news values but with a child's slant (different, funny, exciting, brave, new, largest, smallest, charity ...). Remember the value of what will make good television (like a musical written in Welsh about King Midas which was featured on *Blue Peter*). If it contains music or dancing or wonderful clothes or action, then it will be popular.

Radio too will respond to items like a poetry festival or a music competition or a play – so long as you can promise some child performers, and preferably speakers.

There are also the odd-ball places which may just happen to be interested in something you're doing. A school which had transformed a dead-end corner of the grounds into a water feature with pools, flowers and vegetables was featured on BBC 2's *Gardeners' World* and given 6–7 minutes of air time. We saw photos of the original concrete covered slabs, and then the progress over two years. The cameras recorded the children working in the garden, doing related science projects, art work, etc., and there were interviews. The message given to potential parents and the local community was that this school was imaginative, different, ecologically aware, involved the children in worthwhile and interesting projects, and fostered responsibility. Not bad!

So don't just think in terms of 'education' outlets: you may be doing something with a possibly different slant: architecture, food, music, ethnic minorities, etc., which could be marketed to those specialist niches.

THE OVERALL PICTURE

Doctors and scientists alike tend to be unhappy with the media's tendency to generalise and trivialise. One of the deadliest insults a scientist can bestow is that someone is a 'populiser', yet to communicate via the media you have to be one.

Doctors who are media stars get a rough time too; remember Dr Christian Barnard with the first heart transplants, or Dr Steptoe of test tube baby fame. Whatever the media or the public thought of them, the medical profession tended to turn up their noses. Medical people just don't do that sort of thing.

So it is hard for doctors to put things in layman's language or to simplify an issue in order to make it comprehensible to the public. Their whole training is towards being exact and precise and cutting out the emotional generalisations. And at the back of their minds is always that thought: 'What will my colleagues think?' So out comes the medical language: 'pharmaceutical preparation' instead of 'drug'; 'myocardial infarction' instead of 'heart attack'.

The trouble is that most people get their medical information not from doctors or leaflets but from the press and television. If you have a public health message, or if you are defending your hospital from an attack in the local press saying that it is a cess-pit of infection or incompetence, then you have to go out there and talk to the community. And the media is a very effective way of getting to them.

Some issues may be long term, indeed never-ending, where year after year you are having to say the same message: practise safe sex, don't smoke, drink moderately, get your children vaccinated ... The problem then is to come up with new angles to keep the media interested.

If you are involved in health education, you will have colleagues to convince that acting the fool in some media campaign is worth doing. Keep a press book; write down and keep any anecdotal evidence you can get to show that media coverage works; try to arrange occasionally for some DIY market research, such as getting two or three friendly doctors or health clinics to log enquiries about vaccinations in the days or weeks following a media interview. None of this necessarily 'proves' that media coverage works, but at least it's better than sitting there like a fool when asked to justify your plan to get the whole senior staff dressed up as giant measles.

Other issues are far more short term: a sudden listeria scare; a political row over hospital trusts; a patient's death caused by professional incompetence; mental patients in a new community care hostel. In those cases, it is usually a matter of putting your case across as best you can under pressure. In both situations you'll do better with contacts which are already in place. A crisis is no time to be talking to a journalist for the first time in your life.

It may be worth contacting the medical journalists association if you have any medical specialist stories, as well as fostering health correspondents in local papers and radio.

Another problem that many medical people have with the media is that they feel somehow betrayed if their news is trivialised or sensationalised. Doctors know that what they have to say matters; so why don't the media see it too? The trouble is that a reporter has his own agenda: he is there to get stories which will sell newspapers or put up ratings. He is not necessarily there to perform a public service. It so happens that health stories are often attractive, and important health information will be published, because they affect and interest a lot of people. But his bottom line is different from yours, and that just has to be accepted.

Good relationships between health people and journalists will benefit the whole community. Bad relationships founded on mistrust will benefit no one.

TIPS AND GUIDELINES

Watch your language, whether in press releases or face-to-face. You just have to think out beforehand how you'll put things. Don't use the same sort of terminology as you'd use for a medical journal. Instead of: '53.2% of the case-patients taking 325 mg of aspirin daily significantly decreased their relative risk of suffering a re-rinfarction during the study period', you should say: 'More than half the people taking an aspirin a day greatly reduced their chances of a second heart attack'. Get used to terms like 'most of', 'under half', 'very few'. And use the short layman's terms, not the medical ones.

Particular words to avoid are the easily misundertood ones like 'negative test results' and 'atypical', which will just cause confusion.

Don't forget to publicise successes. It's very easy to forget all about the media when everything is going right; then when a crisis comes along only the negative side is printed. People tend to remember general impressions of what they read, and if they only ever hear about you in the context of ward closures or allegations of ill-treatment, then you'll get labelled as 'the hospital with all the problems'. So it really is worth taking time to push some positive stories too, as an insurance against bad coverage.

It can be difficult to say 'I don't know' to a question when you feel you 'ought' to know the answer. Yet an ill-informed answer is especially dangerous in the medical field; think of the brouhaha caused by the breast screening confusion in 1991 when the Chief Medical Officer was made to appear to be rubbishing all other official advice about self-examination of the breasts. There was very little real difference between 'self examination' and 'body awareness' but some unguarded remarks by a number of bodies made it appear that there was.

You can always ask to think over an answer and come back in 10 minutes. Or if you really can't say 'I don't know', then find another formula, such as 'That's not my speciality' or 'I don't have the exact figures to hand and I wouldn't want to speculate'. Whatever you do, don't go off into the wide blue yonder.

You might be asked to comment an official policy, or, even worse, on a policy you don't personally agree with. Make sure you have thought out your response beforehand. The safest thing is smilingly to fend off the question with: 'That's a matter of policy that is really for the hospital manager to deal with'. If you want to go further, then add, 'But my personal opinion is ...'. If you don't want to go further, then shut up. If necessary, repeat the same formula if you are asked again, but always with a confident cool smile. Anything too tight-lipped will be interpreted as meaning you don't agree with official policy. If you're asked what the official policy is, and you don't know, then either say so, or simply say you'd like to connect the questioner with the person who can best answer the question.

If you are approached to do a press or broadcast interview, find out in what capacity you are being approached and how you'll be introduced. Are you going to be billed as a 'spokesperson' of some kind, e.g. 'a representative of the Society of Public Health'; 'a consultant at the struggling Trust hospital'; 'a typical GP'? If you're happy about that, fine. Otherwise either get the handle removed, or make clear at the start that you are only speaking your own opinion.

For television interviews, it is usually best to dress conservatively and smartly. White coats are normally better avoided unless you are doing an interview actually on a ward round, or if you are trying to emphasise your 'scientific' standing. Usually doctors and health education people should emphasise their professionalism (which means jackets and suits for men, and smart non-floral dresses or suits for women), rather than their friendliness and warmth (shirtsleeves and jumpers for men, floppy necklines and fussy patterns for women). Of course there may be exceptions depending on your message.

If being filmed on location, beware of hospital fluorescent lights which can drain out colour or even worse make you look a queer shade of green. If you have to be filmed in such light (in an operating theatre for instance) be prepared to put on face make-up to restore normal colour.

If you are involved in a crisis – a meningitis outbreak, say – then make sure there is just one person dealing with the media, so that everyone else can get on with their job. Also, that way you'll be communicating just one message, not six. In a complicated situation with lots of different agencies concerned, make sure that the spokesperson is designated straight away, the moment things start to look serious, and not two days later after it's all too late. The first job will be to contact the press and put your point. This will pre-empt questions of the 'When did you know; and why didn't you tell the public straight away?' variety.

Keep the technical people like the microbiologists behind the scenes (unless one of them is the official spokesperson). Their way of looking at things will almost inevitably sound as if it is contradicting the 'official' line. Something as minor as two different totals of the number of cases can be blown up into a story.

Don't play the numbers game at all, if you can help it, in a public health outbreak. Once started: 'We are happy to announce that only six people seem to have been affected by the nitrates in the reservoir', you won't be allowed to stop: 'Well, yes, there have been seven more cases ...' until it becomes: 'Yes, there are now 23 and we did originally say it wasn't very serious, and yes there have been more than we originally thought, and yes I suppose we can't guarantee there won't be more ...'.

FINANCIAL NEWS

THE OVERALL PICTURE

You may hit the financial pages only occasionally, when you are announcing your annual figures or a move to raise capital. Or you may be in the financial world of banking, insurance or property, and your main outlet is through the financial pages.

If you're in the first category, then you don't need especially to worry about how you handle your financial story. All the usual rules apply to drafting your press release and you choose your targets and write your piece in the normal way.

Some public relations agencies will organise AGMs and such for you, but since the dispersal of Fleet Street most financial journalists won't come to routine press conferences, let alone AGMs, so only use a PR agency if you want them to organise the wider aspects of a big meeting.

The other time a specialist agency might help is if you have some very sensitive financial information that might affect share prices. Since the Big Bang in 1986, there are regulations concerning such information to protect the market from insider training, so if you have any concerns you should go to one of the new breed of investor relations agencies for advice.

For those working in the financial world, things are more complicated. Perhaps more than anyone else, they have to use the media to market their products or keep confidence in their standing. A story in the *Daily Mail* about some particular Unit Trusts, just a couple of paragraphs long, brought in half a million pounds' worth of business.

It's not just a matter of letting potential clients know what you are selling; those in the financial world read financial pages avidly every day, and use them for their decisions. An unfavourable article could have an almost immediate effect, and it will be perpetuated in financial analysts' reports to their fund manager clients. As a result, financial journalists probably get more unsolicited press releases and phone calls than any other group, since it isn't just the press officer who is conscious of their existence, but all the marketing people too. This may make life easier for the press person in the organisation, since there isn't the same need to justify your existence as there is in some fields. However, it does mean that there may be many people trying to do your job, and that can be almost as bad, especially when things are tough.

You may have to try extra hard to make sure that you stay as the focal point of media activities, so at least you know what's going on and what is being said to whom.

The time when many organisations may need the financial press is in a crisis. It may be a potential takeover bid, where shareholders need to be informed and influenced. It may be a product disaster, where customers and investors need to be reassured about the company's future. In such situations, it may again be necessary to call in the experts: the City-based financial consultancies who specialise in investor relations. They can advise you on special stunts like the leaks described in Chapter 18.

You have to be careful of over-selling yourself in the financial world. If you overdo your media coverage so that your shares are overvalued, your company is liable for a nasty tumble. Too much hype might even lead journalists and analysts to smell a rat. So the best way is usually a middle course based on one-to-one relationships rather than a constant (or even worse, a sudden) flow of press releases to the business pages.

TIPS AND GUIDELINES

There are many specialisms in financial journalism. It is difficult to keep up with who is who in each paper, and which days each specialist publishes. Yet it's vital if you want to be taken seriously. There's not just the split between City pages and personal finance; there are also correspondents for insurance, property, small business, company reports, pensions, etc. If you just send your news to 'The City Editor', then your chances are slim.

Do your homework before you send out anything. Financial columns will have regular days for appearing so if you have some news about house insurance, for example, then make contact at least three or four days ahead of the publication day of the personal finance page. You will make a better impression if you sound knowledgeable: 'I have some interesting research about the home insurance market, which I think would fit your Tuesday column well …'.

Wendy Elkington, Deputy Editor of 'Money Mail' says: 'I pay a lot more attention to someone with an intelligent approach, who sounds as if he has actually read my paper. We set on Friday for our Wednesday pages, so it's no good phoning on Tuesday with a story. If it's very important, we might be able to do something on Monday, but not later.' It's not just the *Daily Mail* with a fairly long lead-in time for anything other than hot financial news. The Saturday *Financial Times*, for instance, is being set on Monday or Tuesday.

If you know a story is coming up, but you can't reveal the full details to fit in with the papers' normal schedules, then at least let them know the broad picture and tell them when they can have the full facts. With any luck, they'll hold some space ready for you.

City page journalists do look for scoops and shock-horror scandals, as well as general information, which means you should give sensitive information only to those you know and trust. But most specialist financial journalists are extremely reliant on their contacts for their stories, so are unlikely to do the dirty on you. More than other journalists they need a good reputation among their sources, so you can usually trust them.

For the same reason, financial journalists are especially keen on 'rent-a-pundits'. If you can prove yourself a reliable source of comment, you will find yourself used again and again. As Wendy Elkington puts it: 'I look for people who will just give me the information without fuss and hassle, but they are so rare. All I need is somebody whom I can get hold of straight away, or with an efficient secretary who knows where he is and will get him to come back to me in 15 minutes. But there are so few of them; and the ones who do it are the ones I'll always call and quote.'

They are also very approachable for informal contact, especially if you are working in a particular niche and so are they. You may get only 15 minutes over a cup of coffee, but that should be plenty of time to give each other all the necessary information (so long as you think about what you want to impart and find out beforehand …).

Don't be worried if you get coverage of only a few lines; it seems that people read the small stories in the financial sections as thoroughly, or even more thoroughly, than the big stories.

The Sunday papers have a heavy coverage of financial news, set up on approximately Wednesday/Thursday (except for urgent items). They look for solid stories and will give good coverage to those they choose. However it's a gamble, since the dailies will give only a short mention to any stories covered at the weekend.

One way to maximise your chances is to send press releases to the weekend papers to arrive on Thursday, then to the dailies to arrive on Saturday. This means that if the Sundays don't pick up your story, you still have a chance with the dailies on Monday (a traditionally thin day for financial news anyway).

In a crisis you may have to have a two-pronged approach to your press relations. On the one hand, you have to reach customers, shareholders, employees, etc. On the other, you need to reach financial analysts, fund managers, and others with influence in the markets. So don't neglect either target audience; you will probably need a different approach to each.

For the financial pages, your task will be to keep things in perspective, in terms of effect on share prices. Put out the figures that show what percentage of your turnover will be affected by your duff new product, or the ban on tropical hardwoods, to show that it's only minor. Let them know you are fully protected against liability damages or that the earnings lost represent only a penny a share. In other words, you need to explain the limits of the possible impact on your share price – fast!

You also need to persuade everyone concerned that when it's over, it really is over, and there's no ghastly skeleton still lurking in the cupboard ready to jump out. Openness at the beginning will help your credibility when you later say 'That's it'. You don't want the story to drag on for weeks, pulling down prices because of uncertainty.

For a crisis affecting a whole sector, like secondary banks or estate agents, then you have to persuade the journalists (and through them the markets) that you are doing better than most of your competitors.

Where possible address any problems in advance of a crisis. If you know trouble is looming in your sector, even if it won't directly affect you, it's well worth briefing any contacts you have before the whole thing becomes hot news. Then you can hope for coverage of this sort: 'As life assurance schemes come under scrutiny following the collapse of three medium-size companies this week, Rectitude General, one of the largest British insurance companies, were confident that the large companies will remain almost unaffected by the crisis, because …' In such a situation, it's worth pulling out all stops to persuade your chief executive to be readily available to the press, day and night.

Where to Find More

Editors

Published in six volumes (covering national media, local media, international, consumer, etc.). It includes all press and broadcast outlets, plus a readership profile, and forthcoming special features. Published quarterly.

Media Directories Ltd, 9-10 Great Sutton St, London EC1V 0BX
Tel. 071-251 9000   Fax 071-251 3738

PIMS Media Directories

Monthly directories, listing all UK national media, UK local media (with maps), European media, and US media. Also a Financial Directory, which lists all financial media, business and financial associations, UK and EC parliamentary lists, etc. The Directories give named contacts for particular subjects and in particular regions.

PIMS House, Mildmay Avenue, London N1 4RS
Tel. 071-226 1000   Fax 071-704 1360

The Media Guide

An annual handbook covering all sectors of the media in a portable format. A Guardian Book, also available on 0483 268888

Two-Ten Communications (formerly PNA *Media Guide*)
Comprehensive media guide, published every two months. Similar information to PIMS, listing contact names and outlets under regions and under subject areas. Also publishes electronically which means daily updating if wanted, and easy printing out of address labels.

Communications House, 210 Old St, London EC1V 9UN
Tel. 071-490 8111   Fax 071-490 1255

PR Planner
Comprehensive guide to media contacts. Looseleaf format which is continually updated, with over 300 classified lists of magazines and 10,000 editors and specialist writers. Information arranged by region and subject.

Media Information Ltd, Hale House, 290-296 Green Lanes,
London N13 5TP
Tel. 081-882 0155 Fax 081-882 6716

Willings Press Guide
Windsor Court, East Grinstead House, East Grinstead,
West Sussex RH19 1XA
Tel. 0342 326972

GETTING OTHER INFORMATION

Advance
A two-monthly guide to forthcoming editorial features.

2 Prebendal Court, Oxford Road, Aylesbury, Bucks HP19 3EY
Tel. 0296 28585 Fax 0296 436622

Advertisers Annual
Three volumes of information aimed at advertisers. The volume called *The Media Planner* lists all UK publications and broadcasting which accept advertising. Gives circulation, region, advertising rates and copy deadlines for ads.

Reed Information Services Limited, Windsor Court, East Grinstead,
West Sussex RH19 1X9
Tel. 0342 326972 Fax 0342 327100

Benn's Media Directory
Over 2,000 pages listing major media outlets, PR firms, photographers, media training, etc., including cable and satellite outlets. Has three volumes: UK, Europe and International.

Benn Business Information Services Ltd, PO Box 20,
Sovereign Way, Tonbridge, Kent TN9 1RQ
Tel. 0732 362666 Fax 0732 770483

The Blue Book of British Broadcasting
Published annually, listing all UK broadcasting outlets. It is aimed mainly at broadcasting professionals but has lots of useful information about audience reach, figures, etc.

Communications House, 210 Old Street, London EC1V 9UN
Tel. 071-490 1447 Fax 071-490 8595

British Rate and Data (BRAD)
Good source of general media information, such as circulation figures, advertising rates, etc., for newspapers and broadcasting. Updated every month.

Maclean Hunter House, Chalk Lane, Cockfosters Road, Barnet,
Herts EN4 0BU.
Tel. 081-975 9759

Foresight
Rolling calendar of events up to 15 months ahead, cross-referenced and cross-indexed. Includes conferences, arts, social events, political events, major anniversaries, etc.

Profile Systems Ltd, 11 Hatton Garden, London EC1N 8AH
Tel. 071-831 9159

Hollis Press and Public Relations Annual
Excellent for general reference for media work. Over 20,000 contacts in the PR world, listing information sources, sponsors, fund raising, trade and professional associations, sports organisations, PR consultancies, photographers, etc.

Contact House, Lower Hampton Road, Sunbury-on-Thames,
Middlesex TW16 5HG
Tel. 0932 784781/782054 Fax 0932 787844

The Information Bureau

The successor to the Daily Telegraph Information Bureau, but now independent. For a small fee they will check up on facts, diary dates, anniversaries, etc., or help with finding VIPs. For a larger fee, they can do extensive research using their archives and reference library, or help with a speech or press release.

51 The Business Centre, 103 Lavender Hill, London SW11 5QL
Tel. 071-924 4414 Fax 071-924 4456

Expotel

They can provide information about good places to hold press conferences or big media events anywhere in Britain.

Conference Centre, Expotel, Kingsgate House, Kingsgate Place,
London NW6 4HG
Tel. 071-625 0276

MAGAZINES

Broadcast
Aimed at the broadcast industry.

7 Swallow Place, W1R 7AA
Tel. 071-491 9984

Campaign
Aimed at the advertising industry, but worth looking at.

22 Lancaster Gate, London W2 3LY
Tel. 071-413 4570

Media Week
An overview of the whole industry.

City Cloisters, 188-196 Old St, London EC1V 9BP
Tel. 071-490 5500

PR Week
The PR industry Bible.

22 Lancaster Gate, London W2 3LY
Tel. 071-413 4429

UK Press Gazette

The hack's bible, full of general information, gossip, and which journalist is moving where.

Maclean Hunter House, Chalk Lane, Cockfosters Road, Barnet,
Herts EN4 0BU
Tel. 081-975 9759 Fax 081-975 9751

PRESS CUTTINGS AND MONITORING

There are many regional cuttings and monitoring agencies, which will be cheaper and more effective for local press. They can be found in the Yellow Pages or in the general reference books above. Here are some of the best-known national agencies.

Durrants Press Cutting Bureau

103 Whitecross Street, London EC1Y 8QT
Tel. 071-588 3671 Fax 071-374 8171

Romeike & Curtis

Over 1,500 titles covered. Have a special trade and technical service.

Hale House, 290-296 Green Lanes, London N13 5TP
Tel. 081-882 0155 Fax 081-882 6716

Premium Business Information (previously Timms)

Special strength in financial journalism, although also covers all general media.

139 Tooley St, London SE1 2HZ
Tel. 071-403 6033 Fax 071-407 5857

Tellex Monitors

The first monitoring organisation, though there are now competitors. Will send tapes and/or transcripts of any UK programme within the previous month. Will also listen out for coverage or mention of an organisation or a subject area, and notify client.

The Broadcast Reporting Service, Communications House, 210 Old St, London EC1V 9UN
Tel. 071-490 8018

ORGANISATIONS

Chartered Institute of Journalists

The second most important professional body for journalists, broadcasters, press officers, etc.

Suite 2, Dock Offices, Surrey Quays, Lower Road, Docklands,
London SE16 2YS
Tel. 071-252 1187 Fax 071-232 2302

Institute of Public Relations

The Old Trading House, 15 Northburgh Street, London EC1V 0PR
Tel. 071-253 5151 Fax 071-490 0588

National Union of Journalists (NUJ)

The main trade union for journalists, broadcasters, press officers, etc.

Acorn House, 314 Gray's Inn Road, London WC1X 8DP
Tel. 071-278 7916 Fax 071-837 8143

Public Relations Consultants Association

The trade association public relations consultancies. Will provide confidential referral system for choosing a PR consultancy.

Willow House, Willow Place, Victoria, London SW1P 1JH
Tel. 071-233 6026 Fax 071-828 4797

The Labour and Industrial Correspondents Group

For all staff and freelance writers about business and labour relations. They tend to do a lot of cover for each other and pass around information about contacts and stories.

c/o The Daily Telegraph, 181 Marsh Walk, E14 9SR
Tel. 071-538 6104

The Medical Journalists Association

Similar to the above group for those writing about health, particularly in the specialist press.

14 Hovendens, Sissinghurst, Cranbrook, Kent TN17 2LA
Tel. 0580 713920

PHOTOGRAPHY

The Yellow Pages will list local photographers, and there are many London and regional photographers specialising in press work listed in the general reference books above. Some of them will not just take the photos but will also caption them and deliver them to the press direct. The bodies listed below may also be able to help in finding a photographer (as will the NUJ).

British Institute of Professional Photography
Fox Talbot House, 2 Amwell End, Ware, Herts SG12 9HN
Tel. 0920 464011

British Press Photographers Association
c/o The Pound House, Wadstray, Blackawton, Devon TQ9 7DE
Tel. 080421 421

Bureau of Freelance Photographers
Focus House, 497 Green Lanes, London N13 4BP
Tel. 081-882 3315

Royal Photographic Society
The Octagon, Milsom Street, Bath BA1 1DN
Tel. 0225 62841

FINDING VIPS AND ENTERTAINERS

There are a number of agencies which specialise in providing entertainers or Masters of Ceremony, and/or providing famous faces for events. They can be found in the general reference books. If you know who you want, you can also try these routes below.

Equity
The actors' and performers' union. They will tell you a member's agent.

8 Harley St, London W1N 2AB
Tel. 071-637 9311

Contacts
Show business directory. List most actors' and entertainers' agents.

Chanes House, 7 Leicester Place, London WC2H 7BP
Tel. 071-437 7631

MAKING COMPLAINTS

Press Complaints Commission
(Note that the PCC may cease to exist.)

No 1 Salisbury Sq., London EC4 8AE
Tel. 071-353 1248 Fax 071-353 8355

Broadcasting Complaints Commission
Grovesnor Gardens House, 35-37 Grovesnor Gardens, London SW1W 0BS
Tel. 071-630 1966
Broadcasting Standards Council
5-8 The Sanctuary, London SW1P 3JS
Tel. 071-233 0401